Digital Socio

Just because it's called social, doesn't make it social
Emma Uprichard, Summer 2012

Digital Sociology
The Reinvention of Social Research

Noortje Marres

polity

First published in 2017 by Polity Press
Reprinted 2017 (twice), 2018 (twice), 2019

Polity Press
65 Bridge Street
Cambridge CB2 1UR, UK

Polity Press
350 Main Street
Malden, MA 02148, USA

ISBN-13: 978-0-7456-8478-9 (hardback)
ISBN-13: 978-0-7456-8479-6 (paperback)

A catalogue record for this book is available from the British Library.

Library of Congress Cataloging-in-Publication Data

Names: Marres, Noortje, 1975- author.
Title: Digital sociology : the reinvention of social research / Noortje
   Marres.
Description: Malden, MA : Polity, 2017. | Includes bibliographical references
   and index.
Identifiers: LCCN 2016038449 (print) | LCCN 2017005356 (ebook) | ISBN
   9780745684789 (hardback) | ISBN 9780745684796 (paperback) | ISBN
   9780745684819 (Mobi) | ISBN 9780745684826 (Epub)
Subjects: LCSH: Sociology. | Social sciences--Research. | Technological
   innovations--Social aspects. | BISAC: SOCIAL SCIENCE / Sociology / General.
Classification: LCC HM585 .M34567 2017 (print) | LCC HM585 (ebook) | DDC
   301.01--dc23
LC record available at https://lccn.loc.gov/2016038449

Typeset in 10.5 on 12 pt Plantin by Servis Filmsetting Ltd, Stockport, Cheshire
Printed and bound in the UK by CPI Group (UK) Ltd, Croydon

For further information on Polity, visit our website: politybooks.com

Contents

Acknowledgements

If books are the result of collaboration, this applies only more so to a book about the digital. A big thank you goes to my collaborators, with whom it has been a pleasure imagining possibilities and developing ideas, many of which found their way into this book: in particular, Carolin Gerlitz, David Moats and Esther Weltevrede. I am grateful to Celia Lury, without whom there quite conceivably would not have been any Digital Sociology, at least not in the places where I work and write. Thank you to Richard Rogers, with whom I first started working on this and from whom I have learned so much.

Thank you, too, to my old colleagues in Sociology at Goldsmiths, University of London, and my new colleagues in the Centre for Interdisciplinary Methodologies at the University of Warwick, with whom I taught and developed Digital Sociology: Les Back, Jenn Barth, Roger Burrows, Nerea Calvillo, Rebecca Coleman, Andy Freeman, Kat Jungnickel, Dhiraj Murthy, Evelyn Ruppert, Bev Skeggs and Emma Uprichard. I also learnt much from my Digital Sociology students at Goldsmiths, including: Goran Becirevic, Sarietha Engelbrecht, Astrid Bigoni, Hjalmar Bang Carlsen, Sam Martin, Jess Perriam, Nissa Ramsay and Viktoria Williams, and at the University of Warwick, including: Matthias Orliwoski, Swati Metha, Arran Ridley and Thong Zhang.

Chapter 1 was written during a fellowship at the Berlin Social Science Center in the summer of 2014, and I want to thank Michael Hutter and Ignacio Farias for hosting me at the delightfully named Centre for the Study of Newness, and also for helpful discussions with Jeanette Hoffmann and her collaborators. Chapters 3 and 4 draw on published papers: Chapter 3 includes parts of an article written with Carolin Gerlitz, entitled 'Interface methods: Renegotiating relations between digital social research, STS and sociology' and which appeared in *The Sociological Review* in 2016. Chapter 4 builds on 'Mapping controversies with social media: The case for symmetry,' a piece I co-authored with David Moats for the second issue of *Social Media and Society*, and on 'Why Map Issues?' which was published in *Science, Technology and Human Values,40* (5) in 2015. I am grateful for inspiring comments provided on an earlier version of Chapter 4 by Ulrich Beck and his collaborators in Cosmopolitan Methodology during an excellent workshop in Paris in December 2014. I was able finally to finish this book thanks to a fellowship at the Digital Cultures Lab at Leuphana University, and I want to thank Goetz Bachman, Rene Ridgeway and Armin Beverungen in particular for being there to ask the right questions at the right time. I also ben-efited from discussions during events organized by and with: Tanja Bogusz, Andreas Bernhard, Dominique Boullier, Paul Feigelfeld, Martina Leeker, Mark Carrigan, Gian Marco Campagnolo, Endre Dányi, Dana Diminescu, Marieke de Goede, Michael Guggenheim, Steven Hinchliffe, Christine Hine, Bruno Latour, Ella McPherson, Rob Procter, Helene Snee, Tristan Thielmann, Stefan Giessmann, Willem Schinkel, Tommaso Venturini, Robin Williams, Alex Wilkie and Steve Woolgar.

   Thank you to interlocutors in addition to those already mentioned, for sharing their insights and generously engaging with my thoughts on digital sociology, even as I could not face adopting a platform voice while writing this book: Andreas Birkbak, Erik Borra, Anders Blok, Alessandro Brunetti, Michael Dieter, Vera Franz, Ana Gross, Stephanie Hankey, Anne Helmond, Mathieu Jacomy, Christopher Kelty, Monika Krause, Sybille Lammes, Vincent Lepinay, Manu Luksch, Greg McInerny, Linsey McGoey, Evgeny Morozov, Fabian Muniesa, Anders Munk, Sophie Mutzel, Dan Neyland, Tahani Nadim, Sabine Niederer, David Oswell, Mukul Patel, Nirmal Puwar, Bernhard Rieder, Marsha Rosengarten, Sanjay Sharma, Lucy Suchman, Nathaniel Tkacz, Marek Tuszynski, Lonneke van der Velden, Farida Vis and Britt Ross Whintereik. Emma Longstaff and Jonathan Skerrett at Polity were both patient and demanding, and their criticisms and comments provided valuable guidance along the way.

   Finally, I want to thank my family and Krause-Guggenheim for time spent in other places than at my desk, and Darius and Audra for accommodating this project while there were so many important things happening.

Introduction

There is much interest today in transformations at the interface between sociology, computing and media technology, and this book discusses what these transformations mean for our understanding of society. The recent excitement and concern about the changing role of computational infrastructures and devices in social life and social research is commonly captured by the shorthand 'the digital', a term that has been widely taken up. To be sure, this wide uptake reflects the significant investments in digital technologies, architectures and strategies that have been made across many sectors, including government, the universities, business, media and social and cultural organizations. But it is also informed by the conviction that the digital makes possible new ways of conducting and knowing social life. The capture, analysis and manipulation of data, networks and interaction by computational means has produced new interfaces between social life and social research. This book offers a sociological perspective on these latter developments and examines the challenges they pose to our engrained ways of knowing society. It also outlines some practical strategies for conducting social enquiry at this interface. My aim has been to provide an integrated analysis of the practical, methodological, and political problems and opportunities that today's digital infrastructures, devices and practices open up for the analysis of social life, and to situate these in relation to wider questions about the changing role of knowledge in society and public life. I discuss how the digital at once affects social life itself and our understanding of it, and explore its capacities to transform the very relations between social life and research. I argue that this is where the digital challenges our understanding of society most forcefully, and where digital sociology can make its most important contribution to wider public debates about new ways of knowing society.

Covering the contributions of sociologists and scholars from related fields to our understanding of these developments, the book then provides an advanced introduction to the emerging field of digital sociology. It is based on lectures I delivered as part of postgraduate courses on Digital Sociology over the past years: the introductory course of the Masters in Digital Sociology that I convened across the departments of Sociology and Computing at Goldsmiths, University of London, and more recently, as part of the postgraduate offer of the Centre for Interdisciplinary Methodologies (CIM) at the University of Warwick, for students in Digital Media Studies, Sociology as well Big Data and Urban Analytics. The book (like the lectures) serves several overall aims, the first of which is to provide an overview of current debates in sociology, computing and media studies about the new ways of knowing society enabled by digital transformations. As I will discuss in what follows, these debates focused on three main topics: (a) on the general claim that the digital makes possible new forms of knowing the social world; (b) on the concepts, methods and techniques required for the study of today's digital societies; and (c) on the normative, political and ethical issues raised by the new, digital forms of social research. This book covers each of these three aspects. It also serves a further objective, which is to outline an intellectual agenda for digital sociology. Faced with the myriads of problems that digital ways of knowing society open up for social research as well as for the societies of which it is a part, we need to develop new visions of the role of social enquiry in social and public life. The question is then how sociologists can participate actively in the further development of digital ways of knowing, both inside and outside the universities.

In taking up this question, the book advocates an interdisciplinary approach to digital sociology: I sketch out a way of researching digital societies that both draws on sociological traditions and enters into dialogue with media studies and computer science. In so doing, I join others in pursuing an approach to digital social research that is both critical and creative, and engages with the changing roles of technology and knowledge in contemporary social life. I argue that digital sociology is well positioned to address key problems with digital research as it is currently framed across fields: today, digital social research is increasingly defined as a form of data analysis, focused on the detection of patterns in behavioural data. While there are certainly good grounds for the recent surge of interest in digital analytics across science and society – because it confers on social research a renewed capacity to find coherence and intervene in social life – it is limited in other respects. As I will discuss, to equate digital social research with digital data analysis is to go along with an all too narrow conception of the relation of sociology and computing, one that does not equip us to investigate how sociality itself is undergoing transformation in digital societies. It does not enable us to investigate wider possible changes in the relations between knowledge, technology and society for which the rise of 'the digital' serves as occasion. I hope to show that digital sociology *can* address such issues. To see this, however, we must first critically examine the claims for new, digital ways of knowing society, and outline alternative strategies for researching social life with the digital.

The book is structured as follows. Chapter 1 offers an introduction to recent debates about the rise of a new form of social enquiry in the wake of digital transformations of social life and social research: digital sociology. I ask why the term is gaining traction only now: sociologists have studied digital infrastructures, technologies and practices for many decades already, but only in recent years has the term 'digital sociology' come into use. What can explain its rise to prominence? After a discussion of recent uses of the term in sociology, I show how claims for new, computational ways of knowing society were made across fields, in computing, in the media as well as data science, and have become the subject of significant academic and public controversies. The chapter then evaluates different definitions of digital sociology. It can alternatively be characterized in terms of (a) its object of enquiry (the digital society); (b) its methods; (c) its platforms (new sites and techniques for the public communication of sociology). While each of these aspects of digital sociology are important in their own right, I argue that we fail to grasp something crucial about digital sociology as long as we consider them in isolation. In a discussion of relevant examples, I show how the digital affects the relations between social life and its analysis in various ways, and why digital sociology must address these cross-cutting developments.

The second chapter asks: What is 'social' about digital media technologies? I evaluate three prominent answers to this question: (a) the device-centred view that says that social media technologies can be distinguished from non-social technologies by their technical capacities (they allow for social networking, for example); (b) the analytic view that highlights that social technologies make available new sources and forms of social data (for example, social media and mobile, locative data); (c) the critical view that says that media technologies are not social in and of themselves, and only their uptake in social practices make them so. There are then several, mutually inconsistent accounts on offer as to what makes digital technologies social. While some emphasize features like 'user-generated content' or social networking functionality, others foreground the importance of 'contexts of use': it is in the 'doing' of digital practice, that digital media technologies become social. The chapter goes on to discuss a number of problems with these three different views, and then introduces a fourth: the 'performative' – or rather, 'interactive' – understanding of what is social about digital infrastructures, devices and practices. This latter approach highlights that digital technologies do not only facilitate social life, or render it researchable, they also make social life amenable to intervention. I argue that the resulting interactions between social life and digital media technologies require further investigation, and invite us to develop a more experimental understanding of digital sociality, of what makes digital technologies social. If we wish to grasp the relevance of digital media technologies for social enquiry and social life, we must then better understand how the digital changes relation *between* technology and sociality.

The third chapter is concerned with methods. Much recent work in digital sociology has focused on this topic, as questions of method seem to crystallize both the promises and the problems that digital innovation opens up for sociology. This chapter offers an evaluation of these promises and problems, through a discussion of what has become known as the 'digital methods' debate. This debate revolves around the question: should we work towards the digitization of existing methods? Or is it more important to develop so-called 'natively digital' methods – methods, that is, which take advantage of technical features that are specific to digital networked media technologies? I offer a critical evaluation of these two positions, showing how emerging digital infrastructures provide support for both of them. I then make the case for a third approach, which I call 'interface methods'. This third approach builds on the former two, and starts from the recognition that important social research methods are already built into digital infrastructures, devices and practices, even if they currently tend to serve other-than-sociological ends. I argue that it therefore is our task to test and develop the capacities of these methods-devices for social enquiry, so that they may better serve its purposes. While digital architectures constrain social research in many ways, they are also to an extent configurable: the digital application of method requires a continuous mutual adjustment of research question, data, technique, context and digital setting.

Chapter 4 discusses an important methodological problem of digital sociology, which can be summed up by the question: are we studying society or technology? The problem is that sociologists tend to turn to digital social data and platforms in order to study social life, but the resulting research often ends up telling us more about digital technology than about society. I argue that digital sociologists must confront this problem, and I discuss ways of addressing it. First and foremost, it requires that we recognize that there are important problems of bias in digital social research. But we must also move beyond this problem definition, and consider a more fundamental problematic: the object of digital social enquiry is inherently ambiguous, insofar as both technological settings and social practices inflect digital formations, and it is difficult in many cases to disentangle their respective contributions. To conclude, I argue that it would be a mistake to transpose sociological methodologies onto digital settings unchanged. On the one hand, we cannot assume that society and technology can be easily disentangled. But neither can we just assume that digital societies constitute 'hybrids' of the technical and the social. This is because the specification of social problems and media-technological problems is too important and complex a task for sociologists to be able to leave it to others. The solution is to become more flexible in our ontological assumptions: it depends on our research topic, question, research design, chosen methods, and the forms of our data, whether we end up shedding light on digital technology or on digital social life.

Chapter 5 is concerned with digital participation and asks how digital sociology as a research practice and intellectual agenda engages with publics. Do digital media technologies offer new ways for sociology to engage with audiences? Can digital infrastructures, devices and practices help us to imagine new public roles for sociology and sociologists? Across disciplines, it has recently been argued that the digital transforms the role of the public in society: in digital societies, ordinary people increasingly figure as active participants in public life, and not just as audiences. In this chapter, I criticize the idea that the credit for rendering today's media, publics and society more participatory should be conferred on digital technology, and I discuss the contribution that digital sociology can make to the understanding and practice of digital participation. Following Boullier (2016), I argue that classic sociological concepts, like the 'representation of society to society', offer purchase on the empirical challenge and normative promise of digital participation today. Concepts like these offer a different way of understanding the supposed shift from 'audience to participation' in digital societies, and help to identify an alternative normative direction for this project, one that differs from the drive towards ever more active engagement (more participation).

The final chapter discusses the contribution of digital sociology to public life and interdisciplinary debates about the challenges that digital data and analytics pose for our ways of knowing societies. I summarize the main argument of the book: the relations between social life and its analysis are changing in digital societies, and take one step further: these relations are changing today to the point that the role of social research in society has been rendered problematic. Indeed, the digital is today opening up a new 'crisis of representation', as it casts doubt on the capacity of social research to adequately and legitimately represent society. I argue that prevailing conceptions of what computational methods bring to the study of society do not equip us well to understand these transformations and the resulting crisis. However, to address this, digital sociology should not adopt an anti-scientific stance. The main attraction of digital sociology is precisely that it enables the development of experimental forms of enquiry that cut across the divides between the sciences and the humanities. It may develop and inform richer approaches to 'data interpretation', more adventurous ways of introducing social theory into the space of digital research, more playful forms of interaction between social research and social practices. Digital sociology opens up ways to reinvent social research.

1

What is digital sociology?

In social research, as in other fields, the idea has taken root that the digital makes possible new ways of contributing to society. Actual efforts to realize this promise of the digital have proven the initial optimism to be partly misguided. One sobering example is the Samaritan Radar, a social media application that was launched by the Samaritans, an important UK suicide prevention agency, in October 2014. At its launch, the tool was introduced as a way of identifying users at risk of suicide by way of real-time, textual analysis of Twitter data. Once an 'at risk' account has been detected, the Radar would send a message to the followers of the identified account alerting them and 'offering guidance on the best way of reaching out and providing support'.[1] Perhaps unsurprisingly, the Samaritans were forced to close the experimental service after a short time, and it was subjected to harsh criticisms in both news and online media. Many argued that notifying people's social media contacts of their supposed malaise without prior consent amounted to a 'privacy violation', while some flagged the risk of stigmatization of individuals already deemed 'at risk'. Yet others questioned the hubristic presumption that a complex and sensitive phenomenon like suicide risk could be detected and managed using simple methods of data analytics.[2] Indeed, social researchers could no doubt propose different, better methods to understand and communicate with people in trouble using social media, and providing the impulse to do so could be one positive outcome of this episode.[3] However, the Samaritan Radar debacle also sheds light on a wider, rather diffuse phenomenon, namely the remarkably strong expectations, in our societies, that digital technology will make it possible for social research to help solve social problems.

Digital technology presents an important societal phenomenon today, as popular online platforms like Facebook, smart phones and 'intelligent' computational systems have been taken up across the full breadth of society during the last decade or so, from transport to education, from family life to activism, from prison management to wildlife conservation. Whereas the digital used to refer to a fairly special set of practices, those that early adopters, experts, the 'tech savvy' and the young engaged in, today it touches on most aspects of social life. This development has important implications for sociology. But the ongoing digitization of society does not only present an important topic of investigation, it also has the potential to transform the very role that social research itself plays in society. Across society, digital infrastructures, devices and practices are widely seen to offer important, new opportunities for making social research relevant to social life (Back, 2012), for turning knowledge about society into action.[4] As I will discuss in this chapter, what distinguishes the digital technologies of today – what sets them apart from the 'Web' and 'information and communication technologies' (ICT) that went before – is their extensive capabilities for monitoring, analysing and informing social life. Today's digital infrastructures, devices and practices collect an abundance of data that can be used to analyse people's interactions and movements, from the SMS exchanges captured by phone companies to the location data amassed through smart phone apps. They also make it possible to translate data analysis into targeted feedback in everyday settings and user activities, from the query terms suggested by search engines, to the personalized updates that are offered by transport and weather apps and other digital services. It is these interactive capacities of digital technology, in combination with its ubiquity in society – the fact that digital technology can appear to be everywhere – that today feed the conviction that the digital makes it possible to re-connect social analysis with social intervention, as in the example of the Samaritan Radar app above.

What makes the digital such a relevant phenomenon for sociology then goes beyond its importance as a research topic. Its contemporary significance must also be understood in terms of the transformations of social research, and of its role in society that it makes possible. These transformations have been described in various ways, but they can be summed up in the belief that social research, through its implementation in computational infrastructures, may gain the capacity to intervene in social life and thereby to address or even solve social problems. The Samaritan Radar project was presented as a way of taking advantage of the widespread uptake of a social media platform like Twitter across society for a progressive purpose, and it did this by outlining a new way of using methods of textual analysis to act on the issue of suicide risk. As such, this project offers a clear demonstration of the belief in the power of the digital to confer onto the analysis of social life the capacity to help solve social problems. However, once the project was underway, multiple challenges to this ambition came into view, such as the risks of privacy violation and stigmatization. Furthermore, as a blogger speculated a few months later, the fact that a suicide prevention agency is monitoring social media might even lead users to practise self-censorship, thereby affecting the very fabric of interaction in these settings.[5] As such, the Samaritan Radar episode can also be interpreted as a kind of 'critical' test of progressive hopes invested in the digital. This is partly what makes it such a relevant case from a sociological perspective.

I would like to argue that the digital today does offer fresh opportunities for connecting social analysis and social intervention, but not in the way in which this promise is usually understood. This is because digital societies are marked by far more complex interactions between social life and knowledge – between social research and social action – than tends to be recognized when data analysis is put forward as a way of acting on social problems. The Samaritan Radar episode highlighted some of these more complex dynamics. This tool did not only facilitate interaction – feedback – in the technical sense of sending a notification to an identified user's social media contacts. It also brought into relief more comprehensive forms of interaction between social research and social life. When the monitoring and analysis of everyday activities is used as a basis for intervention into these activities, a complex set of exchanges between knowledge and behaviour is set in motion, as the public debate that followed on the launch of Samaritan Radar also highlighted. When users are identified as a 'suicide risk', this designation may initiate a dynamic in which social concepts – like 'suicide risk' – and social life inter-react: once individuals (as well as others) are 'aware of how they are classified', this produces a situation in which these actors are likely to 'modify their behavior accordingly', to quote the description that social theorist and philosopher Ian Hacking (2000, p. 32) has provided of what he calls the 'interactivity' between social research and social life. This type of transformative effect, by which the description of a social situation transforms that situation, has long been of special concern to sociologists and philosophers (Thomas and Thomas, 1928; Becker, 1963). As I will discuss in what follows, one of the key questions that arises in digital societies is how computational forms of interaction at work here combine with sociological dynamics of interactivity between knowledge and social life.

In this book, I would then like to propose that the digital opens up new occasions for interaction and interactivity between social life, technology and knowledge, and that these form a central challenge for sociology in a digital age. The proliferation of computational infrastructures, devices and practices across society has given rise to new forms of exchange and mutual adjustment between social research and social life, a development in which social, technical and epistemic processes fuse in ways we need to understand much better than we do now. On a general level, it means that if we are to grasp the significance of the digital for sociology, we must recognize that interaction is not just a notable technical feature of digital technology today. Interactivity – in the broad sense of exchange and traffic between the analysis of activities and those activities themselves – presents a crucial sociological dynamic. Indeed, in the classic view of the early twentieth-century sociologist Max Weber (1905/1968), this is the defining challenge of social science. As Weber famously noted, what distinguishes social enquiry from other forms of research is that it must contend with the fact that the ideas people have about the social world interact with what happens in it. As sociologists have since argued, social research presents a special form of knowledge insofar as it is *inherently interactive*: social research must expect, and indeed anticipate, that knowledge about social life and social life itself mutually influence one another (Cicourel, 1964). This is also to say that social dynamics of interactivity are not at all new in themselves. However, in today's digital societies, technology must increasingly be factored into these complex processes. Remarkably, however, while there has been much interest in the new ways of knowing society that digital technology makes possible, both inside and outside the university, the complex interactions between digital technology, social research and social life have received much less attention. As I will discuss, the debate about digital social science has largely proceeded within a *representational* framework – one focused on the capacity of digital data analysis to represent adequately given social phenomena and patterns – and not an interactional one.

Over the last decade, however, sociologists and scholars in related fields such as digital media studies, geography and computing have been hard at work to develop the concepts, methods, and methodologies that we need in order to understand the complex interactions between digital technology, sociality and knowledge, and the aim of this book is to offer an introductory account of these important if challenging efforts. In this opening chapter, I will provide an overview of this emerging work on digital sociology, with a special focus on the claim that the digitization of society makes possible a new way of knowing and intervening in society. The chapter situates this claim in relation to longstanding engagements in sociology with computational technologies, as both an object and instrument of social enquiry. By considering recent interest in digital sociology against this historical backdrop, we are able to move beyond two equally dissatisfying claims: the claim that the digital ways of knowing society emerging today present a radically innovative form of knowledge, as some advocates of the 'new' computational social science have suggested; but also beyond the claim that there is nothing new about digital sociology, that it is basically 'old sociology' with a few new 'sexy' but superficial and unconvincing technological features built in.

Rather, the research practices that today go by the name of 'digital sociology' contain both old and new elements – old and new techniques, methods, concepts, sources of data, and forms of intervention (Latour et al., 2012; Watts, 2004; Law and Ruppert, 2013; MacKenzie et al., 2015). This insight will allow us to confront a different set of questions from those pushed into the foreground by the opposition between the old and the new. The question for digital sociology is not only whether today's digital societies give rise to new social forms or give us more of the same, or whether digital sociology presents a new or an old way of knowing society. We must equally consider whether and how 'the digital' entails changes in the relations *between* technologies and social life; *between* knowledge, society and technology. Indeed, I want to argue that it may be ultimately more productive to adopt the latter, relational perspective. We will need to come to terms with these changing relations if we are serious about deploying digital technologies for progressive purposes. Today's digital transformations invoke important debates from sociology's past and about the role of ideas and technology in social life. I would like to show how digital transformations render these sociological traditions newly relevant to contemporary problems. And that they do so in ways that challenge us to develop a more 'technology-aware' way of understanding social life.

The 'rise' of digital sociology

One of the puzzles of 'digital sociology' is that the label has come into usage only relatively recently: it only started appearing in print towards the end of the 2000s.[6] This is strange because sociologists have studied the role of computational technology in social life and society at large for many decades (Athique, 2013). It was in 1976 that the sociologist Daniel Bell (1976) announced the coming of the post-industrial society, a societal transformation in which the computer and its uptake in industry, government and organizations played a central role. In the new society that was announced by Bell, it was no longer the production of material goods, but information- and data processing that would function as 'the engine' of social transformation. Not just grand theories of society, but also empirical studies of social life, have for many decades already insisted that computational technologies play a formative role in social life. It was almost thirty years ago that Lucy Suchman published *Plans and Situated Actions* (1987), a classic fieldwork study of the interactions between people and computational systems, most notably a 'smart' photocopier, in everyday work places. Suchman's book made the case for a more-than-technological, 'socio-technical' understanding of computational practices and arrangements. Her field studies showed how capacities that are often ascribed to digital technology – such as the ability to represent reality, or to coordinate action – in actuality are the outcomes of social and technical interactions *between* people and machines, as well as with everyday environments and objects.

To be sure, the rise to prominence of personal computing and the widespread uptake of Internet technologies from the 1990s onwards meant that the analysis of the computational society, and of computational social practice, had to be updated. But this job was largely done in the late 1990s and early 2000s, with the appearance of Manuel Castells' *Network Society* (1996) and Miller and Slater's *The Internet: An Ethnographic Approach* (2001). These classic studies broadly followed in the footsteps respectively of Bell and Suchman but showed that after PCs, the Web and e-mail, computerization no longer primarily affected the professional spheres of industry, organizational life and state bureaucracy, as earlier accounts of the computerization of society had argued: computing now came to transform social relations, practices and structures, *in everyday, cultural, political, and public life.* In this same period, sociologists were also turning to the Internet and the Web as sites of research, taking up established methods like ethnography and network analysis to conduct social research online, studying online communities and researching so-called socio-technical networks – hybrid formations involving human and non-human elements (Hine, 2000; Slater, 2002; Rogers and Marres, 2000). Importantly, however, in this period, it was the concept of the 'network' – closely connected to the figure of the Web – and the distinction between online and offline, rather than the digital as such, that dominated sociological thinking and research on the computerization of social life (Woolgar, 2002).

Since the early 2000s, PCs and the Internet have been joined by popular social media platforms, smart phones, and large-scale investment in 'intelligent' computational systems in such sectors as transport and energy. These infrastructures, devices and associated practices build on and extend the capacities of previous incarnations of computing in (and as) social life – they are networked, interactive, designed for non-expert users, and so on – but there are some important qualitative differences. Previous studies of the computerization of social life tended to focus on specific social domains – such as commerce or activism – or specific sectors and communities, like the implementation of computational systems in 'air traffic control' (Suchman, 1997) in the 1980s, or hacker culture (Riemens, 2002) in the 1990s. Even as sociologists studied computational practices and forms of organization that extended across time and space (such as diasporic networks (Diminescu, 2012)), and their uptake among different social groupings (elderly engineers; adventurous teenagers; activists), these digital forms of life were nevertheless described as special – the domain of the young, the savvy, migrated, the radical. Today, however, 'the digital' touches on most aspects of social life. It is no longer special, and must be addressed as part of most if not all substantive areas of sociology, from citizenship to intimacy, the relations between the state and the economy, the changing role of contractual labour in society, to the experience of self and nature, from gender relations to the city (Orton-Johnson and Prior, 2013; Lupton, 2014). As such, the digital can be understood as a new kind of *total social fact* (Fish et al., 2011; Lury and Marres, 2015). This term coined by the anthropologist Marcel Mauss, Adam Fish and others have argued, is perfectly applicable to the Internet: just as in Mauss' description of the total social fact, the Internet today touches on 'every aspect of organized human life', and qualifies as a 'phenomen[on] which extend[s] to the whole of social life' (Mauss, 2005: 70, cited in Fish et al., 2011). What Fish et al. say about the Internet, we can extend towards the broader category of the digital:

it must be understood as irreducible, as affecting most if not all areas of social life, and as itself generative of new social practices, ties and relations, a point to which I will return.

Why do we speak of the digital today? As computerization takes on the aspect of a total social fact, prior pre-occupations with its special effects – what happens when social life becomes networked? when culture moves online and becomes virtual? – are replaced with concerns with more sobering societal effects, such as: what kind of influence are digital industries gaining over societal arrangements? As I will discuss, projects to re-configure society's infrastructures, forms of organization and practices by way of the digital have multi-faceted implications, but there is one outstanding feature I want to highlight at the outset, and this is the critical importance to these projects of social research, broadly conceived (Marres, 2012a). As digital technologies are embedded ever more widely into societal infrastructures and social practices they generate an abundance of information about social life, enable the application of analytic tech-niques and make possible new forms of feedback (Savage, 2009). The ubiquitous use of smart phones and digital platforms and the grafting of 'intelligent' computational systems onto existing trans-port, communications and energy architectures – in the form of travel cards or smart energy meters – have resulted in what is often called a 'digital deluge': a wealth of digital traces that can be used for research and other practical purposes (Given, 2006; Savage and Burrows, 2007; Edwards et al., 2013). As the digital increasingly inflects both large-scale infrastructures and our most intimate practices, these social arrangements become connected by an ever-expanding pool of devices for data capture, analysis and feedback, whether it is in the form of new methods for consumer credit rating that take into account social media data, or the reputational scores of Twitter users that are monitored by these users themselves, as well as, potentially, their employers (Kitchin, 2014; Gerlitz and Lury, 2014; Deville and van der Velden, 2015). The range of fields and potential applications is vast, but, as the journalist and novelist John Lanchester put it suc-cinctly, what matters is that it is digital.[7]

Today's widespread use of the short-hard term 'digital' may then be taken to refer to the loose and diffuse set of capabilities that derive, not just from the 'computerization' of society in general, but, more specifically, from the equipment of social arrangements and prac-tices with devices for data capture, analysis and feedback (Amoore and Piotukh, 2015). Arguably, indeed, wider projects to re-make societies by way of the digital *critically* depend on the embedding of new empirical instruments for research and intervention into social practices, environments and infrastructures. This circumstance can help to clarify an important distinctive feature of the forms of social enquiry that over the last years we have started to refer to as 'digital sociology'. While computational arrangements, processes and practices have for many decades served as topics of sociological research, the 'digital' presents sociology with something that is qualitatively different, as the digital transformation of society today involves the configuration of a vast, evolving, potential 'empirical apparatus' for social research across social life. Digital devices have been taken up so widely that they can today be configured as instruments for analysis of and intervention in, not just this or that special practice, but society.

However, there is one important, stubborn detail that goes unmentioned in this story about the rise of 'the digital' as a machine for knowing and transforming society. Many sociologists remain unconvinced that the sources of data and methods made available by today's digital infrastructures present something new, or that they are even usable for social enquiry. Some of this scepticism is mild and takes the form of playful reminders that if we *really* want to know what the 'digital' refers to today, we should consider its promotional, sensationalist and hype-like quality, as suggested, for example, by a Twitter message sent by the British sociologist Mike Savage in July 2013: 'wow! The rise of digital sociology!'[8] The tweet included a link to a Google Trends visualization of the key-word 'digital sociology' and the related terms 'digital anthropology' and 'digital cultures' (Figure 1.1). Under the heading 'interest over time', the figure compares the number of times people have searched for these phrases since 2009, suggesting that the term 'digital sociology' came into use around January 2011, a good few

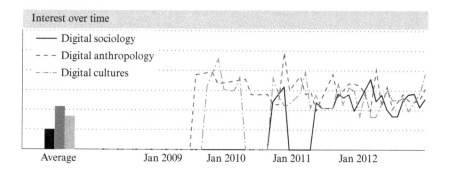

Figure 1.1   Savage's Google Trends query, July 2013

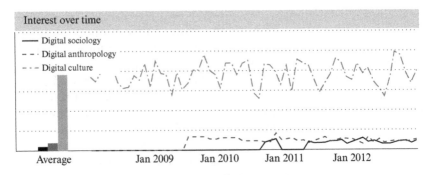

Average   Jan 2009   Jan 2010   Jan 2011   Jan 2012

Figure 1.2   Savage's Google Trends query, with an 's' removed,
July 2013

years later than digital anthropology, and at least ten years later than digital culture. As Savage is surely aware, it is easy to question the accuracy of such figures: for example, when we remove the 's' from digital cultures, the picture changes, showing how the academic disciplines, among them sociology, are dwarfed by 'culture' when it comes to their ability to make the connection with 'digital' (Figure 1.2).[9]

Around the time Savage wrote this message, hype-ish and inflated claims about digital social science were still doing the rounds of the more serious media. In an especially exuberant article that appeared in 2011, the *New York Times* described recent efforts of social scientists 'to mine the vast resources of the Internet – Web searches and Twitter messages, Facebook and blog posts, the digital location trails generated by billions of cell phones' – as realizing nothing less than the aims of universal social science, citing 'social scientists who believe that digital data will for the first time reveal sociological laws of human behaviour – enabling them to predict political crises, revolutions and other forms of social and economic instability, just as physicists and chemists can predict natural phenomena'.[10] In sociology, this grand narrative about a 'new science' that will uncover the eternally valid laws of society has a name – it is called sociological positivism and is most commonly associated with the nineteenth century sociological theory of August Comte, and, it has to be said, tends to be regarded among serious sociologists as too naive and/ or hubristic an idea to seriously entertain. Sociological scepticism also extends to the practical challenges of digital social enquiry. One major issue here – to begin at the top of the iceberg – is that most digital systems today are privately owned: significant parts of the emerging apparatus for social analysis are located beyond the public Internet, and remain inaccessible for most social researchers (Savage and Burrows, 2007; Wagner-Pacifici et al., 2015).

Should it then really surprise us that, as the computational social scientist David Lazer and his co-authors (2009, p. 721) observed, 'leading journals in economics, sociology, and political science show little evidence of this field?' They went on: 'but computational social science is occurring – in Internet companies such as Google and Yahoo, and in government agencies such as the US National Security Agency (*sic*)', and all this still appears to be largely true today, even as the 'foresight' of the NSA to use digital data for social research purposes today, after the recent controversies about Internet surveillance, qualifies rather less as a shining example than Lazer and colleagues suggested back in 2009. Indeed, a broad range of problems have been identified with the use of digital infrastructures, devices and data for social research purposes, as I will discuss in what follows. But before doing so, I first want to examine in more detail the general claim that the digital makes possible a 'new way of knowing society.'

From vision to controversy

Notwithstanding the continued scepticism of many, over the last decade scholars across the disciplines of sociology, computing, media studies, geography, anthropology, and related fields have formulated intellectual visions of a new digital form of social enquiry. As already suggested, many of these visions focus on data: sociologists have argued that digital infrastructures inaugurate a new age of the 'traceability' of social life (Latour, 1998; Thrift and French, 2002). The outstanding feature of digital technologies, from this vantage point, is that they render everyday activities recordable and monitorable to a new degree, and with unprecedented intimacy: your phone traces your movements, your thermostat knows when you are asleep, search engines know what you think. Some sociologists have characterized the data collected by digital means as 'transactional' or 'naturally occurring' social data (Edwards et al., 2013). In contrast to the purposefully collected data that sociologists used to rely on, such as surveys or interviews or focus groups, the argument then goes, today's digital data are not produced in artificial situations. They are generated as a by-product of already occurring interactions and processes across social life. However, as we shall see in Chapter 2,

many other sociologists have criticized the idea that digital environments, such as for example Facebook, qualify as 'natural' (Derksen
and Beaulieu, 2011; Lewis, 2015).

A second vision of a new, digital way of knowing society focuses
on the new analytic techniques that digital infrastructures enable.
Most spectacularly, some sociologists have claimed that the digital
makes possible a 'scaleless' form of social enquiry, as it allows us to
zoom from a particular 'data point' out to the whole (data-set), and
back again. This claim is of key importance for sociology, because it
suggests that the digital may help to bridge a long-standing divide in
sociology, that between the detailed description of social life on the
micro-level and the analysis of whole populations on the macro-level
of society (Latour et al., 2012; Conte et al., 2012). As Latour et al.
(2012) put it, digital infrastructures allow us to 'navigat[e] data sets
without making the distinction between the level of the individual
component and that of the aggregated structure' (p. 590) Indeed,
Latour has gone a step further, as he generalizes this claim about
digital methods to make a wider argument, arguing that the digital
allows us to sidestep one of the foundational problems of sociology,
that of the 'great divide' between society and individual, between
structure and agency. Less extreme, but gesturing in a similar
direction, is the argument by Savage and Burrows (2007) that the
digital data deluge makes possible a shift from theory-driven causal
'explanation' to a more empirical style of 'description' as the dominant mode of sociological analysis, as digital data analysis enables
the fine-grained description of social life on the granular level as
well as extrapolations towards wider 'patterns of living' (Savage and
Burrows, 2007; Adkins and Lury, 2011; Mackenzie et al., 2015).

A third vision, finally, proposes that the 'game-changing' feature
of emerging, digital infrastructures does not consist of either digital
data, or digital forms of analysis, in and of themselves, but instead
derives from the ways in which data capture, analysis and feedback
are combined in the digital arrangements that are configured across
society today. Social media, mobile and other 'smart' infrastructures
have a double-faced nature, in that they present at once an instrument for the analysis of social life and a device for intervention in
it (Edwards et al., 2013; Healy, 2015; Law and Ruppert, 2013;
Marres and Weltevrede, 2013). As such, digital infrastructures have
the capacity to reconfigure the relations between social research
and social life, as it has long been assumed by many sociologists
and philosophers of science that society cannot be studied with
interventionist, experimental methods, such as those associated

with laboratory science: most prominent sociological methods like sample-survey analysis, interviews and fieldwork are not experimental but observational. This third perspective, then, highlights what I referred to in the introduction as the new forms of 'interactivity' that mark the relations between social research and social life in digital societies. It pays special attention to the ways in which the proliferation of digital devices across social life has been accompanied by the uptake of social concepts and methods, such as the 'social network' and 'network analysis', across society (Mayer, 2012; Healy, 2015). The digital then directs our attention anew to the 'social life' of methods (Law and Ruppert, 2013) and makes it necessary to reflect not only on how the digital enables sociologists to understand the world differently, but also on how the social world itself is transformed by digital ways of knowing society (see also Knorr-Cetina, 2014; Marres, 2012a).

I will examine these three visions of new digital ways of knowing society in more detail in what follows, but striking about each of them is that, *to a greater or lesser extent, they ascribe to the digital the capacity to solve sociology's problems.* Indeed, sociologists like Bruno Latour (Latour et al., 2012) explicitly argue that digital infrastructures provide a way out of one of the long-standing problems in sociology, that of the rift between the study of society as a whole, on the macro-level, and the investigation of social practices in their particularity, on the micro-level. As he puts it: because digital traces allow sociologists to follow 'the action' from micro to macro, they suspend the need to posit different levels on which sociality unfolds (see also Manovich, 2011). Although arguably in a less extreme fashion, this capacity of the digital to (dis)solve sociology's problems is also invoked in sociological discussions about the 'data deluge'. As noted, some sociologists have characterized the data that digital infrastructures make available as 'naturally occurring', and this too suggests that the digital may help us to solve a recognized, methodological problem, namely that of the 'artificial quality' of generalizable social data. The data that are classically used to analyse societal dynamics on the macro-level, such as survey data, are not like laboratory data, but neither are they exactly 'natural': they depend on a machinery of 'survey-sample analysis', including the design of questionnaires, the selection of discrete moments in which to conduct the survey and so on (Cicourel, 1964; Savage, 2010). Thirdly, and finally, the claims that 'new' forms of interactivity between social research and social life are arising in digital societies also contain a promise to solve one of sociology's problems, namely the problem of a sociology that is perceived and/or perceives itself as 'out of touch', as not sufficiently engaged with society (more about this in Chapter 6).

It is then not just social organizations like the Samaritans, or 'susceptible' journalists at the *New York Times*, who believe that the digital can solve problems of social research. (It is not just out-there in society, that 'the digital' is capable of conferring problem-solving capacities onto social research.) However, as noted above, problems with the 'new', digital approaches to knowing society have been formulated with equal conviction if not zeal. Lee et al. (2008) have argued that the more sensational claims for new computational ways of understanding social life tend to overstate the differences that separate the 'new' from 'old' forms of social research, and they suggest that such claims to innovation tend to depend on the forgetting of previous advances in sociology (p. 5; see also Watts, 2004; Chapter 3). Others have highlighted more specific problems with the claims for a new digital sociology. Zynep Tufekci (2014a) and others have pointed at the biased nature of much digital data, as social media and smart phone users tend to over-represent people from some segments of the population and some locations (see also Murphy et al., 2013). Furthermore, digital data tend to be inflected by the technical features of digital platforms, applications, devices. Even if the issue of private ownership of digital data is to an extent circumventable, for example by using automated techniques for online data capture (see Chapter 3), it remains the case that digital architectures tend to leave their mark on data collected by these means, in ways that are moreover notoriously opaque (boyd and Crawford, 2012; Driscoll and Walker, 2014). Scholars have also taken issue with the empiricist ideal of data-driven research (Gitelman, 2013; see also Marres and Weltevrede, 2013), which has become newly fashionable in the wake of the digital deluge, inside and outside the university: these critics point out that analytic techniques that are advertised as 'data-driven' – as enabling 'emergent pattern detection' through the analysis of search engine, or phone, or transport data – do not do what it says on the tin: they are in actual fact highly theory-laden, as they tend to heavily rely on models, and a limited set of data formats (such as query terms), and as such come with conceptual assumptions build in, as highlighted by Bowker's (2005) slogan that 'raw data is an oxymoron'. Relatedly, Emma Uprichard (2013) has criticized the claim that digital analytics can be applied to 'whole data sets', pointing out that, in practice, data analysis almost always relies on some form of 'data reduction' and, indeed, prior categorization.

In this book, I will also take issue with those visions that assume that the digital, in and of itself, can solve sociology's problems. As I would like to show, the emerging field of digital sociology is marked by proliferating controversies about the forms and directions in which to develop social enquiry by way of the digital. However, in flagging problems that trouble digital ways of knowing society, I do not want to argue that the more enthusiastic claims for a new digital sociology are wrong. Rather, I think the significance and potential of the digital for sociology is that it presents a positive, constructive occasion for us to engage with problems in and of social research, broadly conceived – that is, as it is practised across academia, the media, government, business, politics and everyday life. The digital, then, presents an important new site for the negotiation, contestation and imagination of different ways of knowing society, raising many troubling but important and relevant questions in the process that we should take time to explore and discuss: who is capable of social enquiry? who owns the means of its production and distribution? what are useable data? what techniques of intervention can sociology use? what relations between researchers and research subjects should we strive for? The digital does not solve sociology's problems, to the contrary, it unsettles and exposes the troubles and difficulties of social research, and, we should strive to ensure, makes these available for collective exploration.

Importantly, this debate about digital ways of knowing society is not just conducted among sociologists: it has emerged as an important topic of wider, interdisciplinary and public debates over the last years. I have already quoted a well-known contributor to these debates, David Lazer, who in the 2009 *Science* article, together with co-authors from computing, physics and social science, sketched the outlines of a new 'computational social science'. Their vision favoured a quantitative data science of behaviour, which would 'compile [digital traces] into comprehensive pictures of both individual and group behavior', and in this way 'transform our understanding of our lives, organizations, and societies' (Lazer et al., 2009). Earlier, one of the co-authors of this piece, Alex Pentland had used the term 'Sociology of the 21th Century' (Manovich, 2011)[11] to describe his computational social science project using mobile phone data, in which he and his colleagues ran semi-controlled experiments to capture and analyse large sets of smart phone data, analysing interactions such as 'who shared apps with who' and claiming that social behaviours can be inferred from this type of data (Eagle et al., 2009). Striking about this work is not only the appropriation of the label 'sociology' to describe a project in data science, but also

the readiness of the researchers involved to advance claims almost
as hyperbolic as those reported in the *New York Times* above. In his
book, *Social Physics*, Pentland (2014) says that digital data 'give us
the chance *to view society in all its complexity*, though the millions of
networks of person-to-person exchanges' (p. 11; italics mine), and
that the 'digital breadcrumbs we all leave behind as we move through
the world – call records, credit card transactions, and GPS location
fixes, among others' –make possible new ways of 'analysing patterns
of human experience'. To be sure, in some respects these claims
are *not* so unlike some of the visions advanced by digital sociologists
above, but in other respects they are very different. They re-activate
a universalist vision of social science, one which much sociological
training and literature precisely teaches us to qualify.[12]

One important task for digital sociology is to clarify and help us
understand what is problematic about such claims, not just ethically,
in view of the spectre of a surveillance society raised by such statements, but also methodologically, in terms of whether and how these
knowledge claims hold up. A crucial issue here concerns the relation
between technology and society: whereas the computational social
science narrative above suggests that digital data open a window on
the social world, social and cultural researchers have pointed out
that digital platforms presents first and foremost socio-technical
arrangements (Gillespie, 2010), in which human and computational
elements combine to structure social action. For this reason, Lewis
(2015) has argued that 'digital data cannot be interpreted indepen-
dently of the technologies through which they are imprinted'. Such
data, that is, are likely to express features of digital systems and
devices as much as they are expressive of 'human behavior'. For
example, if a particular app is frequently downloaded by a particular
group of users, does that tell us something about those users, or does
it rather tell us something about the auto-suggest and rankings of
apps on the platforms they use? (More on this question in Chapter 4.)

Another important topic of debate between disciplines is the use of
digital platforms to conduct experiments on society. As noted, many
sociologists have ethical and epistemic problems with experimental
methods: they believe these methods are only of limited use if the aim
is to understand society, as experiments tend to create highly artificial
circumstances and are likely to involve the deliberate manipulation
of human subjects (Guggenheim, 2012; Gross and Krohn, 2005).
But many computational social scientists are not concerned by these
issues. As Duncan Watts wrote in a recent newspaper article: 'it's
unreasonable to insist that the behavior of humans and societies is

somehow an illegitimate subject for the scientific [experimental] method'.[13] A self-described 'in-house sociologist' at a popular social media platform has famously used this platform to conduct large-scale experiments, among others by installing buttons on selected pages encouraging users to register as donors or to vote.[14] As he claimed: 'Facebook is not above using its platform to tweak users' behavior [. . .]. Unlike academic social scientists, Facebook's employees have a short path from an idea to an experiment on hundreds of millions of people' (Simonite, 2012). Facebook has since come in for serious public criticism for the so-called mood manipulation experiments conducted on this platform, which tried to determine the influence of social media on people's happiness by manipulating the news feeds of millions of Facebook users (Crawford, 2014). Much of this criticism rightly focused on the ethical problems raised by deliberate attempts to affect people's feelings without their consent, or even knowledge. But there are also important methodological questions. For one, many social media experiments serve the narrow objective of finding out how 'real world behaviours are amenable to online intervention' (Bond et al., 2012). But there are many other possible ways of understanding social life through intervention, by combining analysis and feedback, in ways that may be applicable in digital settings, as I will discuss in Chapter 3.

Digital ways of knowing society, then, present crucial topics not only for academic, but also for interdisciplinary and public debate today. Not only that, digital social research, broadly conceived, has become the subject of public and societal controversy in recent years. Digital ways of monitoring, analysing and influencing activities across social life raise serious social, ethical, legal and political issues, perhaps most prominently in the case of the controversy around data surveillance in the wake of the leak of NSA files in 2013, and their revelation of mass data capture, monitoring and analysis by security and intelligence services. Other recent controversies about digital methods reflect the state and character of digital societies themselves, as technologies like search algorithms and Twitter bots are revealed to both express and perpetuate biases (of gender, race, politics): search engine queries like 'women' and 'blacks' bring defamatory content to the surface. Such cases raise the question of whether the problem lies with the algorithms that favour this type of dubious content, or with the content itself, instigating important debates about the 'politics of algorithms' in both academic and popular publications (Ziewitz, 2016).[15] To give yet another example, recent discussions about 'creepy apps' (Shlovski et al., 2014) have highlighted problematic infringements, as free-to-download smart phone apps as innocuous as a 'flashlight' app collect a broad range of data from the phones on which they have been installed, including movement-related geo-locative data and phone-traffic related meta-data. Such scandals lift the lid on a dodgy world of data commerce (Rohle, 2007). As a last example, take the public leaks of personal information, such as those following the release of search engine query data by Yahoo. While Yahoo presented this data leak as a positive contribution to 'open' science and public knowledge, it was quickly established that the anonymized query data it had made public could fairly easily be de-anonymized, as geeks and journalists set out to identify users in the search engine data, a discovery that led to public debates about what should and should not be included in the definition of 'personal data' today (Gross, 2015; see also Rogers, 2013). Such public controversies and debates highlight that digital research, far from being removed from the concerns of society, touches on important societal and political processes (Boellstorf and Mauer, 2015). It also suggests that the manifold questions that digital social research has unleashed in recent years are irreversible, as these questions cannot be un-asked: what data is it permissible to extract from embedded infrastructures and personal devices for purposes of social research? What societies are revealed by data, and what kinds of knowledge claims can they support? Who owns the 'findings' and what does social research 'owe' its subjects and society at large?

What then does the 'digital' in digital sociology refer to?

The claims for a radically new, digital way of knowing society cannot simply be accepted at face value. But how *then* should we understand the implications of recent digital transformations for social enquiry? It is difficult to provide a simple answer to this question, partly because digital technology presents such a long-standing topic of sociology. In order to get a handle on the methodological and ethical issues flagged above, I believe we need to consider a fundamental ambiguity surrounding 'the digital' in the phrase 'digital sociology'. The 'digital' in digital sociology may denote at least three different things: it may refer to (1) the *topics* of social enquiry; (2) the *instruments and methods* of social research; (3) *platforms* for engaging with the audiences and publics of sociology. Depending on which of these aspects of the 'digital' we consider, we arrive at a very different understanding of what digital sociology is, and I therefore want to briefly introduce each of these three incarnations of the digital separately. A more general point also follows: given the broad range of uses and meanings of the 'digital' in sociology, it would be unwise to close down the question of 'what digital sociology is' too quickly, as would surely happen if we would attempt to give a single, 'total' definition of digital sociology in this first chapter. The following answers to the question 'what does the 'digital' in digital sociology refer to? are then not intended as a way of forcing a quick settlement of the definition of digital sociology. Rather, they are a way of opening the black box of digital social enquiry, in order to formulate an approach that can address at least some of the methodological and normative issues flagged above.

Phenomenon

First and foremost, 'the digital' presents sociology with an important societal phenomenon that requires investigation. As noted, the digitization of social life is itself nothing new. But as the digital touches on most dimensions of social life, from the most intimate details (how we wake up) to the widest global systems (the undermining of 'supply chain models' by ubiquitous computing; shifts in migrant travel routes), it takes on the aspect of what we called above a 'total social fact'. As a consequence, important new questions arise: the rise of social media platforms, mobile applications, new forms of data, and 'smart' infrastructures, inflect modes of practice or ways of living in distinctive ways. As an emerging architecture of social life, the digital has the capacity to transform ways of being, including processes and practices of transacting, knowing, sharing, electing, caring, travelling, campaigning, decision-making and so on. To return to the phenomenon with which I started this chapter, suicide, it seems that the digital has occasioned potentially complex changes in its associated practices and forms. Recuber (2015) has shown that the 'suicide note' is no longer what it was in digital societies: it is increasingly common for these last notes to be published online, with the consequence that what was previously a highly intimate form of communication, addressed only to close ones, is today becoming a more public-facing genre. The Samaritans are not the only ones experimenting with digital forms of intervention – there are multiple projects underway that seek to deploy digital analytics for mental care, as in the 'automated flagging for psychological health', developed by the Durkheim project, with funding from the US military. Such projects turn to social media platforms as potential sites for social care, bringing this sector into direct and intimate relations with digital industries (Davies, 2015a, p. 227).

As such, the example of 'digital suicide' brings into relief another critical feature of today's digital infrastructures, devices and practices. Insofar as they cut across existing social domains, digital arrangements do not only affect existing sectors and practices, they have the capacity to change relations between them.[16] There are abundant examples in many different sectors: in the area of health and well-being, so-called self-tracking technologies are changing relations between digital industries, the insurance sector and the care of the self, as insurance companies now offer discounts to customers who agree to use wearable devices like Fitbit to track their own health (Neff and Nafus, 2016).[17] In the area of civil society and social movements, connections are proliferating with a third domain, that of tech and digital innovation, as non-governmental organizations working on social and political causes like urban regeneration, have come together with the start-up sector, to give rise to a new 'civic tech sector' and new ways of social problem-solving, as in the 'FixMyStreet.org' project by MySociety, which allows citizens 'to discuss local problems like graffiti'.[18] Finally, in the area of transport, digital industries have been teaming up with car companies to develop new forms of 'intelligent mobility', such as the self-driving vehicles that bring together, not just automotive innovation and computing, but equally the governance of transport systems and everyday navigational practices in potentially new ways (Dennis and Urry, 2009; Forlano and Halpern, 2015). The digital then has the potential to transform relations among social sectors and practices, and this raises not only important social, political and ethical issues but is also likely to entail broader societal transformations.

We also need to consider something else: as digital infrastructures, devices and practices cut across existing domains, they have the capacity to give rise to new organizational forms. Across government, civil society, business, culture, education, politics, and everyday life, the 'digital' has been taken up as an occasion to develop and test new forms of coordination and mobilization, such as the 'collaborative economy' that combines social and economic forms of organization, as in services that facilitate house and car-sharing (Gill and Bialski, 2011); the 'data labs' that now sit in organizations from government to the media, or the 'hackatons' and 'data sprints' organized by activist, cultural, educational and commercial organizations (Irani, 2015). Finally, as these organizational forms and formats enter into wider circulation, it becomes increasingly clear that 'digitization' has specific societal effects, affecting particular forms and relations constitutive of social life (see also Clough et al., 2015). The digital dimension of social life is no longer well-captured by *general* distinctions that used to be prominent in digital social research, such as those between online and off-line, networked or not networked, embodied or dis-embodied, virtual and actual (Woolgar, 2002; Castells, 1996). Whereas earlier literatures highlighted these metaphysical transformations, todays digital transformations are giving rise to notable sociological effects: the digital is now associated with a variety of social transformations beyond virtualization and networking – such as experimentation, flexibilization, participation, privatization, optimization, radicalization and creativity. Each of these effects are fundamentally marked by normative ambivalence – they have both positive and negative dimensions, good and bad sides.

Part of the reason for this lies in a fundamental trope that accompanies projects of digital transformation, namely the widespread tendency to confer on the digital the capacity to solve social problems discussed above. Today there seem to be few if any problems – whether it is toxic waste or police violence – of which it is not claimed that it can be solved by digital means. As the saying goes: 'isn't there an app for that?'[19] To be sure, this belief in 'technological fixes' is not new: sociological studies have long directed critical attention to the logic by which technological innovation is privileged as an operator or 'engine' of change in modern societies: here, technology is routinely imagined as active and society as passive and 'to be acted upon' (Waijcman, 1991). From this perspective, the widespread investment of capacities for social change in the 'digital' in contemporary societies – the expectation that digital innovation can solve many if not most of our problems, from how to do the weekly shop to patient care and the organization of developmental aid – must itself be investigated, in terms of what broader changes it makes possible and impossible (Mackenzie, 2005). However, while 'solutionism' – the association of technical innovation with social problem-solving – is a long-standing phenomenon in knowledge-intensive societies (Popper, 2002 (1945); Morozov, 2013), in today's societies it is deployed towards specific effects. Some of these are listed above, but they also fundamentally include the displacement of responsibility for what were previously defined as public problems towards private actors: digital industries, NGOs, communities, selves. This is however far from a simple story: as digital arrangements cut across domains, they have the potential to unsettle *wider* distributions of authority and agency between the state, industry, civil society and other actors. The digital is today taken up by a *diversity* of actors as an occasion to bring about a re-distribution of capacities, privilege and power among actors and domains.

Method

We arrive at a rather different understanding of 'digital sociology' when we take 'digital' to refer, not to the topics, but to the *instruments* of social enquiry, to the methods and techniques of sociological research. Much of the recent writing and debates about new digital ways of knowing society treat the digital in this way: they investigate whether digital infrastructures make possible new ways of researching social life (Ruppert, Law and Savage, 2013). Recent debates about computational social science also presume that the digital presents essentially a new set of computational *methods and techniques* for researching society. This work proposes that the digital brings techniques and methods not traditionally considered part of the sociological tool-box into its purview, including automated data extraction and interactive data visualization (Halford et al., 2013; Mützel, 2015). It also usefully highlights a key feature of the new digital networked infrastructures and devices for social research: their programmability and adjustability (Weltevrede, 2015).[20] As we will see in Chapters 3 and 4, digital devices do not just make available *ready-made* data and tools for social research, they can and often need to be *actively configured* to capture some data and not others, deploy some measures rather than others, and so on. Partly for this reason, the development of practical and technical computing skills assumes special importance in digital sociology (Brauer, 2011). However, to accept the idea that computational techniques, in and of themselves, are 'new' to sociology, is to indulge in some serious forgetting of history.

Sociologists have been using computational techniques and methods for at least as long as they have been studying computational societies. Quantitative sociologists have been working with the statistical software package SPSS from the late 1960 onwards (Uprichard et al., 2008), and before that sociologists used punch cards, in which they inputted their data in order to get them processed by a 'supercomputer' which, as Sally Wyatt (2008) remembers, involved a long process of preparing the cards and then walking over to the building that housed the supercomputer (see also Driscoll, 2012). In the 1980s, the invention of the computer already figured on the list of the most important advances in the social sciences of the twentieth century (Deutsch et al., 1986). Sociologists have then been 'tooling up' for many decades, and importantly, this interest in using digital technology to study social life has been shared across many different methodological approaches and traditions, from the sample survey analysts crunching statistical data to the more 'qualitative' conversation analysts who have long used audio software to transcribe 'social talk' into written form (Ashmore et al., 2004). Going further back, it is clear that calculative technologies similar to todays digital research techniques have served as instruments of social research since at least the early twentieth century. This includes the design of survey questionnaires (Didier, 2009), opinion polling (Osborne and Rose, 1999), and the use of visual techniques in network analysis (Mayer, 2012). It is also important to recognize that not all digital ways of knowing society are primarily about computing in the narrow sense, i.e. coding, as for example in the case of virtual ethnography (Hine, 2000) and 'unobtrusive methods' (Lee and Fielding, 2008) – methods that aim to observe interaction and wider social phenomena online and to offer interpretations of these.[21]

The 'digital' in digital sociology can then neither be reduced to a simple story of the 'becoming computational' of social research, now that researchers have at their disposal programmable 'social' technologies from online platforms to smart phones. Sociology's methods became digital a long time before the rise of today's digital methods. But at the same time it seems fair to say that in recent years none of sociology's methods has remained unaffected by digitization, from the conduct of ethnographic fieldwork by digital means (Murthy, 2008), to the analysis of social networks and actor-networks that are now maintained and sometimes formed by digital means (Newman et al., 2007; Latour et al., 2012). As already noted, sociologists believe that the ever-expanding range of digital infrastructures for data capture and analysis available across social life do make possible the development of new methods for knowing society (Savage and Burrows, 2007; Rogers, 2013). But it is not the digitization of methods as such, but rather the digital re-mediation of established social research methods in contemporary society that raises new methodological questions, as I will discuss in Chapter 3.

There is also a more complicated problem with attempts to define digital sociology in terms of the uptake of new digital research instruments: the digital devices that some believe make possible a 'new' way of knowing society in many cases do *not* satisfy the definition of an 'instrument' of social research. They do not facilitate the kind of transparent deployment that is presumed in the idea of the digital as 'tool' for researching social phenomena. As I will discuss, it is far from self-evident that today's digital infrastructures make available 'society' or even 'social life' as an object of research. At least from the mid 1990s onwards, researchers in the social sciences and humanities have sought to harness the Internet for social and cultural enquiry, and much of this work is grouped under the label 'Internet research', a helpfully ambiguous term which precisely leaves *un-decided* whether the Internet constitutes an object or method of social enquiry. Indeed, many social media researchers and digital sociologists would reject the ambition to 'purify' the object of digital social research: in studying Web content, online forums, email, RSS feeds, social media platforms and so on, these researchers refuse to decide unequivocally whether their object of enquiry is social life or media technology. Instead, they refer to digital platforms and devices as *both a topic and resource of social enquiry* (Housley et al., 2014; Burgess et al., 2015).

Platform

There is third and final referent of the digital that deserves our attention: it also includes the channels, settings and instruments that sociologists use to communicate their knowledge and engage with research participants, communities and publics. Remarkably (but not coincidentally), much of the work that comes under the term 'digital sociology' has a public-facing quality. In Britain there is an active digital sociology study group, which hosts regular public events and maintains a lively online presence (Carrigan, 2016), and much of the international debate about digital sociology has been a debate about public sociology: it has focused on the question of whether and how digital infrastructures, devices and methods make possible new ways for sociologists to make their knowledge public and engage with audiences (Carrigan, 2016; Healy, forthcoming). The Australian sociologist Deborah Lupton (2014) lists the public promotion of sociology 'using social media and online tools' as one of the three 'core' activities of digital sociology. One of the first articles to use the phrase 'Digital Sociology' (Wynn, 2009) discussed how sociologists could use digital devices like blogs in their teaching. Generally speaking, it seems that 'digital sociology' first entered the sociological lexicon as a marker *not* of a new empirical approach – a new way of collecting data or implementing social research methods – but as a new way of communicating sociology, using digital 'tools' such as blogging to present sociology in more creative, interactive, engaging and practice-based ways (Back, 2012).

One consequence of this emphasis on the practical, pedagogical and public aspects of social research is that much work on digital sociology adopts the perspective of a user of digital technology. By virtue of this alone, digital sociology reduces the distance between researchers of and participants in digital social life. However, the increasingly common use of social media, apps and the like by sociologists does not only affect the relations between sociology and its external audiences, but also the research process itself. As I will discuss in Chapter 5, digital platforms make it easier for sociologists to involve research participants more closely and actively in their ongoing projects. As such, work in digital sociology re-activates older, participatory approaches in social enquiry, such as action research and the interactive research styles developed by the early proponents of social network analysis, for example, that of Jacob Moreno in the early twentieth century, who notably used social network visualizations to involve research participants in discussions about their social positions (Mayer, 2012; Giessmann, 2009). Digital platforms also arguably enable new forms of interaction between researchers and participants, and this especially insofar as these platforms present *a shared infrastructure* of social life and social research. For example, in her sociological study of the valuation of 'data' in social media, the British sociologist Bev Skeggs (Skeggs and Yuill, 2016) did not simply keep her respondents informed about the progress of her study, or solicit their view on the findings. The research project as a whole was premised on exchange: while respondents allowed the researchers to log in to their accounts and ongoing social media activities, the project in return provided participants with access to the ongoing analysis and visualization of their personal data, performed as part of the project via the project website.

The uptake of digital tools by sociologists for publicity and participatory purposes may also result in a noticeable blurring of the boundaries between what are traditionally defined as separate phases in the 'research cycle' (Marres and Weltevrede, 2013), such as the collection and analysis of data, and the communication of findings to communities and wider audiences. An example of this can be found in an article published by Les Back and Shamser Sinha (2013) in which they report on their research on asylum seekers in Britain, and the use of SMS phone texting by the UK Home Office to notify people they have no 'right to remain'. The article includes screenshots of the actual content of the text messages – including a 'go home' message that one recipient received while already on the plane, and reports on 'regular data drops' of asylum seekers' mobile phone numbers by private data brokers to the UK Border Agency.[22] The publication of these findings became the starting point for new social research: as Back and Sinha's findings were reported by the *Guardian* newspaper, they became the subject of exchanges on Twitter, and Back and Sinha's article thus served as an 'elicitation device' (Back and Sinha, 2013; see also Lezaun and Soneryd, 2007): eliciting online conversations among relative strangers about the issues involved, the initial research gave rise to a new kind of social research object. Far from signalling the end of the research process, the publicization of results served as an occasion for further enquiry.

Whether as object, method or platform, 'the digital' then presents not one but several important dimensions of sociological enquiry: it is a central topic of sociological investigation, occasions projects of methodological innovation, and helps to realize engagement initiatives, and it has done so for many decades. While it is true that different sociologists have tended to concentrate on the one aspect or the other (on the digital as object, method *or* platform), it's important to note that the three different dimensions of digital sociology are non exclusive. Arguably, indeed, now that the digital is becoming a total social fact, *all* digital sociology projects must somehow address each of the three 'digitals', and ask the question: how does the digital inflect my object of study, my methods, and the communication of my work? The different elements – object, methods, platform – can also be taken to refer to different aspects of research design in digital sociology: what is this study about? What methods do we use? How do we communicate our research? The commitment to engage actively with these questions rather then bracket them could be a useful working definition of digital sociology. However, while each of the above three aspects of digital sociology is important in its own right, we fail to grasp something crucial about digital sociology as long as we consider them in isolation. This is because many of the observations about a possible new, digital way of knowing society that I introduced in Section 2 and 3 straddle the boundaries between the objects, methods and platforms of sociology, and point towards developments that operate across this distinction.[23] What is more, many of these cross-cutting digital developments affect digital social research and digital social life simultaneously, and this raises further challenges for social enquiry, which remain out of view as long as we approach the digital as *either* a topic *or* a method of social enquiry.

Problems with digital ways of knowing society:
bias, instrumentalism, interactivity

The recent interest in 'digital sociology' cannot simply be explained in terms of the emergence of radically new, 'digital' objects or instruments of social research: 'the digital' does not, strictly speaking, present sociology with a new phenomenon, and neither does it enable research techniques that are strictly 'new' in and of themselves. But this doesn't mean that nothing important has changed. The 'rise' of digital sociology is the result of a peculiar set of cross-cutting developments. If the empirical and analytic capacities and scope for intervention of social research are being transformed today, these changes *are strongly dependent on complex technological changes happening across society*, whether it is the popularity of social networking tools or the embedding of GPS tracking technologies in mobile phones. Considering the dependence of digital social research on such wider socio-technical transformations, what is striking about many pitches for a new digital way of knowing society is the *highly instrumental* coding of digital technologies they imply. Digital data, notwithstanding their origins in socio-technical infrastructures, are expected to act as 'windows on the social world':[24] to record social life without the digital leaving too much of a mark on the data. As French parents allegedly tell their toddlers, the methodology of computational social science demands of the digital that it does not make itself noticed ('ne te fait pas remarquer!'). Most of this work assumes a representational framework.

While computational social scientists were quick to take advantage of the data that digital infrastructures made available, they left undiscussed some of the large methodological challenges of studying society with digital technology: how exactly can we assume that digital infrastructures disclose societal phenomena, given the partial roll-out of these infrastructures, their interactive features, and the general opacity of these vast machines? As noted, sociologists, as well as social, cultural and media researchers in other fields, have long highlighted problems with this instrumental deployment of digital networked data and tools in social enquiry, including problems of digital bias (boyd and Crawford, 2012). However, in doing so, these critics also introduced into the discussion an understanding of bias that differed from that assumed in representational methodologies: in their view, bias does not just involve a negative, distorting influence of the research apparatus on the 'social phenomenon' under investigation; rather the very constitution of digital data involves dynamics that are at once social and technical, their 'content' is a consequence both of how digital technologies work and what people do with them, *in ways that are difficult to dis-entangle* (Wagner-Pacifici et al., 2015). In part, these critiques of digital bias must be understood as arguments for better, more robust empirical research designs, calling on sociologists to clarify how we can extract sociologically robust data from messy socio-technical assemblages (Ruppert, Law and Savage, 2013). But some of these critiques also take aim at the wider methodological frameworks of digital social science: In positing that their object of analysis is 'society' (or 'behaviour'), this research is limited in its ability to illuminate the interaction between technologies, social practices and knowledge in digital societies. From this perspective, then, the problem with the new digital ways of knowing society is not just that they tend to overstate their capacity to produce new knowledge about the social world. The problem is the very framing of the object of enquiry: as long as the object of computational social science is defined as human behaviour or experience, it is not well-positioned to address – as a positive, empirical topic for digital sociology – the question of how technology, sociality and knowledge – and much else besides – interact in digital societies.

This, however, is a long-standing topic of enquiry for sociology; as noted in the introduction, sociologists working in interpretative traditions have long taken a special interest in the interaction between technologies, social practices and knowledge, and so have social studies of science and technology.[25] This interest goes back to the Weberian insight that social action stands out for its orientation towards ideas, and the classic, pragmatist-inspired Thomas theorem of 1923, which highlights the importance of interactivity between concepts and social life: 'When people perceive things to be real, they will be real in their consequences.' In digital societies, such dynamics of interactivity notably involve feedback between people, information and technologies, as well as environments (Suchman, 2007a). Furthermore, these dynamics become only more consequential, given the interactive nature of digital technologies themselves, and the ways they involve ongoing, dynamic loops between users adjusting actions and infrastructures adjusting information feeds: socio-technico-epistemic dynamics of interactivity – between people, technology and knowledge – then seem of undeniable importance to the study of digital social phenomena (Mackenzie et al., 2015). Strikingly however, precisely these dynamics risk to fall by the wayside when narrow definitions of the empirical object of computational social research are upheld, which tend to assume a strict

separation between the human action to be studied and the technological bias which has to be 'corrected for'.

Part of the problem with the new digital ways of knowing society is,
then, that they tend to disregard the positive phenomenon of interactivity, focusing mainly on addressing the negative problem of bias.[26]
And this highlights a difference in perspective between sociology
and computational social science. However, it would seem a mistake
to understand this difference mainly in terms of a 'divide' between
qualitative and quantitative approaches, or as an expression of the
'two cultures' (Snow, 1959) marking the humanities on the one
hand, and the sciences on the other. To be sure, differences between
'hard' scientific or quantitative approaches and 'soft' interpretative
or qualitative ones are a familiar trope in both academic and public
debates about knowledge but, as many scholars have argued, the
'digital' may precisely provide a way *out* of this all-too-familiar opposition. These scholars flag, for example, the potential for art-science
collaboration in digital research, and the mixture of interpretative
and calculative forms of analysis that occurs in computationally
enabled research (Latour et al., 2012; Myers, 2006). Indeed, it seems
necessary to move beyond this opposition, if we are to bring within
the scope of social enquiry the dynamics of 'interactivity' between
digital technology, knowledge, society. In the social sciences, the
study of interactivity, such as the effects of classification on behaviour described in the introduction, has classically been thought of as
requiring a qualitative approach, and thus, a rejection of calculative
methodologies. But this may no longer be the case. In digital societies, dynamics of 'interactivity' notably include non-human entities,
such as algorithms and computationally equipped environments.
Furthermore, 'interpretation' here is *not* an exclusive feature of
'human' knowledge or experience, but increasingly can be taken to
include the computations of technology and environments (Lury,
2012).

Indeed, in many ways the empirical ambition of digital sociology –
to study society with digital technologies – equally goes against
established methodological frameworks in qualitative research.
Today's work in digital sociology deviates from the analytic frameworks on which qualitative sociologists previously relied in the study
of the Internet. Many qualitative sociologies of the Internet were
highly critical of the instrumental deployment of the Internet for
social research. Slater (2002), for instance, argued that the Internet
must be studied as either a 'social artefact' or a 'social space' in its
own right. This perspective affirms that the 'digital' inflects and

enables social life, but it explicitly excludes the possibility that digital technology may be the source of 'representations' of a pre-existing social reality, at least insofar as the rigorous representation of social phenomena is concerned that is required by sociology (Slater, 2002; see also Hine, 2000). From the mid 2000s onwards, there has been a discernable broadening of the 'research methods' taken up by qualitative researchers in the social sciences and humanities, bringing the empirical deployment of the 'digital apparatus' within purview of social and humanities approaches (Snee et al., 2015; Lee et al., 2008). However, specifically digital and Internet-based methods developed in the social sciences and humanities – such as virtual ethnography (Hine, 2000) and online content analysis (Herring, 2009), – are most commonly considered 'Internet methods', *meaning methods for studying Internet-related phenomena*, such as 'virtual communities' or 'digital media spheres'. They were not generally accepted *or even framed* as methods for researching social phenomena.[27] In contrast to this, digital sociology affirms the empirical capacities of distributed computational arrangements, i.e. the ability of digital infrastructures, technologies and practices to render analysable social phenomena transcending these technological arrangements. At the same time, however, I will argue in this book that if we are to accomplish this re-orientation in digital social research without restricting its scope or otherwise impoverishing it, we must nevertheless continue to strive for a methodological objective adopted by Internet research, namely to affirm the constitutive role of digital technology in the mediation of social life.

The coming out of the technology of sociology

What, then, should we make of the provocation that is digital sociology? Where to go from here? There are at least two scenarios for the development of digital sociology which each have their drawbacks and advantages, but I have a clear preference for one of them. The first, tempting but in my view ultimately unsatisfactory option would be to work towards the re-instatement of the above, established division of labour in digital social research: to uphold a strict division between two different analytics approaches, those that frame the digital as an *object* of social enquiry, and those that deploy it as an *instrument* for researching social life. This 'road map' for the further development of digital sociology has much going for it, not least that it is in line with wider institutional divisions in sociology, between substantive fields such as the sociology *of* technology and the sociology *of* media (digital as topic), and methodological approaches like statistics, discourse analysis, social network analysis and so on (digital as instrument). This choice would also be broadly in line with established, disciplinary framings of digital social research: qualitative methods like ethnography can be used to study digital communities as a topic, while quantitative methods like statistical analysis rely on digital technology to study society.[28]

This approach translates the provocative claim for new, 'specifically digital' ways of knowing society into a much less provocative, more easily acceptable claim to knowledge, one that depends on 'the digital' as an infrastructural condition of possibility for knowing society, but is largely in line with existing methodological frameworks. However, there is also another choice, one that says that the early visionaries got it exactly right when they claimed that what is emerging today is a *specifically digital* way of knowing society. This digital way of knowing society unsettles established methodological frameworks, insofar as it includes technological effects in the social phenomena to be interrogated. When analysing a network of Facebook contacts, we are studying both the effects of particular digital media practices, but potentially also, a broader social phenomenon. We then recognize and indeed affirm that digital infrastructures, devices and practices pose highly provocative and interesting challenges for social enquiry, as they call into question the very convention according to which the digital is to be framed either as object or as instrument of enquiry, but not as both.

In this book, I will propose that we need to get deeper into this trouble, before we can get out of it. If we are to grasp the methodological implications of 'the digital' for social enquiry, we must begin by recognizing that in many cases the digital does not feature as either object or instrument of social enquiry, but precisely as a bit of both, and in many other capacities as well, which we must interrogate. I will then propose that we must stay with the trouble (Haraway, 2010) implicit in the proposition that 'specifically digital' ways of knowing society are emerging today. To be sure, there are many moments in which it makes complete sense to treat 'the digital' as either an object or an instrument of enquiry, and to switch frames between them as necessary, but such frame-switching will not do as an overall methodological strategy in digital sociology. As long as we keep switching between approaching the digital as topic and as method of social enquiry, we will remain dissatisfied with digital sociology. We are now in a position to specify what the source of this dissatisfaction is. Many define digital social research in terms of the uptake of 'new data' and 'new techniques' for understanding and intervening in society – and this 'instrumental' definition falls short on at least two fronts. First, the instrumental definition of digital sociology in terms of new data and tools is *incomplete*, because it has very little to say about the changing role of digital technology in social life. While theorists and researchers across fields have made *big* claims about the type of knowledge and interventions the digital makes possible, many nevertheless end up offering *disappointingly narrow* definitions of digital sociology. As Dourish and Bell (2011) point out: they mostly define it as a sequence of data capture, analysis and feedback. However, digital infrastructures, practices and devices are also enabling wide-ranging changes in social practices and relations themselves. The instrumental definition of digital sociology does not equip us very well to investigate these changes: it invites us to 'step inside the box' of digital data capture and analysis, asking that we accept digital technology as *the frame* of social enquiry, but this does not enable us to investigate the changing roles of digital technology *in* social life. These latter transformations should surely be on the research agenda of digital sociology.

Second, instrumental definitions of digital social research not only have a tendency to overstate the newness of digital sociology, they also risk misrepresenting it. As Duncan Watts (2004) has argued, most of the methods of the new computational social science tend to consist of combinations of older and newer techniques, architectures, methods, and ways of doing things. Recent work in network analysis and visualization, for example, draws on long, well-established methodological traditions in social science (see Chapter 3). But the problem with overstated claims to newness is not only that they are inaccurate. They also blind us to the possible failures of digital social research to innovate: while the sources of data and some of the analytic techniques may be new, the methodological and theoretical frameworks of much digital social research are deeply familiar (Healy, 2015). While celebrating a 'new' form of knowledge of society, propositions put forward under this banner as a matter of fact *re-establish* methodological frameworks that in many areas of social science are considered outdated, such as the idea that there exists such a thing as 'naturally occurring' data in society. Work in digital social science, then, does not just pose the risk of overwhelming us with innovation, but far more seriously, it puts us in danger of reverting to outdated methodological frameworks, that is, of failing to advance sociological agendas.

But how then should we define digital sociology? I would here like to offer a minimal description, to be elaborated over the chapters to follow. Digital sociology, by its very name, foregrounds the computational dimension of social enquiry as well as social life. From this vantage point, 'digital sociology' not only entails a shift in our ways of "knowing society', but also in the ways sociology relates to digital technology (Back, 2010): the digital no longer features as either object or method of social enquiry, but refers to the setting, or field, from which social enquiry operates. Adrian Mackenzie and colleagues (2015) provide an especially helpful account, proposing that to practise digital sociology is to locate social enquiry 'in the field of devices', which they describe as a 'complex weave of technical elements [..] inhabited by people who react to, who experience and are affected by durable and transient calls to order their actions with and through devices (Mackenzie et al., 2015, p. 367). To assume this kind of definition is to break with a long-standing habit in sociology: most sociologists aren't used to characterizing their own practice in terms of its technological or material dimensions (Wakeford, 2016). There has never been something like 'electronic' or 'magnetic' sociology, not even in the period that sociologists started recording their interviews on tape recorders, to give one example (Back, 2010). Indeed, the 'technology of sociology' used to be a derogatory term: the phrase was used by the post-war sociologist Paul Lazarsfeld (1975) to characterize dull, un-imaginative sociological studies, research which did not tailor its questions and methods to the topic at hand, but simply applied generic, ready-made research protocols to whatever topic presented itself.

Of course this does not mean that imaginative and inspiring sociological studies in previous times did not involve the use of technology. But the technological dimension of social research tended to be 'bracketed' in the reporting and narration of this research in written publications. Indeed, the bracketing of the technologies of knowledge has long served as a powerful *methodological convention* in sociology and many other fields (Latour and Woolgar, 2013 (1979); Ashmore et al., 2004): academic writing in sociology tended not to say very much about how, practically, 'they did it', that is, about their technological and material practices. Often, of course, this reticence has good reasons, namely to maintain a focus on the empirical reality under investigation. However, as social researchers are today increasingly engaging with digital data and tools, this methodological convention is becoming less and less tenable. *Partly because of their complexity and relative opacity, the uptake of digital data and tools directs attention to social enquiry as a socio-material-technical practice* (Marres and Weltevrede, 2013). As a consequence, almost the opposite of Lazarsfeld's definition of the 'technology of sociology' applies today: if we are to avoid generic research and successfully tailor our approach to the phenomenon at hand, we must take more of an interest in the technological dimension of social enquiry (see also Lury and Wakeford, 2012).

The 'rise' of digital sociology, then, signals a 're-valuation' or 'un-bracketing' of the role of technology in social research: it indicates a different way of appreciating the technological dimensions of social enquiry, one that questions the separability of method and technique in social research.[29] Speaking only partly tongue in-cheek, we could say that digital sociology signals the 'coming out' of technology as a significant dimension of social enquiry (Marres, 2012c [2015]). It signals a transformation in the attention paid to the role of technology in social enquiry. Defined as such, digital sociology is rather like 'environmental sociology': most if not all sociological phenomena have an environmental dimension (and so does most sociological work), but we would certainly **not** characterize all sociology as 'environmental sociology': it depends on whether we *make something of* this – digital, environmental – dimension of the phenomenon, method or practice (Back, 2010). In many cases, to be sure, the digital like the environmental dimension of sociology is best treated as 'forgettable' and this also means that digital sociology presents an inherently partial perspective, and certainly is not inherently relevant to the whole of sociology. Defined as a form of attention, however, digital sociology is the opposite of a sociology that treats the digital as a mere instrument – as a pure means to an end, which does not affect its purpose. A device-aware sociology, that is, is the opposite of a sociology that claims that the digital specification of its topics or practices is of little interest. To be sure, this is a rather fluid way of characterizing the field, but it places a specific requirement on sociology: we should render more explicit the role of digital technology in social research, and attempt to develop sociology not just 'of' or 'by means of', but 'with' the digital (Back, 2010): to practise a device-aware sociology. That is also to say, the un-bracketing of the technology of sociology is far from already accomplished. Some time ago, social theorists made the important argument that in information-intensive societies, enquiry into social life cannot remain separate from society's infrastructures, but must become immanent to its informational circuits (Lash, 2002). But since then sociologists have been searching for ways to translate this insight into viable research practices. There are at least two risks here: The first is that we bow to the myth of technology-driven research. The second risk is 'reflexivity', or rather the wrong kind of reflexivity, one in which an awareness of the technological dimension of social research translates into inward-looking, self-regarding forms of enquiry.

Regarding the first risk, this is best known by the name of 'technological determinism', and consists of the belief that technology is the principal cause of – or more minimally the 'driver' – of innovation, a belief which then gets extended into the assumption that it must be privileged as a driver of advances in knowledge. Sociologists of science and technology, while interested in the relations between the former and the latter, have been critical of this general belief, most importantly because it fails to recognize the active contributions made by other entities – people, ideas, environments, and so on – to the realization of innovation or the advancement of knowledge (Bowker and Star, 2000). Deterministic ideals of techno-science promote a vision in which 'knowledge' stands at the receiving, passive end of innovation, with 'technology' taking the credit as 'a force of innovation' while, in actual practice, advances in knowledge and understanding tend to be a collective accomplishment, of people and machines, and much else besides (Suchman, 2007a). As noted, the critique of technological determinism has been around for many decades, but many narratives about a new 'data-driven' research present only thinly veiled variations on this old theme, and these narratives, to be sure, deserve another round of critical analyses from sociology, exposing technology-driven forms of progress for the partly false myth that they are. Indeed, as today not just science – or the economy – is placed at the receiving end of the 'technological drivers', *but sociology itself*, it becomes ever more important to offer constructive alternatives to the deterministic vision: our task is to imagine ways of practising sociology *with* technology, an approach that recognizes the *participation* of technology in the doing of social research, but refuses to inflate its role to that of the principal 'driver' of sociological knowledge. We need to clearly establish, then, the difference between tool-driven social research and device-aware sociology.

However, this reconstructive project brings with it further risks, including those associated with 'reflexivity.' A call for more device-awareness in social enquiry may easily be misunderstood as a call for an inward-looking investigation of sociological practice itself, one that takes a disproportionate interest in sociology's own technological operations. This is not an insignificant risk, but it is smaller than might appear, insofar as it would be a mistake to assume that the devices of digital sociology are somehow located inside sociological practice: digital devices of social enquiry are not internal to sociological practice as conventionally conceived. The outing of digital technology as a notable dimension of social research, precisely *cannot be understood as an event 'internal' to sociology*. Indeed, it is far more accurate to say that wider apparatus' of social research are *being outed* today: digital transformations of the societal infrastructures for social data capture and analysis are not 'spearheaded' by sociology or even the university sector, but arise from developments across organizations, industry, governments and everyday life, i.e. all those fields across society involved in the configuration of digital platforms, mobile and 'smart' systems for social research, broadly conceived. Digital ways of knowing societies are emerging across social research and social life, they are being negotiated and contested between disciplines and fields – between the university, industry and society – and not reducible to a singular, determinate cause or practice.

Conclusion

To determine the salient features and issues of emerging digital ways of knowing society is the task I take on in this book, but we are now in a position to give a provisional answer to our question 'what is digital sociology?' First, we can be clear about what it is not. It is not a completely new way of knowing society, made possible by new data and new research techniques which in turn are made possible by new technology. Not only do the new data and new methods – in more ways than tends to be acknowledged – resemble the old data and old methods. They also are more unstable and more contested than the declaration of their newness allows us to recognize. The claim that the digital enables a 'new way of knowing society', it is now clear, overstates the capacity of digital infrastructures to solve sociology's problems. We are faced instead with proliferating controversies about what are the correct methods, what is the right scale, who can know, who should be able to access what data, and who has the right to appropriate data and author findings? These questions are shot through with ethical and political issues, including accountability, discrimination, privacy, ownership and autonomy, as I will discuss in the next chapters, and many of these issues have to do with the displacement of 'social research capacity' to private, digital industries. But many of the above questions present, at the same time, genuine problems of research. At least some of the visions of the new digital sociology falsely presumed that digital infrastructures were already configured for sociological analysis. As we shall see, these infrastructures are configured for many purposes, including those of marketing research, but social enquiry, alas, is not self-evidently among these. The configur-ability of digital arrangements for sociological purposes is contested, at stake, and needs to be tested and demonstrated.

This is why we need to investigate how digital infrastructures can be re-purposed for social enquiry (Rogers, 2013; Weltevrede, 2015). The 'rise' of digital sociology puts at stake far more than only the data, techniques and methods of social enquiry. 'The digital' does not just present sociology with new data sources or instruments, but has the potential to displace the very relations that constitute social enquiry. As I will discuss in the next chapter, the digital has the capacity to reconfigure relations between researchers and researched, between research and its 'contexts of application,' and between society and social science. To conclude with one last example of such changing relations, we can think here of the Creepy Facebook Graph Search. This search function has been released (and re-released) on a number of occasions over the last years, and renders social media user profiles searchable by attributes. This first of all presents a forceful example of the embedding of a social form of analysis in popular digital platforms. But equally important are the ways in which this application puts 'social methods' into the hands of social media users, and the problems that flow from this. Within hours of Facebook launching the new feature, users started running and capturing problematic queries, such as 'girls who are single, live nearby and like getting drunk'.[30] A range of such problematic queries was soon catalogued and viewable on the blogging platform Tumblr,[31] something which clarifies how pivotal the role of user communities becomes for successful 'digital critique' in quick-paced digital societies. (What slow, sociological analysis has to offer in return, I will discuss in Chapter 6.)

Digital sociology, as I would like to show, involves the experimental re-configuration of relations between social research and its publics, between data and methods, knowledge and intervention, in ways that are both highly problematic and offer the promise of renewing social enquiry and its role in society. While this too, is a rather open-ended definition, it certainly does not follow that the *tasks of digital sociology are open-ended.* Insofar as 'the digital' operates upon the relations between social life and social analysis, it presents a determinate matter of concern for sociology, a problematic situation in which sociology is directly implicated. As digital infrastructures, devices and practices emerge as one of the primary settings in which social life is rendered researchable today, the relative capacity of sociology to know society, as well as the relevance of sociological knowledge to social life and society at large is directly at stake. To formulate and place pertinent requirements on this evolving digital research infrastructure – how do these machines need to be configured in order to serve sociological enquiry? – is an urgent project, and one that requires engagement with specificities.

One of the specificities that will concern me in this book is that of the relations between different competencies in social research, not least between those of computing and sociology. As noted, for some digital social research places new demands of literacy on sociologists, who must learn computing skills in order to take advantage of the programmability of research infrastructures for purposes of social research (Munk, 2013). As I hope this chapter makes clear, the requirements are more varied and more symmetrical: we need communication of skills and sensibilities in both directions, between sociology and computing. Otherwise, demands for sociologists to learn computing skills become just another instance of the asymmetric myth of technology (computing) as driver of knowledge (sociology), figuring the former as new and active, and the latter as old and passive. Indeed, both sociologists and computer scientists have criticized asymmetrical approaches to the relations between their disciplines: both have refused to enter into a service relationship with the other (Dourish and Bell, 2011). This then raises the question: what sociological sensibilities should inform digital ways of knowing society? My answer in this book will be to emphasize methodological skills. However, we should at the same time not shy away from recognizing *how difficult it is to separate computational and sociological ways of knowing*: computer scientists have been involved in the 'analysis' of society at least as long as sociologists have been working with computational technologies (Procter et al., 2013). The most important question is then not how sociology and computing relate, but instead: how does the digital occasion the reconfiguring of relations between social life and social analysis across disciplines? How can sociology participate in this wider process of experimental re-configuration of relations between social science, computing and society? These are the questions of digital sociology, and they are explicitly partial questions. Digital sociology is ultimately a form of awareness, nothing more, nothing less.

2
What makes digital technologies social?

'I'd like to augment this tool with an online community – This will give us more data.'

Thus spoke a developer of a software application for data-driven learning, during a presentation to an interdisciplinary audience, in March 2014. No doubt, the confident assertion that it is possible to design, 'program' or generate social arrangements like community can also be found in other settings, as when architects or artists are called upon to create a sense of community through neighbourhood interventions, like the design of a play area (Marres, Guggenheim et al., forthcoming). Nevertheless, the development of digital ways of knowing and engaging with social life across fields and disciplines has brought with it some remarkable assumptions about what makes up the 'social': today, digital technologies are ascribed strikingly powerful capacities when it comes to the creation, manipulation and elaboration of social bonds, and the above quote can serve as an indication of this. More generally speaking, in recent years a widening circle of experts, commentators and critics have claimed that a new, close relationship is forming in our societies between the 'digital' and the 'social'. The two are now often equated in professional and public parlance: digital platforms are called social media and platform-based services – from car-sharing to freecycle initiatives – are known as the social economy. We should keep in mind that a tendency to rhetoricize technology – to cover it over with non-technical vocabulary – has long been a defining feature of the computerization of social life (Woolgar, 2002). But in the last decade or so 'the social' has taken pride of place among other useful labels (such as participation, and new services).

An especially significant event in this regard, of course, was the branding of new, online platforms as 'social media' in the mid 2000s, as companies like Facebook led the way in re-labelling digital communication and engagement as 'social networking', and developed technical architectures and highly popular applications in support of this objective, to the point that the social media scholar Bernhard Rieder could playfully observe in 2007: 'Facebook: that's the social!' (see also van Dijck, 2013).[1] However, while online platforms have played a critical role in forging connections between the digital and the social, it is *not* limited to them, but extends to other digital arrangements, and other domains. Digital industries such as IBM have in recent years made the development of what they call 'social technology' their stated objective, which they explain as the project to 'connect[..] people across all levels of an organization' or to 'engage directly with customers to build lasting, meaningful relationships'.[2] The forging of a connection between digital innovation and sociality also affects domains beyond innovation, like the economy and public politics, and indeed, the capacity to transform these other domains by way of the digital seems partly the point, i.e. what this connection is meant to enable. For example, the commentator Will Hutton has opposed the social entrepreneurship of Palo Alto to the 'anti-social' economy of austerity Britain,[3] and in doing so, he too seemed to sign up to the argument that what makes the digital economy different from other economies is that the former is more 'social', that it is more committed to investment in and maintenance of community. Policy think tanks like Demos in the UK, furthermore, have written reports advocating a new form of 'social' government, which they characterize as a government that is more responsive to and engaged with publics, and achieves this by making use of digital platforms like Twitter to communicate with them (Davies, 2015b). These arguments can be called into question, but we can observe a tendency, in public and promotional discourse, to evaluate the contribution of digital technologies to any sector in terms of their ability to make it 'more social', which means something like 'more engaging', but also 'less dependent on formal institutional frameworks', and much else besides.

We are dealing here with a complex development, and no doubt, the fortunes of the 'social' framing of the digital may wane, even if momentarily, as happened with other frames, such as 'cyberspace' and 'virtual worlds' – which drew on metaphysical and anthropological ideas about exotic other worlds. But the social phase in digital innovation poses a special challenge for sociology: it namely has brought into circulation ideas about the 'social' which are at odds with sociological understandings of what is after all their core concern. As I will discuss in what follows, prevalent discourses about social media and social technology suggest that digital technology has only recently 'become social', and from a sociological perspective, this is decidedly strange, and indeed simply implausible. As discussed in Chapter 1, social and cultural researchers have been studying the social aspects of computational technologies for many decades. They have relied on computational tools and data to study social life for at least as long or even longer (Uprichard et al., 2008). From the perspective of social research, then, both digital technology and media *were* already social, well before the advent of 'social media' (Coleman, 2012; Papacharissi, 2015).[4] However, even if social researchers across disciplines believe that the labels 'social media' and 'social technology' are based on misunderstandings, this of course does not mean that they can dismiss the importance of these phenomena. As suggested above, the widespread efforts to approximate digital technology and sociality have significant implications for everyday life, for the economy and politics, and indeed, for the very status and role of the social in digital societies.

As I will discuss in this chapter, the approximation of the digital and the social has significant potential implications for sociality itself. A crucial objective of social media and social technology is to enable particular operations upon social life, such as the generation of new social ties, or as the parlance has it, to 'augment' sociality. In the digital context, social relations are not treated as 'given', but as something that can be 'enhanced' or 'generated' and 'deployed' towards practical purposes. Many sociologists and media scholars have been highly critical of this instrumental coding of sociality, as it goes against deep-seated assumptions and values, such as the notion that to sustain social relations is an 'end in itself' (Marres and Gerlitz, forthcoming). Couldry and van Dijck (2015) have argued that social media aren't 'social' at all, and must in fact be called antisocial: digital arrangements tend to frame sociality in instrumental terms, as something that is deployable to secure other goods (influence, data, attention, wealth, and so on), and, Couldry and van Dijck argue, this organization of sociality first and foremost serves the ends of digital industries and their clients, and not primarily those of communities and other social groupings. As such, the approximation of the digital and the social, in our societies, may well signal an unravelling of social logics (Couldry and van Dijck, 2015; Goldberg, 2016). However, there are not only important differences, but also similarities and resonances between specifically digital framings of sociality and sociological understandings of what makes technology social. For example, social media platforms like Facebook and Twitter are remarkably well-aligned with certain sociological theories, such as performative perspectives that highlight that social life is not 'natural' but enacted (Thielmann, 2012; Hogan, 2010; Healy, 2015). As long as our critique of digital sociality remains limited to the descriptive level, treating it as a given – but *that* is not the social! – we fail to grasp something important about both the digital and sociality. In this chapter, I will examine various understandings of sociality that have become common and relevant in todays digital context, by reviewing different answers to the question: what makes digital technologies social? I will argue that today's digital media technologies not only challenge sociological understandings of the social, they also provide an important occasion for sociology to contribute to societal debates.

Platform-centric perspectives: technology makes the social?

Asking the question 'what makes digital technologies social?' today, we face a puzzling circumstance. The answers that are provided by prominent experts of 'the digital' tend to highlight *technical* features of digital infrastructures, devices and practices. Literature on 'social media' technologies provides especially clear examples of this. Prevailing accounts of social media platforms in public, tech, as well as academic discourses, foreground two features in particular: 'user-generated content' and 'social networking' (boyd and Ellison, 2007; Mandiberg, 2012). From this perspective, social media technologies must be distinguished from other digital technologies by the distinct types of user activities they enable: (1) social networking or the making of 'connections between users' own profiles and those of others' (boyd and Elison, 2007),[5] and (2) the creation and exchange of content between users (van Dijck, 2013). What makes (some) digital media technologies 'social' is then that they enable everyday people to be participants in, and not simply spectators of, media (Mandiberg, 2012; Beer and Burrows, 2007): users can now create and publish their own contributions, often thematizing their own everyday experiences; by connecting with other users, they can organize and create communities; and through sharing and commenting platforms enable the collective validation, promotion and evaluation of knowledge, events and actors (Bruns et al., 2013). One example is vinepeek.com, a site that amalgamates short videos uploaded by users of the mobile service Vine under the slogan 'watch the world in real-time'. While Vine enables users to create and post short video clips (with a maximum length of six seconds), 'for their friends and family to see', Vinepeek aggregates these feeds, streaming random snippets for a potentially global audience, providing viewers with a composite view of everyday moments recorded by unknown individuals.[6]

These definitions probably come closest to 'common sense' understandings of what makes digital technologies social. The platforms that fit these definitions are among the most well-known and familiar digital applications today. Indeed, social media are a key example of the successful mainstreaming of digital technology, and it has been argued that it was only with their rise to prominence that the computational technologies formerly known as 'ICT' – information and communication technologies – became fully 'domesticated' in society (Berker et al., 2005), or 'socialized' (Lupton, 2014; Lury and Marres, 2015). However, *from a sociological perspective this familiar answer to the question of what makes digital technologies social is highly puzzling, insofar as they are technology-centric*: even if prevailing definitions of social media use social terminology to characterize digital media technologies – such as community and participation – they use these terms to describe features of these technologies themselves, and only in the second instance, what people do with them. Thus, Mandiberg (2012) points out that a notion like 'user-generated content' is inherently technical, and offers a 'machinic', and 'technocratic' perspective on everyday digital media practices. 'Content generation' after all frames users as 'generators' – rather than as authors – of 'content' – rather than of 'stories' or 'art' or 'knowledge' (Mandiberg, 2012). Accordingly, social researchers, whose interest by definition goes beyond the technical dimensions of the digital, have not at all been inclined to accept the above understandings of what makes digital technologies social.

The techno-centric definition of social media technologies can be traced back to a particular source: tech industry and business literatures. The idea of the 'social Web' is often attributed to Tim O'Reilly, who in 2005 proposed to define 'Web 2.0' as adding 'an architecture of participation' to the Web. (Suitably, O'Reilly first proposed this definition on an online forum, stating rather informally ('socially'?) that he had woken up with that definition in his head that very morning.)[7] In the following years, O'Reilly's definition was widely taken up in order to distinguish the 'new' online platforms like YouTube, Twitter, Facebook and Weibo from the 'old' Worldwide Web. His definition, that is, enabled the *periodization* of digital networked technologies: from this perspective, 'sociality' is what distinguishes the interactive platforms launched in the early 2000s from the 'static', 'less user-centred' Worldwide Web of the 1990s. While 'Web 2.0' has entered common parlance in sociology too, it should be noted that many social researchers and theorists are sceptical about O'Reilly's definition. As Gabriella Coleman (2012) pointed out, the two main features highlighted by the techno-centric definition of online platforms – 'posting content' and 'sharing' – in many ways pre-date the rise of the very large for-profit platforms like Facebook, and the designation of these platforms as 'Web 2.0' and 'social media', wrongly suggests that the use of email, discussion lists, internet relay chat (IRC) and other online forums before the rise of big commercial platforms somehow wasn't fully 'participatory' or 'social'. Even if these pre-existing digital practices weren't 'mainstream', and were less popular and more 'minoritarian' in their orientation, this does not mean they were any less social. Surely we don't want to go along in the fiction that digital technologies only acquired a social dimension with the rise to prominence of commercial platforms?[8]

Social and cultural researchers, then, have offered critical analyses of the understanding of sociality advanced in literatures on social media. According to the media scholar Jose van Dijck (2013), the rise to prominence of techno-centred understandings of sociality in the wake of digital platforms must be understood as first of all a commercial, political and cultural project, one that social and cultural researchers should investigate and contextualize in relation to wider societal dynamics, such as privatization. As she puts it 'making the Web social', in reality means 'making sociality technical', and thereby making it available for intervention, manipulation and control (see also Gerlitz and Helmond, 2013). As social researchers challenged the definition of digital sociality in terms of technical features, they have also advanced alternative perspectives, and this includes those that highlight the critical role that data play in the re-branding of digital infrastructures, devices and practices as social.

Data, traces, materials

The recent proliferation of digital technologies across social life have also brought into relief a second, very different answer to this chapter's question: the view, briefly put, that it is *data* that make digital media technologies social. This is the understanding that emerges from recent literature on digital sociology, which as we saw in Chapter 1, singles out the ongoing capture and analysis of vast amounts of data about social life as a key feature of the digital today. Digital data capture arguably makes social phenomena available for analysis in new ways, enabling the monitoring and analysis of activities, movements, transactions and populations in real or near-real time (Housley et al., 2014). While this is not always explicitly stated, the suggestion is often made that these 'data-intensive' approaches to social analysis somehow provide better or 'truer' access to social life than older social research methods (Ruppert, 2013). Rather than the old 'top-down' methods, which impose their pre-defined categories on social life, digital data strengthen bottom-up forms of analysis, where classifications and categories are derived from the data themselves, for example by way of cluster analysis (Webber et al., 2015; see also Callon, 2006). As such, digital data are said to make possible a type of social enquiry that is less dependent on generalization: instead of a sociology that reasons along the vertical axis of moving between particular phenomena and more general categories, it is then argued, 'digital' ways of knowing society move along the horizontal axis of following circulations and the distribution of activities, transactions, attributes. Another way of putting this is that *digital networked technologies operationalize a distinctive social ontology*, a way of structuring the social world that is not so much focused on the 'summing up' of the general population using a limited number of fixed categories (gender, age, education, ethnicity), but rather on the dynamic, lateral, granular description of distributed groupings (Castellani, 2014; Uprichard, 2012).

But what is it about digital data technologies that they make possible this type of 'high-resolution' access to social reality? The answer provided by Housley and colleagues is that digital media technologies may 'facilitat[e] the generation and analysis of 'naturally occurring' mediated data, as contrasted with findings from experiments, surveys and in-depth interviews, which are necessarily the artefacts of social researchers' (Housley et al., 2013). Digital networked data, according to this view, are different from the 'designed' data that have long been central to sociological research, such as data collected via questionnaires, focus groups and interview methods. These latter methods can be characterized as 'single-purpose': they have been developed by social researchers in order to generate data for the express and sole purpose of social research. By contrast, digital media technologies render available for analysis a broad range of trace data (time, place, etc.) and materials (text, photos, videos, tags) that are produced as part of social life, and both of these serve many purposes besides social research. Highlighting this latter feature, others have characterized digital data as 'by-product data' (Kitchin, 2014; Savage and Burrows, 2007), but we can also call to mind here the type of 'data about social life that are produced as part of social life' in which adherents of the sociological approach called ethnomethodology have for so long taken a special interest (Thielmann, 2012; Passmann and Gerlitz, 2014). Whatever the term, it implies a distinctive understanding of the 'special relationship' between digital technologies and social life: *The digital technologies that today help to facilitate social life – like online platforms or smart phones – at the same time generate data about social life and render it analysable.*

Housley et al.'s above account of 'naturally occurring' data draws on well-established sociological approaches: it is in line, for example, with the work of the early twentieth-century sociologist W. I. Thomas, who preferred to work with 'un-designed' materials (for a helpful discussion see Lee et al., 2008). However, other sociologists have challenged precisely this idea of the 'naturalness' of digital data, and they advocate a different explanation for why today's digital data offer such rich sources for sociological analysis: platform-based and other forms of digital data are formatted in ways that agree with specific social methods, like network analysis and conversation analysis. From this vantage point, digital data stand out for their artificiality, not their naturalness. As Shaw (2015) points out, platform data tend to be strongly marked by platform effects, such as search terms suggested by auto-complete functions, or users taking up hashtags that are trending on the platforms in question. This 'influence of the (technological) setting' on the activities recorded on digital platforms presents a complex sociological question, as it challenges the notion that social behaviour and technical artefacts can be easily separated out in our understanding of digital technology. Sociologists of technology have long debated this issue (Latour, 1998), but digital platforms arguably take the socio-technical formatting – or 'scripting' (more on this below) – of action one step further: much activity here is mediated by pre-fab action formats such as 'liking', 'faving' and indeed 'clicking', which all at once make it easy to perform social action and to capture these actions in data (Gerlitz and Helmond, 2013; Rieder, 2013; Crawford and Gillespie, 2016).

The debate about the 'naturalness' of digital data has implications for the methodology of digital social research (see Chapters 3 and 4), but it also has implications for our answer to this chapter's question. From the above perspective, we must concentrate on the capacities of todays digital architectures to establish continuities, not only between sociality and technicity, as usefully highlighted by van Dijck above, but between sociality, technicity and knowledge. What makes digital technology social is their triple-edged nature: digital architectures are sufficiently *open-ended* to enable social interaction, expression and organization, yet they are *controlled* enough to facilitate intervention and manipulation of these activities, and they provide the *artificial* conditions required for the recording and analysis of these actions (Derksen and Beaulieu, 2011). Or, to formulate this differently: on the one hand, digital technologies equip users to conduct, organize, document and research social life, while on the other hand, these technologies actively structure and format social life in ways that render it available for large-scale monitoring, analysis and intervention by selected actors.[9] That is also to say that there are important asymmetries in play here, which I will discuss below.

What is remarkable, from this vantage point, is the extent to, and ease and intensity with which data analytic technologies have become embedded in social practices and infrastructures. This has led some, like Patricia Clough, Karen Gregory and colleagues (2015 – see also Haber, 2016) to argue that digital data is becoming a primary mediator of sociality in our societies, as the most diverse sectors and practices latch on to data – not just Web and social media data, but phone data, traffic data, purchase data, any data – as the key instrument and medium through which to conduct, valuate, know, coordinate and manipulate social activities. As Clough puts it, this turns data into 'a primary interface and circuit of our societies', something she describes as the 'data-logical' turn in contemporary society. Others have spoken of the 'datafication' of sociality. This, according to Couldry and van Dijck (2015) has been one of the primary results (or purposes) of the re-framing of digital technology as social technology over the last decade or so: 'When Mark Zuckerberg vowed in 2010 that Facebook's mission in life was 'to make everything social', he really meant: to move social traffic onto a networked infrastructure where it becomes traceable, calculable, and so manipulable for profit' (p. 3).

However, some sociologists take issue with the emphasis on 'data' as the outstanding feature, good or 'currency' of digital societies. Drawing on holistic understandings of knowledge, they have argued that strictly speaking there is no data without analysis – insofar as data are always already formatted and structured – by way of classifications, concepts, ontologies (Bowker and Star, 2000). When we investigate the uptake of data-intensive technologies across social life, this turns out to be accompanied by the uptake of particular data formats, classifications and measures, from the more technical format of 'comma separated values' to popular measures like the hashtag trend (Castelle, 2013; Kennedy, 2016). As such, the so-called *datafication* of social practices and arrangements amounts to their *analyti-fication*: as the digitization of infrastructures, arrangements and practices renders them more data-intensive, they do not merely have more 'data stuff' passing through them, but acquire particular data formats and measures, which may then constrain and format activities, actions and events. Others have taken issue with the very concept of 'data': Bruno Latour and others (2012; see also Latour, 1998) propose to use the term 'traceability' instead. Whereas the concept of data presumes a particular architecture (such as the data-base), the notion of trace is more minimal, positing merely the detection of a thing or movement and the recording of this (see also Boullier, 2016). And whereas the notion of 'data' entails a belief in the 'extractability' of information from the setting that produced it, the notion of trace preserves a reference to the device by which it was detected (Marres and Weltevrede, 2013). However, whether sociologists choose the one term or the other – data or trace – to account for the significance of digital technologies to social life, in both cases the generation of informational patterns as part of social life is shown to play an important role in the organization of social life.

Practice, the situation: the sociological serum, but does it still work?

We shouldn't forget, however, that for many sociologists the idea that sociality can be understood in terms of 'users generating data and interacting with each other's content' simply lacks plausibility, and the same goes for the idea that this could offer an adequate basis for understanding social life. Many sociologists and anthropologists argue that we must look beyond digital platforms, data and content if we are to understand life in digital societies, and that we need a different starting point. An important alternative is provided by those who advocate the study of *digital practices* (Dourish and Bell, 2011; Slater, 2002; Suchman, 2007a). As Don Slater (2002) put it succinctly: 'we cannot identify the features of digital media technologies without considering how people use and understand them in practice'. This approach entails yet another answer to the question in this chapter's title. From this vantage point, what makes digital technologies social is what is done with them: that they are practised in and as part of a situation. Sociality extends *above and beyond* the features, outputs and effects of the technologies themselves, and is precisely not reducible to patterns that have been retained in data. The ephemeral, untraceable, the unsaid constitute crucial dimensions of social life, and indeed many social interactions and ways of doing – from coded ways of speaking to contextual gestures – are precisely concerned with this dimension.[10] More generally speaking, this approach relocates sociality from 'inside the machine' to its outside: rather than doing an analysis of 'baby pictures on Facebook', we should strive to understand the practices involved in people turning to Facebook to post photos soon after their babies are born (Licoppe, 2004).

Practice-centred approaches argue that understanding digital technologies in their social dimension requires *a situational perspective*: when people are social 'with technology', they are so in inevitably *located, situated or embedded* ways. From setting up a not-for-profit Internet service provider in Amsterdam (Rommes, Van Oost and Oudshoorn, 1999); Web use by HIV AIDS positive migrant women in and around London (Mazanderani and Brown, 2011), to Mumsnet debates about different possible treatments of head lice (Hine, 2012) – each of these presents very different ways of taking part in social life using digital technologies, and the studies cited above each in different ways aim to demonstrate that these practices can *only* be understood by taking into consideration their social, cultural and political contexts. Importantly, practice-centred studies do not only aim for a celebration of diversity of use, their claim is more fundamental: technology is always and inevitably practised as part of specific situations, and consequently we cannot adequately understand either technology or sociality if we fail to consider the modes in which they are practised. As Lucy Suchman and colleagues (1999) put it: 'Technologies, in this view, are constituted through and inseparable from the specifically situated practices of their use.'[11] The classic empirical example Suchman gives is the use of computer systems in airports for purposes of air traffic control: to understand what's going on when the departure and arrival of aeroplanes is managed with such systems, we need to consider these systems in-use. For example, we need to consider how Nick the operator deliberately feeds in the 'wrong time' in order to give his colleague on the ground some space – a few more minutes – to get things ready (Suchman, 1999). The argument is then that we simply cannot understand airport ground operations by studying the formal features or empirical outputs of the system – e.g. by analysing its architecture or 'logs' – but only by analysing the interactions between humans, machines and settings *in situ*.

The practice-centred approach to digital technologies is a well-established social research perspective, going back to the 1980s, but it continues to be relevant in today's digitizing societies, among others because it de-centres the focus on single digital media technologies. Platform-centred and data-centric approaches have a tendency to focus on a single digital device or setting – say Facebook, or smart transport cards – but a practice-centred perspective can help to sensitize us to the fact that the conduct of social life involves many different devices – from phone and SMS to email and social media – and is spread out over various settings. As Christian Licoppe (2004) put it, 'one needs to take into account the way the management of a given social relationship will rely on the whole available technoscape' (see also Moats, 2015; Postill and Pink, 2012). This is, then, one important reason that sociologists give for adopting a social perspective on digital technology: we will never grasp the 'ecology of practice' as long as we analyse only what happens 'inside the box' of a given digital platform or data set, say that of Facebook. As Madianou and Miller (2013) and Postill and Pink (2012) also propose, this practice-centred perspective has only become more relevant in recent years, insofar as recent digital transformations (social media, mobile, smart infrastructures) precisely entail a multiplication of digital applications and devices 'beyond the Web' and the specification of distinct social practices – from group texting to responsive transport management and digital street art.

At the same time, recent digital transformations pose important challenges to practice-centred perspectives. For one, digital infrastructures, platforms and devices are increasingly designed with the express purpose of capturing more elusive phenomena that are traditionally thought of as being 'beyond the technical', and belonging to context. Platform design explicitly favours practice-centred or mundane perspectives: Twitter famously asks 'what did you have for breakfast this morning?'; visual platforms like Instagram encourage the production of photo diaries that capture the extraordinary in the ordinary. More generally, online interaction favours informal styles of expression as a way of being brief, funny and 'non-boring', and one result is the proliferation of contextual information online (what was the colour of the dress, that plastic bag hanging in a tree?). Furthermore, algorithmic technologies built into digital infrastructures are famous for their ability to detect the un-said: supposedly Facebook knows you're gay before you do. In his article, 'The nice thing about context is that everyone has it' Seaver (2015) gives the example of music listening – what is the right music for you during a ride home from work? While a few decades back, we might have been inclined to say that this question can only be answered 'from the standpoint of the situation', today's algorithmic services like Spotify are able to determine this on the basis of the analysis of large-scale patterns in music listening. Seaver's article raises an important question: Is the domain of social moments, truths and effects that can only be grasped from a practice-centred perspective shrinking in digital societies? Are today's digital technologies increasingly equipped to grasp contextual factors and to attune intervention to this?

Arguably, the appeal to 'contexts of use' isn't quite as critical a gesture today as it was twenty years ago: back then, it was offered as a way of derailing the positivist framing of both technology and social reality, the reduction of the social to what can be clearly counted and labelled. Also arguably, however, contextualist arguments pose much less of a challenge in today's digital societies, as one of the primary aims of digital innovation over the last decades has been to bring contextual and locative factors and dynamics within its purview. This does not make the 'untraceable' or that which is 'beyond inscription' any less relevant a sociological category. Indeed, the evasion of traceability is still what social ways of doing and talking are very much about, but this sociality now becomes researchable by a variety of means, including coded exchanges in digital settings (Boyd, 2014). Indeed, online platforms are *designed* to enable and coordinate distributed social activity across settings, while at the same time rendering contextual utterances, interactions and events analysable and deployable (as mediated through photography, informal talk, geo-location, and so on) across settings. As a consequence of this, the opposition between, on the one hand, the qualitative and contextual, and on the other, quantitative and anti-contextual becomes harder to sustain. Does an ethnographic video clip posted on Twitter count as content or context? More generally speaking, we can ask: What do we mean by the 'context' of digital media, when millions of social media users themselves are documenting their surroundings *using these very media*: do their observations constitute social media's context or content? Is it by definition only the ethnographer or social and cultural researcher who has access to 'context'? Does the notion that social and cultural researchers have privileged access to social context become harder to sustain in a context of mass observation?

This question requires investigation, but it is important that we appreciate that the practice-centred approach does not simply limit our attention to human experience, the embodied practice, the immediate situation. Foregrounding the 'incalculable' aspect of social life is not its only aim. When sociologists say 'practice' or 'situation', not all of them are referring to action that is contained in a setting, or the 'face-to-face', or even, to the human perspective on things. Thus, the sociologist Knorr-Cetina (2009) insists that from the practice-centred perspective, too, the relevant circumstance is that 'many areas of everyday life have now migrated to the Internet, as an increasing portion of banking, travel booking, shopping, [..] reading or what substitutes for it, are now no longer handled face-to-face but electronically'. As Knorr-Cetina puts it, in digital societies social life increasingly happens in synthetic situations: these are situations that notably involve informational devices that 'establish channels towards other contexts' (Knorr-Cetina, 2009, 2014). One of the questions practice-centred approaches to digital social life are today grappling with is how to account for 'multi-contextuality'. While the outstanding feature of practice-centred approaches to digital media technologies is that they locate sociality beyond the machine in situations, what counts as a situation – its very composition – may be undergoing transformation in digital societies. This work calls into question a long-standing assumption of qualitative studies of social life, namely the idea that the 'face-to-face situation' is somehow fundamental and logically prior to mediated and/or distributed situations.

Interlude: how do social 1, 2, and 3 add up?

There are, then, at least three different answers to this chapter's question – which raises the further question: how do they add up? To an extent, the technology-centric, the data-centric and the practice-centric understanding of what makes digital media technologies social are complementary. For example, the former two approaches assume a perspective that is largely 'internal' to digital infrastructures, arrangements and devices, inviting us to look at sociality and society through the lens of digital architectures and data. The latter proposes that we adopt an 'external' perspective on digital, that of the situation. One could say that they approach the question of what makes digital technology social from opposite directions. However, there are also tensions between the three perspectives, and they can be said to pull in different directions. Data- and technology-centred approaches challenge the situational understanding of sociality insofar as they are mainly concerned with wider processes of distribution, aggregation, interactivity (Uprichard, 2012). While practice-centred approaches tend to underscore the ordinariness of digital ways of doing things, and tend to be sceptical about sensational claims about the radical innovations claimed for new digital technology. Whether it is the Web, or mobile or social technology, they tend to emphasize that digital technologies are configured differently in different places, settings and situations, and therefore resist being summed up into one over-arching slogan or narrative, about what is new in our age. By contrast, the techno- and data-centred perspectives to a degree go along with the sensational claim that digital media technologies have acquired important new 'social' and socio-logical capabilities: for example, because they enable the organization, coordination and participation of and in social life on a new level and extend its scope (Gerlitz and Lury, 2014).

However, while the differences and similarities between approaches are important, we should beware of assuming too static an understanding of digital sociology. Indeed, striking about this emerging field is the relative ease with which concepts and methods are exchanged – or appropriated – between different theoretical perspectives. One example of this can be found in the sociological concept of the 'script'. This concept has long been used by sociologists to highlight the conventional, dramaturgical character of social life (Goffman, 1978) – the way we stage our entrance when arriving in a room full of people, for example. However, the concept was used to a rather different purpose when it was taken up by social studies of technology in the early 1990s, which used it to build the argument that the use of technology in practice tends to involve the execution of 'action programmes' – which involve both humans and non-humans (Akrich and Latour, 1992). Latour and Akrich give the example of the hotel key with a metal weight on it. This device distributes action between hotel receptionist and hotel guest in a particular way: because of the weight the guest will be inclined to bring back the key, without the receptionist needing to remind her. (Importantly, this idea that the execution of a script depends on contributions from both technology and people – that it involves both humans and non-humans 'acting in concert' – went against the technological determinist idea that the technology 'makes' people act in particular ways (Akrich and Latour, 1992).) Building on this work, digital sociologists are today developing yet another application of the concept of the script. *As mentioned, a key feature of digital platforms and applications is that they make available a 'grammar of action'*, 'action formats' – or inform-actional formats (Marres, 2015) – designed to make certain activities 'more doable' in digital settings – 'like liking', 'following' and 'flagging' – and in one and the same go, these formats render these activities available for analysis and intervention (see also Gerlitz and Helmond, 2013; Passmann and Gerlitz, 2014). The question is – who or what participates in the execution of these scripts and how?

Alexander Halavais (2013) has offered an insightful analysis of the role of 'inform-actional' formats in the digital platform Twitter, which may shed light on this. Recounting how the 're-tweet' emerged as a socio-technical script in this setting, he describes how it began as an informal practice, as early Twitter users copied and pasted other user's tweets into their own to pass on the message. Subsequently this practice was formalized when the convention emerged to insert 'RT' before the message in question. Twitter then further formalized the gesture by embedding an RT button into the Twitter interface,[12] and Halavais shows that this latter intervention had significant transformative effects on the very activity now known as re-tweeting (Passmann and Gerlitz, 2014): with the introduction of the button, users became less inclined to add comments of their own in re-tweet messages. That is, re-tweeting became more like a practice and process of 'diffusion' – with the same 'content' passed on to lots of users – while prior to the introduction of the button, it was more like a process of translation – in line with the dictum that there is no displacement without transformation (Latour, 1999). On this basis, Halavais offers a powerful critique of the ideal of 'user-driven innovation': it was not simply that Twitter took up an innovation developed by users. By automating user practices, by way of the button, Twitter robbed this practice of some of its generative capacities, namely the inclination to participate actively in the modification (modulation) of content. As a consequence of the formalization of re-tweeting, individual users' activities became less creative and the overall functioning of the platform became more inclined towards large-scale promotional activity. Halavais focuses our attention on the *formation of a script* as a distributed process, showing how an emergent practice may translate into an infrastructural feature and, from there, into a constraint on practice.

Examples like these help to make clear that it's probably a mistake to think that we need to make a strict choice between the three different perspectives of what makes digital technology social. Indeed, attempts to understand digital social life are likely to produce awkward encounters between diverse sociological traditions, competences, sensibilities (Carrigan, 2016; Castellani, 2014). However, while the above three perspectives are especially influential today, I do not think that they are sufficient in and of themselves if our aim is to address this chapter's question adequately. There is a particular aspect of digital infrastructures, devices and practices that we need to examine in more detail: the type of interventions in social life that they make possible.

Representing and intervening: rendering social life (and analysis) deployable

Digital technologies do not simply facilitate the *conduct* of social life, and they do not just render it *recordable and analysable*. In part because of the interactive capacities of computer systems, the combination of these two features enables a third type of operation upon social life: digital technologies make social life available for intervention. There has been no lack of attention to this third feature in popular and academic narratives about social media platforms, where it is claimed that social media 'augment' and 'enhance' social life, in line with the rhetorics used by social media industries themselves (Bucher, 2013; Riedl, 2011). Digital technologies do not just make it easier to maintain existing or given relationships between people, they enable the creation of new ties (Licoppe, 2004). However, what makes social media platforms stand out is that they have been expressly designed in order to serve this purpose. As Gerlitz and Helmond (2013) have shown, a digital innovation like Facebook's 'Like' button is designed to intensify and amplify connections between users, digital objects, and Facebook itself. The technical term for this is 'social graph enhancement': the idea that social media technologies allow users to maintain more relations more intensively than would be possible without them (Bucher, 2013).[13] Generally speaking, social researchers have been rather critical of the definition of social relations assumed and promoted by such terminology: they call into question whether 'making connections' on digital platforms – in and of itself – really qualifies as sociality at all. As discussed in this chapter's introduction, sociologists have criticized social media for infusing sociality with logics that seem antithetical to or corrosive of it, citing the widespread commercial deployment of social media and the general 'flattening out' of interaction. Interventions legitimized as the 'enhancement' of sociality, then, actually result in its impoverishment, degradation or even annulment (Couldry and van Dijck, 2015; Davies, 2015b).

From this critical perspective, the combination of the doing, knowing and intervening in social life in digital platforms has as its overriding consequence the *instrumentalization* of sociality. As Gerlitz and Lury (2014) note, the 'social connectors' of the digital world – likes, shares, stars – are easily treated as resources, a currency to trade, or a market one 'games' (see also Arvidsson, 2011). It is tempting to conclude that social relations here are not an end in themselves, but are made to serve different economic and political purposes. While much about this critique seems to be plausible and appropriate, there are some aspects of the mediation of sociality by digital platforms that it fails to capture. Insofar as digital technologies invite a broadly interventionist approach to sociality, they do more than making it subservient to other purposes: in treating social relations and activity not as something given and un-changing, but as a set of activities, patterns and forms that may shift, expand and are thus transformable, digital technologies can be said to invite an *experimental approach* to sociality. This difference between instrumental and experimental approaches to sociality is somewhat elusive, but a key difference is that the former treats the ends – to which sociality is treated as the means – as more or less given, while in an experimental approach certainty about purposes, too – what is sociality for? – may be suspended (Marres, 2012b). We do not quite know what social forms, patterns and processes will be invented with digital technology.[14] In view of this, we should consider that sociologists have long argued that the relation between technology and sociality is first and foremost a transformative relation. Scholars across fields have drawn on this fundamental insight to make sense of transformative relations between the digital and the social. According to Sonia Livingstone (2008) 'the very language of social relationships is being reframed today, as people construct their "profile", make it "public" or "private", they "comment" or "message" their "top friends" on their "wall", they "block" or "add" people to their network, and so forth'. The question here becomes how the digital inflects the very categories people use to make sense of social life: what counts as a 'friend' today arguably differs from what a 'friend' was some decades ago. As a colleague told me, when he asks his students at the start of his class on social networks 'how many friends do you have?' some say five, others say 500.

Furthermore, in order to understand the transformations of sociality in digital societies, we should look beyond the relation between technology and sociality. We also need to consider the relation with knowledge. Indeed, the invention of what we today think of as 'social media' are partly the result of concerted efforts to make the Internet more accessible for social research, and, indeed, to better adjust Internet architectures to sociological understandings of human interaction and communication dynamics. The rise of social media platforms did not just yield masses of so-called 'social data', which could be used for marketing and other research purposes. The very development of these platforms explicitly involved the *implementation* of sociological ideas in digital architectures. Take 'People You May Know', the algorithm developed by the professional platform LinkedIn and subsequently implemented by Facebook, which suggests users to follow or 'friend'.[15] As the LinkedIn Web site states clearly, this algorithm implements the sociological concept of 'triangle closing', which was first developed by the early twentieth-century sociologist Georg Simmel, in his work on 'tryadic closure', which described the phenomenon that if one person knows two people, *they* are likely to know each other (see also Bucher, 2013).[16] In social media settings, then, the concept of 'tryadic closure' no longer presents a description of inter-personal relations, it here serves as an instrument for the organization of actors and content.

On a more general level, Kieran Healy (2015) has described the increasingly important, generative roles that social networking technologies perform today in the valuation of content and interaction across social domains. Foregrounding the importance of what he calls 'affiliation engines', Healy notes that today's dominant platforms like Amazon and Facebook 'typically embed various network techniques in their software service, and make an effort to reveal the structure of the network to users or otherwise harness structural properties in order to do something useful'. Importantly, Healy (2015, p. 199) also emphasizes the diverse provenance of the analytic methods built into digital infrastructure:

> The methods [. . .] at the heart of Web 2.0 sites [from PageRank to the clustering and equivalence methods], have diverse roots. Some come from computer scientists in the world of machine learning; some from researchers in library or information science; some grew out of statistical methods for the identification of clusters and the reduction of high-dimensional data; some are based on the analysis of complex systems; and some are rooted in social network analysis as practised by sociologists. Formally, many of these methods are very similar. All of them have been given a big push by the rise of cheap computing.

Insofar as we can say that the Internet is being configured as a 'sociological machine' today, this is clearly an inter-disciplinary endeavour. Nevertheless, it is striking how many sociological references one can find among the technical descriptions of platform algorithms (another case is the Matthew effect first described by the American sociologist Robert Merton (see Chapter 3)). Furthermore, 'social' vocabularies are very much part of the *language* deployed by digital industries, policy, research and public commentators to frame the rise of digital platforms. Birkbak and Carlsen (2015) have analysed descriptions of the Facebook's Newsfeed by industry experts and commentators, arguing that these involve the formulation of a distinctive 'social grammar': for example, they present the Facebook version of the PYMK algorithm as enabling a distinct type of sociality, and way of valuating the social, one focused on the activation of 'weak ties'.

Finally, we must pay closer attention to the ways in which digital technology does not only operate upon the categories, forms and practices of sociality itself, but allows sociality to be brought into relation with other registers of action, such as the economic and the political. To be sure this phenomenon is not limited to digital platforms, as discussed in recent literature on social marketing (Moor, 2011), but as noted, digital platforms have occasioned a fusion of social, economic and political vocabularies. Some conclude that digital technology facilitates the 'economization' of social relations, but others propose that we fail to understand something important about digital sociality if we analyse it in reductive terms. Digital platforms perform a more complex operation than suggested by the idea that they reduce – or colonize – the social to and with the economic: they enable different registers to be *brought into relation* in multi-faceted ways. David Stark has argued that social media only work insofar as they leave enough room for sociality to unfold on its own terms.[17] From this perspective, something different from the 'colonization' of the social by commercial or economic logics is going on today. Instead, digital technologies enable the inter-articulation of sociality and other registers of action, like economy, politics, and morality: they bring these registers into relation precisely *without* subsuming the one under the other (Marres, 2011). This does not mean that there is no commercial bottom line to social media industries, which there is, but rather, that this bottom line does not in and of itself present an adequate sociological principle. Distinctive about digital platforms is they make available a range of different registers of action to different audiences: from the standpoint of users, social media are supposedly about 'keeping in touch'. But from the standpoint of social marketing, social media are first and foremost platforms for knowing and coordinating markets (Gillespie, 2010). One person's social world is another actor's market, and yet another's political audience, *and the other way around.* Carolin Gerlitz has proposed we draw on the concept of commensuration (Espeland and Stevens, 1998) to understand the ways in which measures such as social media likes, hits, and shares are deployable across fields – everyday, professional, activist – and bring these fields into changing relations.

Over the last years, digital sociologists have studied the unsettling effects of the deployment of digital analytics in a variety of sectors, showing how fields from journalism to consumer finance are transformed in both radical and subtle ways by new types of digital interactivity. Christin (2015) has studied the introduction of dashboards in newsrooms in the US and France, examining how the live monitoring of audiences affects status hierarchies in newsrooms, among others through the display of live audience metrics (hit rates) on newsroom displays. Christin's study shows that these effects are highly variable across settings, as in Paris newsroom practise enlightened indifference, while in New York gaming the numbers is considered a pleasurable pursuit. Joe Deville and Lonneke van der Velden (2015) have described how practices in consumer finance are being transformed by social media analytics as payday lenders rely on the analysis of Facebook behaviours to assess the credit worthiness of individuals. As Deville and van der Velden note, uptake of such digital methods does not only affect the back-end operations, but may transform the very relation between lender and borrower: as payday lenders rely on social analytics, your 'personal' credit rating is redefined from a financial score into something more akin to a social assessment (see also Deville, 2015).

As these authors also note, our understanding of digital transformations, not just of social domains but of relations between domains (journalism and audience research, payday lenders and social media users and non-users) is in need of further development, and this is an important task for future work in digital sociology. But recent studies have highlighted that insofar as digital infrastructures, devices and practices cut across social settings, they open up an intermediate zone, which does not simply belong to one social domain or another. A critical feature of this zone I have already mentioned, namely that it enables the creation of new connections between social analysis and social intervention. Accordingly, this zone can be characterized as a space of 'interactivity' – in both the technological and sociological sense of the term. On the one hand, interactivity is one of the outstanding technical features, of computational technology, and of the Internet as a social infrastructure: it is marked by constant feedback between user actions and interactions, content streams, selective disclosure and continues deployments of analytics, from most reads to trends and influence scores. On the other hand, sociological dynamics of 'interactivity' are prominently at work in digital networked settings.

The sociological idea of 'interactivity' highlights that the concepts, measures and instruments that are used to document social life, do not just offer neutral descriptions, but may actively influence the phenomena in question. I mentioned the example of the category of 'women refugee' in the previous chapter (Hacking, 2000), but other famous examples include the labelling of 'young offenders' by social workers and the legal system (Becker, 1963): labels like these work as self-fulfilling prophecies, as they lead actors who are classified thus to act in accordance with this classification. Sociologists of science and technology have taken up this sociological idea to argue that 'technologies of knowledge' act in the world in similarly prophetic ways (Law, 1994). They have shown that instruments for 'knowing society' such as opinion polls and focus groups or survey questionnaires, not only produce descriptions of society and social life, they 'enact the social' (Law and Urry, 2004): they actively contribute to the organization of society, inviting people to present themselves as 'individuals with views', organizing these views and translating them into aggregate forces that politicians and journalists, for example, must contend with (Osborne and Rose, 1999; Lezaun, 2007).[18] These kinds of sociological dynamics of interactivity seem to abound in digital infrastructures, devices and practices (Law and Ruppert, 2013). Take the 'auto-suggest' functions that have been built into search engines over the last years. Social researchers, journalists and other commentators have drawn attention to some especially disturbing interactive effects produced by this technology: When typing a racist query into a search engine, such as 'why are Blacks. . .?' the engine will suggest popular queries to complete this query, which reconfirm the racist message. Auto-complete functions put on public display existing Internet users' prejudice (Baker and Pots, 2013), but they also work to confirm – and indeed risk to amplify – racial prejudice.

In digital infrastructures, social and technological dynamics of interactivity work in tandem, and they both display disturbing discriminatory effects, and risk to aggravate these effects in so doing. In another example of this, Kate Crawford (2013) has described socio-technical dynamics of interactivity demonstrated by smart phone apps, in this case an iPhone application designed for communities to report problems to local authorities, like pot-holes in the pavement. In a trial of this app on the US East coast, this digital service, too, brought to light discriminatory logics: Uptake of this app resulted in a data-base of reports which mostly concentrated on affluent areas – areas where more people own an iPhone. As Crawford shows, the app raised the spectre of an 'interactive' policy of pot-hole fixing that would be skewed towards neighbourhoods with a high incidence of smart phone users. And there are many more examples, some of which have been reported in the mainstream media, under loud headlines such as 'being wasted on Facebook may damage your credit score'.[19] While many of these news stories – rather predictably – tend to focus on 'young offenders', they usefully highlight that interactivity between digital and social life – the intensifying movement from representation to intervention and back – is not just a feature of digital infrastructurs, devices and practices themselves, but has the capacity to affect social, political and public life much more widely.

Changing relations between technology, sociality and knowledge

While some of the interactive features of digital infrastructures are no doubt new, they bring into play dynamics that have long been core concerns in sociology (Thielmann, 2012; Law and Ruppert, 2013). One can think here of the work of Anthony Giddens (1987) on 'double hermeneutics', which drew attention to the circulation of sociological concepts in social life, as people are today likely to explain their behaviour in reference to social concepts like 'class'. Sociologists, then, are not alone in deploying concepts and methods to make sense of society. In making this argument, Giddens drew on Harold Garfinkel's classic studies in ethnomethodology (1984 [1967]) which proposed that a formative aspect of social life is the production of methodical accounts about it. Garfinkel argued that everyday and professional actors use methods to render social life accountable as they go about their everyday and professional lives (see also Cicourel, 1964). That is, the ethno methodologists argued that social life itself has a 'methodical character', and this claim chimes well with many aspects of digital social life. Digital practices from email to Twitter render social life 'increasingly self-documenting and self-archiving' (Lee et al., 2008; Beer and Burrows, 2013), and they also render it increasingly 'self-analysing' and 'self-accountable' – as examined, among others, in social studies of the use of self-monitoring technologies for health and well-being (Lupton, 2014; Neff and Nafus, 2016).

Indeed, Tristan Thielmann (2012) has argued that digital media technologies have granted new empirical plausibility to the propositions of ethnomethodology: 'digital infrastructures, settings and occasions enable everyday and professional actors to account for social life as part of social life'. However, digital technologies do this in a more literal sense than at the time that Garfinkel and colleagues developed their arguments: in digital societies, it is not only mundane and professional practices that render social life accountable, it is done through the introduction and modification of mundane and professional devices (Button and Dourish, 1996).[20] Indeed, 'digital' culture offers some delightful examples of the accountability practices, and 'methodical enactments of social life' that ethno methodologists used to study, such as the website hetexted.com, where girls share SMS messages send to them by potential boyfriends, and collectively attempt to interpret what they might be trying to say.

The resonance of today's digital infrastructures, devices and practices with sociological ideas developed in previous times usefully reminds us that we can't simply 'blame the technology' for what can seem like an incredible expansion of practices of social accountability in digital societies. Indeed, sociologsts have shown that the rise of 'accountability regimes' is a crucial feature of post-industrial societies (Miller and Rose, 2008; Woolgar and Neyland, 2013). What is more, social theorists have suggested that accountability is at the very heart of social life itself. In his classic *Economy and Society*, Max Weber (1968 [1905]) defined sociality as 'the curation of our actions with an eye towards their interpretation by others': action is social when it is performed in view of the accounts others might provide of this action (for a discussion, see Halewood, 2014), and today the connection with social media technologies is hard to miss: is this not exactly what they are for? Importantly, such a sociological understanding of social media technology further problematizes the idea that these technologies provide empirical access to social life as it occurs 'naturally' out there in social reality. Instead, they enable the curation of social life, as many other technologies for rendering social life accountable did before (the photo album, the wedding list . . .).[21] Which is also to say, social life *is* curation, at least in part, and it follows that we cannot treat the 'staging' of social life in social media as a 'source of bias' – one that obscures social life as it is 'really' happening. The naturalistic conceptions of social 'behaviour' that tempts us to think this remains blind to a formative dynamic of social life: social life is done by way of the production of accounts about it. But just as importantly, the connections between social media technologies and ideas from the sociological literature serve as a reminder that it is not just on digital platforms that social life acquires a 'methodical character'. While computational technologies appear to play an increasingly important role in structuring this relation between accountability and sociality, we should remember that digital media technologies present one instantiation of a much wider feature of technology and sociality: that there are deep, mutual implications between the practice of being 'social' – of orientating action and experience towards others – and that of rendering action accountable in a more formal and indeed technical sense.

The configuration and contestation of the social

What then makes digital media technologies social? This chapter has surveyed a range of answers from the sociological literature to this fundamental question. But it should now be clear that these various answers are also in tension, if not all-out disagreement, with one another. Is sociality scripted *into* technology, or practised *with* it? Do digital media technologies facilitate and record social lives that extend *beyond* digital settings, or do they enrol users into the enactment of *medium-specific* forms of sociality? Rather than offering quick answers to these fundamental questions, it is crucial that digital sociologists retain an active interest in them, and cultivate an awareness of how the sociological concepts, methods and instruments that we take up in digital research orientate our inquiries towards one answer or another (Marres and Gerlitz, 2016). In the next two chapters on methods and research design, I will discuss what methodological approaches can enable us to cultivate this awareness. However, it also remains the case, as I argued earlier, that the different answers are to a degree complementary: it is *never* just the platform, the data, the practice or the context, in and of itself, that makes digital sociality what it is. Sociality is not reducible to either one of these elements in isolation. To appreciate this, we need a holistic view on digital social life, one that recognizes that sociality is enacted with digital media technologies in various ways, varying across different settings and occasions (see on this point also Postill and Pink, 2012), and that multiple entities participate in the configuration of sociality with digital media technologies: settings, data, contexts, methods. A stronger version of this claim leads us to recognize what Lucy Suchman has called the 'configurability' of relations between the digital and the social (Suchman, 2007b). It is not only the case that multiple entities contribute to the doing of social life with technology. Different *forms* of sociality are enacted with digital technologies, and sometimes 'the digital' matters more and sometimes less to it.

To recognize this 'configurability' of digital ways of being social certainly does not make digital sociology any easier. On the one hand, it requires that we recognize that there exists significant variability in how digital technology matters in and to social life. On the other hand, configurability can under no circumstance be mistaken for optionality: digital sociality is *not* whatever we want it to be. Indeed, if social enquiry into digital technologies over the last years has demonstrated one thing, it is that social life is constrained in a thousand ways by architectures, interests, protocols, principles, affects, habits, standards and so on.[22] Digital sociality is also NOT optional in a different sense, highlighted by the remark by Emma Uprichard that serves as this book's epigraph: 'Just because its called social doesn't make it social.' The label 'social' has been much abused in digital discourses in recent years, where it has been used as a front – for instance, as a way of not saying 'marketing' or 'mainstreaming' – and where there has been a remarkable lack of curiosity and lack of interest in following through whether and how this term is applicable to digital technology. In this context, it becomes an important task for sociologists to investigate empirically and critically what 'sociality' is turning into in digital societies. One notable item on the sociological 'to do' list, in this regard, is to examine not only the extent to which the meaning of 'social' is subject to drift, but also the extent to which it is contested and put at stake by digital projects, strategies and campaigns. There are many areas in which this negotiation and contestation of digital ways of being social currently takes place, but I would like to conclude this chapter by flagging three important issues of contention of special relevance to sociology.

Power laws

The first and probably most important issue here is the re-validation of hierarchical forms of social, political and public life – but also their contestation – in digital societies today. Arguably the most ubiquitous figure of digital analytics today is what is usually referred to as the 'power law'. This figure shows a highly uneven distribution in which the largest share or activity, resources or goods befalls to a few actors, followed by a signature 'long tail' in which a majority partakes only modestly in said activity or goods. The figure is often presented as an 'empirical' discovery, that is, as a way of showing that democratic visions of the Internet as an egalitarian space are refuted by patterns in the data. Many of the more common digital and social media statistics follow this pattern: number of tweets per user, volume of traffic per page or site, the distribution of numbers of followers, and so on, they all show the concentrated peak in combination with the long tail. In many ways, these figures present sociologists with 'nothing new', as many have consistently warned that notwithstanding the dominant narrative that the 'digital' is a force of good (democracy, innovation, prosperity), digitization reproduces asymmetric power relations (Sassen, 2002; Terranova, 2006; Sharma, 2013). However, sociologists have also noted that the analytic figure of the 'power law' is the product of a highly particular knowledge practice, one that plots frequencies for an 'entire population' in a two-dimensional space (Lury and Marres, 2015).

When it comes to digital platforms, it is not at all an 'abstract' point to claim that statistical methods play a role in the production and re-production of the 'power law': social media actively rely on the measurement of power law-like patterns to determine who or what is 'hot or not', which terms, users, content, to display or not. As such, the power law presents a clear example of a socio-technical interactivity: Digital platforms feed power laws back to users in the form of trend lists and/or rankings ('top tens'), thereby further encouraging users to follow these. The power law then does not just offer a description of what goes on in digital settings, but informs it – not as a 'law' that governs action from above, but as an instrument that influences collective action. Platforms actively promote the 'happy few' (top ranked) through their interfaces, and user practices are actively orientated towards these platform measures, as they attempt to make their profiles or content rise to 'the top', or actively evade detection, something which has been going on since Google implemented its hierarchizing Pagerank algorithm at the end of the

1990s. But social media render these logics only more visible and prominent, with their dynamic feeds and follower counts (Gillespie, 2010).

In this context, it becomes a key challenge for both social actors and social analysts to orient their activities towards other types of distributions. Taking on this task, social media researchers have documented more horizontal forms of engagement and content circulation in social media, as in studies on retweeting by Erik Borra and David Moats (for a discussion, see Moats, 2015), which highlights re-tweeting patterns that follow the many-to-many 'grassroots model', as an alternative to the one-to-many 'broadcast model'. In collaborative work with Esther Weltevrede, we also examined alternatives to the asymmetrical, hierarchical measurement of popularity (liveness) in social media analysis, exploring relational measures for the detection of relevance (liveliness) (Marres and Weltevrede, 2013): this latter measure proposes a focus not just on currency of use (how often is this term used?) but on variation in relations: how often is it used in relation to new terms? From this perspective, terms and actors becomes interesting not when they are popular (find broad uptake), but when they are brought into relation to actors and terms they were not connected to before.

Bots, or the arte-factuality of the social

A further object of negotiation and contention in digital social life today is the role of 'bots', and other programmed entities. Automated content is increasingly prominent in digital environments: bots assist in the management of online platforms, as in the case of Wikipedia's bots which help to detect and sometimes correct new edits on this platform (Niederer and van Dijck, 2010). So-called 'social bots' and all manner of automated accounts are increasingly prominent in social media from Twitter to the dating app Tinder, as bot accounts follow users and tag or re-post content in an effort to gain an audience for their own – usually commercial – content (MacKinnon, 2015; Gillespie, 2013). This expanding presence of bots online can be partly understood as a consequence of the aforementioned dynamics of popularity that are so influential in digital platforms: given the value placed on volume as a way of rising in rankings, it may become a logical step to buy Facebook likes from a click farm in Bangladesh (Lury and Marres, 2015). However, there are many further reasons, such as the multiplication of digital channels, from SMS to Instagram and so on, which make it practically necessary for intensive users to 'copy' and 'paste' among these channels. As such, automation of digital interaction and content is likely to become increasingly acceptable, and expert users today routinely rely on automatic alerts, feeds and posting services to manage their digital lives.

The deployment of bots in human interaction goes back many decades, and includes the famous chatter bot Eliza who was designed in the 1960s. What is remarkable about the presence of bots online, however, is not only their prominence – in 2014 Twitter acknowledged that '23 million active users are actually bots'[23] – but also how little their presence factors into popular accounts of digital social life. Even as the presence of bots expands online, with fully automated profiles showing up anywhere from dating apps to text messaging (Licoppe, 2016; Licoppe et al., 2008), the idea that we interact as humans in digital settings is firmly upheld in public discourse surrounding social media and the digital society. The phrase 'digital sociality' invokes things like the social network, online communities, friends liking each other, and this remains very much the language of digital sociality today, rather than the story of users interacting with spam, of bots sending other bots advertising materials. It can be taken as indicative of one of several paradoxes that mark digital sociality: on the one hand, recent waves of digitization have meant that technology has come to play an increasingly prominent role in the conduct of social life today, but at the same time the very proliferation of these technologies across social life has served as an occasion for the re-affirmation of *'human' forms of sociability* online: digital platforms are commonly refered to as social media; when texting, tweeting and so on, people invest energy in humane forms of communication – joking, praising, supporting, et cetera. It is not just the commentators on social media, then, but users and social actors themselves, who have worked hard to respect the 'please ignore' sign that hangs over the contribution of automated entities to digital social life.

Today, this habit of bracketing the bots may be changing as AI is widely welcomed as the next big thing in digital worlds. But the ongoing bot-ificaiton of digital sociality is likely to continue to cause trouble, as it poses a threat to the widely shared project to uphold a human-centred social ontology in digital environments and inter-action. This has been the objective of many digital industries and government initiatives so far, as the identification of 'real persons' seems critical to the economic and political viability of digital services, and it is hard to see how this wider project could change, a point I will return to in Chapter 6. However, we should also consider how far the digital society has already come: the Internet used to be known as the place where 'nobody knows that you are a dog', as the famous New Yorker cartoon had it, but today's digital platforms have turned it into an environment in which 'nobody knows that you are a bot', and for very different reasons. In the New Yorker cartoon, the reason for the not-knowing was online anonymity, but what's going on today is more like a stubborn commitment to human interaction and disavowal of its machinic qualities. Today nobody wants to know as knowing would disturb the prevailing idea that the socialization of digital platforms has been largely successful. To rephrase the paradox in yet another way: *the very technologies that have granted the language of sociality – 'social connection', 'engagement' and 'community' – a renewed currency in our societies, are at the same time the technologies that have made the role of robots and other artefacts in social life much more prominent.* The question is: will the contribution of technology to social life continue to be treated in instrumental terms, as a necessary condition but not a formal feature of social life, or will technological entities be allowed to make a recognizable difference to the forms that social life takes in our societies (Marres, 2012c)?

Methodological individualism and other ontological assumptions

A final issue I want to highlight concerns ontology: as social concepts, methods and measures are being deployed with special intensity in today's digital environments, one of the key questions is what anatomies of social life will be consolidated by these means. As discussed in Chapter 1, sociologists are far from the only interested parties here, as issues around anonymity, collectivity and personhood have been at the forefront of public debate about the digital society in recent years. However, for sociologists, these issues do not only have ethical and political importance, they also have methodological and epistemic relevance: how these issues play out will have implications for the type of social forms that will be doable and analysable by way of the digital in decades to come. A key point of concern here is the assumption of 'methodological individualism:' the idea that society is ultimately reducible to a population of individuals with stated attributes (e.g. preferences, opinions). Many of the measures implemented by digital platforms like Facebook or Amazon invoke this assumption, as in the case of the algorithm that shows that 'people who bought X also bought Y'. It also has a respectable intellectual pedigree: Methodological individualism has been advanced in the last century by figures like Max Weber and Karl Popper. However, it has also been contested by other social theorists like Theodor Adorno and holistic philosophers like W. Quine, and it may well be time to have this debate again. It would require that we shift the debate about digital social life to a more fundamental, architectural level, and discuss the social ontologies scripted into digital infrastructures today. What are the implications of organizing interaction according to a 'preference-based' framework?

Another fundamental ontological assumption that requires critical interrogation is what Karin Knorr-Cetina (2014) has referred to as the 'scopic regimes' that reign in digital societies. The metaphor of 'watching' is highly prominent in both public and academic discourses about the digital society: social media have been called 'voyeuristic' and the public problem of digital surveillance is discussed in terms of users 'being watched'. However, in at least some respects this visual metaphor is problematic itself, insofar as the figure of the 'seeing eye' suggests an empirical clarity and purity which is not at all in agreement with the opacity of much digital infrastructure. It obscures the key role played by restrictive data formats and analytic operations in the organization of digital data, and as such presumes a transparency of the digital apparatus which it precisely lacks (Pasquale, 2015). This problem is captured well by Karin Knorr-Cetina in her thought experiment entitled 'when the screens go black' (ms.). Even if no one would be watching the screens, and indeed, even if there was not just no seer, but no seeing, computational systems would still be running across society. To be sure, Knorr's thought experiment also raises questions about the 'autonomy' of digital machines, but it highlights the limits of the metaphors of watching to capture the drama of the digitization of social life – it is *the analytic operations* inside the box, not just the watchers outside it, or the watching, that require critical attention.

Conclusion

What makes digital media technologies social? This chapter has foregrounded a paradox: the more social concepts and methods play a role in digital infrastructures, devices and practices, the less we can take for granted that we know what 'the social' refers to. Digital media technologies have been re-designed in order to support social interaction, connection and exchange, but they do this at the cost of rendering social life analysable and influencable. This growing analys-ability and manipulability of sociality, too, has paradoxical effects. It has the capacity to destabilize social life as well as the conceptual category of the social. Rather than intensifying or 'enhancing' social life, social technologies may also 'erode' sociality or 'downgrade' it, by translating sociality into something else, such as marketability. However, the digital is also occasioning experiments in sociality, as new ways of relating and new forms of exchange are being invented, as in the case of the use of bots and automated accounts. In this context, it becomes important for sociologists to study what is happening to the social itself, and this is currently the subject of lively debate among sociologists. As we have seen, while some argue that the 'social' is currently being colonized by logics that are alien to it, principally economic ones (Davies, 2015; Couldry and van Dijck, 2015), others argue that the success of social technology – as well as social innovation, social media, social journalism, and so on – is precisely that it does not *reduce* the social to the economic, but enables 'multi-valent' action – action that operates according to multiple logics at once (Gerlitz and Lury, 2015; Marres, 2011).

One of the notable features of digital technologies designated as 'social', I have argued, is the prominent role that *knowledge technologies* play in their day-to-day functioning. As we have seen, digital devices come with concepts, measures and methods built in that derive and resonate with sociological knowledge – from Georg Simmel's concept of 'the triad' to the heuristic of the like (which seems a pretty direct translation of 'preference'). This uptake of social categories in digital architectures is a complex development, which can be interpreted in terms of the ongoing socialization of digital technologies, but another relevant factor is the growing role of analytics in digital infrastructures. In this chapter I have argued that it is crucial that *sociologists investigate the resulting interactions between knowledge, technology and practice in digital societies.* This is only more crucial in view of a circumstance discussed in the first chapter: the emerging field of computational social science so far has had fairly little to say about the interaction between social analysis and social life. Much of this work derives its methodology more or less ready-made from the natural sciences, and does not express much interest in methodological challenges specific to the social sciences: the question of how ideas about social life influence the conduct of social life, and more precisely, the interaction between categories used to make sense of social life and the enactment of social life.[24] As we have seen, the 'naturalism' of what goes on in digital settings is increasingly called into question, and the formative role of digital technologies in the conduct of social life is becoming increasingly apparent. As a consequence, socio-technical dynamics of interactivity are likely to become more and not less relevant in and to digital systems (Bowker and Star, 2000). Sociology has excellent resources to contribute to our understanding of these dynamics. The circulation of research methods in society has been a longstanding *topic* of social enquiry, and work in sociology and related fields has long cultivated an interest in the intimate relations between social methods and soci-ability. Another important question today, however, is how sociology can make a practical difference to the conduct of social research with digital instruments. Should our insights into socio-technical dynamics of interactivity make a difference to how we conduct digital social research?

3

Do we need new methods?

'It's a sociological machine!'

It was early in the academic year, the time when students and lecturers don't know each other very well, when a student suddenly came out with this insight during a seminar on Digital Sociology. Our theme that day was 'digital analytics', and the topic of conversation a popular online data tool for the visualization of trends: projected on the wall was a graph showing the rise and fall of two search engine queries over time, 'burn fat' and 'room for rent' (Figure 3.1). It was produced with one of the better known of these tools, Google Correlate, which plots the volume of queries over time, and allows users 'to find search engine queries with a common pattern', and to discover 'search patterns which correspond with real-world trends'. Our particular graph showed how the queries 'losing weight' and 'apartment for rent' follow the same seasonal cycle, as they pick up and fall away in the same months (November, March), and I had indeed chosen it for its distinctively 'sociological flavour': the figure is suggestive of a complicated, distributed dynamic by which geographically dispersed actors become jointly inspired in Spring to change the way they live, or more specifically, their spatial arrangements, as they seek to expand the spaces they live in and reduce the size of their own bodies.[1] But, being the teacher, I asked: What's so sociological about this? The students did not miss a beat: 'It's just what people type in as part of their daily lives'; 'words they use of their own accord'; 'it's not a controlled measurement, as in a clinic or a lab'. And: 'these are collective expressions, we see queries in the aggregate'; 'it is not about individuals, as in psychology'.

The features of sociological research and digital methods that we discussed during this seminar have been extensively debated among

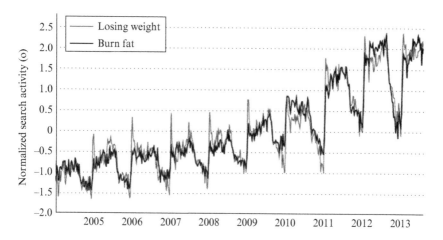

Correlated with losing weight
0.9705   burn fat
0.9695   workouts
0.9690   burn calories
0.9679   houses for rent
0.9668   houses for
0.9665   in shape
0.9660   2 bedroom
0.9656   3 bedroom
0.9643   4 bedroom
0.9616   how many calories are burned
United States Web Search activity for **losing weight** and **burn fat** (r=0.9705)

Figure 3.1   Correlated queries for 'losing weight' over time (Lury and Marres, 2015)

Source: Google Correlate

social scientists, media scholars, computer scientists. As part of these debates, many of the above suggestions as to what makes online data capture and analysis 'sociological' have been criticized. As we have seen in previous chapters, many sociologists have been sceptical or critical about the more sensational claims made for a radically 'new' digital way of knowing society. In particular, they have criticized as simplistic the idea that digital networked technologies make social life available for analysis. Sociologists emphasize that online data is not 'natural' data, insofar as digital content and digital action is often highly *formatted* (Lee et al., 2008). The structuring effects of techno-logical 'settings' – such as like and fave buttons – together with the conventional character of much social life result in a proliferation of 'artificial' expressions in digital settings. This also applies to search engine query data, which as we have seen are very much inflected by the workings of search engines themselves. One can't really say, then, that search engine query data consists of 'words actors use of their own accord', *but this does not mean that the students quoted above weren't onto something:* in spite of the problems just noted, there is something about the rawness, or directness, or indexicality of actual search engine queries unfolding through time that strongly appeals to the sociological imagination.

As we have seen, the new techniques for social research that are enabled by digital, mobile and smart infrastructures and practices are the subject of widespread debate, not just in sociology but across the social sciences and humanities, computing, and public life. Google Correlate has served as a poster-child of sorts for these debates: the data tool was developed not just to showcase nifty findings like the correlation between dieting and moving house, but to demonstrate that digital infrastructures enable *methodological innovation* in data analysis. In a well-known paper about Google Correlate, the company's scientists claimed that it presents a new type of predictive analytics, or anticipatory science, as this method was able to predict the outbreak of the Flu well before other, established research institutes, like the United States Centre for Disease Control and Prevention, could do so (Ginsberg et al., 2009). This particular claim to methodological innovation, in turn, was widely taken up by commentators across the social sciences, humanities and public debate in order to advance a further set of claims about the 'rise of big data' and 'natively digital methods'. These commentators, too, claimed that the digital enables forms of analysis that were not feasible or even conceivable before (Mayer-Schoenberger and Cukier, 2013; Rogers, 2013). Others, however, have taken issue with the very idea that today's digital infrastructures facilitate methodological innovation, arguing that the 'new' tools heavily rely on old forms of analysis, such as co-occurrence analysis (Abbott, 2011). These critics have also offered political and ethical critiques of digital methods – arguing that research techniques and tools that build on digital infrastructures are fundamentally opaque, in part because of the proprietary status of much of the data they generate. Furthermore, while a method like Google Correlate is presented as a contribution to knowledge, it has much wider ramifications for research, as it in effect configures online data analysis as a private form of enquiry.

This is also to say, whether digital instruments for data capture, analysis and feedback qualify as 'sociological machines' is very much *in question* today, and much of the wider debate has centred on the claim that these instruments enable the development of new methods of social enquiry (Diminescu, 2012). In this chapter, I will provide an overview of arguments for and against this possibility, and will offer an argument of my own: to adopt a phrase used by the philosopher Paul Feyerabend, my position is *firmly for and against* the idea that digital methods are new. But I will first provide an overview of the interdisciplinary debate about the supposed newness of digital methods, and review more detailed accounts of the type of methodological innovations in social research enabled by digital devices. I will then make the case for a particular approach to digital methods, which I call 'interface methods' (Marres and Gerlitz, 2016). This approach emphasizes that digital methods are not simply new or old but highly *ambiguous* as to what methods and methodologies they embody and enable. Because of this, I argue, the question that sociologists should be asking is not so much whether or not digital tools *are* new or old, but whether they can be *configured* to further develop methods of social enquiry.[2] To be sure, there is much today that prevents digital instruments from operating as 'sociological machines', and they lack many capacities that are crucial to the successful conduct of social enquiry. But this should not only lead us to critique these instruments, it should also inspire practical efforts to adjust them to serve sociological purposes. Rather than dismissing digital methods, we must ask: what is required before digital devices can serve as sociological machines? Finally, I will take up the political critique flagged above that the configuration of digital infrastructures for purposes of social enquiry is about much more than 'method' – it is about knowledge culture – and I will argue that that this is another place where sociologists can make a valuable contribution to digital methods development.

The digital methods debate

As noted, the claim that digital research presents a next frontier in methods development in the social sciences has been taken up widely, by sociologists and computer scientists, media scholars, ethnographers and statisticians, as well as by university managers, policy makers and funding bodies, and others. This widespread support for methodological innovation in digital research, however, is accompanied by even more widespread disagreement about the form and direction that this project of innovation should take. This disagreement is not just limited to sociology, but extends across disciplines, including anthropology, media studies, computing and geography (Halford, Pope et al., 2013; Procter, Vis and Voss, 2013; Kitchin, 2014; Kelty et al., 2015). Across these disciplines, enthusiasm about new methodological possibilities encounters knowing scepticism about the booms and busts of innovation cycles, which today affect knowledge and technology, theory and methods alike, inside and outside the university. To make sense of this encounter, Richard Rogers (2009) has elaborated a helpful distinction, namely that between the development of 'natively digital' methods and the 'digitization' of methods. Advocates of the former project argue that digital technologies make possible, or even necessitate, the development of 'intrinsically new' methods, which take advantage of distinctive features of digital infrastructures, devices and practices (Rogers, 2013; see also Lee et al., 2008). Adherents of the latter approach, by contrast, stress *continuity* in methodology development across different media and technological settings. They stress the similarities between today's digital data and techniques and their 'pre-digital' equivalents, and conclude that our main challenge is the implementation of existing methods, such as content analysis or survey research, in digital settings (Herring, 2009; Savage, 2010). The digital then presents social researchers with a basic methodological choice: in conducting digital research, do we seek to translate established methods like ethnography or content analysis into digital forms, or do we seek to develop more experimental, 'new' methods that seek to take advantage of the inherent features of digital technologies and practices?

Below I will give two concrete examples of these different approaches to digital methods, but I first would like to make a more general point: while the digital methods debate is centrally concerned with 'the new', it nevertheless signals the return to a classical framing of social enquiry, one that assumes that social enquiry can be defined in terms of its 'methods'. This is in some ways remarkable, as over the last decades several sociologists declared that we had entered an epoch 'after method', to use the title of John Law's (2004) book. Drawing on work in the sociology, philosophy and history of science, this work asserted the primacy of research practice as the mode in which we 'know' social life. Highlighting the unpredictable, tacit and messy nature of 'doing' and 'making' social research in field sites like farms and fisheries, sociologists like Law followed philosophers of science like Paul Feyerabend and Thomas Kuhn to question the value of the overly formal and tidy accounts of knowledge production that result when research is narrated and described in terms of the 'application of method' (see also Woolgar and Neyland, 2013). In this respect, it seems ironic that as soon as sociologists declared that 'method is dead', digital researchers developed their projects of methodological innovation, effectively saying 'long live method'! This return to methods, however, is not simply a matter of sociologists renewing their dedication to formal procedure in social research. It also has to do with the changing role of social methods in social life in digital societies. As I argued in the previous chapter, 'the digital' has focused attention anew on what the very same John Law and others have called the 'social life of method' (Law and Ruppert, 2013). It has occasioned a wider (re-)valuation of social method in the facilitation, analysis and elaboration of social life.

Partly for this reason, we do well to adopt a broad perspective on digital methods and ask: how do the different approaches – 'natively digital' methods and the digitization of methods – make a practical difference to how social enquiry is practised? For Richard Rogers (2013), 'natively digital' methods stand out for their emphasis on what he calls 'medium-specificity': a term taken from art history, it has been used to highlight the material and socio-technical qualities of the media technologies used to implement method, and to argue that such qualities make a difference to the forms of knowledge produced by these means (see also Lury and Wakeford, 2012; Guggenheim, 2015). To give an example, using tape-recorded interviews to understand people's social networks – asking people to describe their networks – will result in a different kind of network analysis than a study that relies on online methods of hyperlink analysis (using software to crawl and analyse links connecting Web pages).

Furthermore, the idea of 'natively digital' methods highlights that digital devices already come with specific methods built in: when we rely on Google to locate relevant materials, for instance, we introduce, by virtue of this seemingly trivial fact alone, an element of network analysis into our study: Google itself relies on hyperlink analysis to rank sources on its query return page, among several other methods (Rieder, 2012). However, rather than viewing these 'methods-of-the-medium' only negatively, as arrangements that threaten to distort our research perspective, and thus a source of bias, Rogers proposes that social and cultural research can find in these 'methods-of-the-medium' a positive source of methodological innovation. For example, Rogers has proposed a method for analysing 'source distance' with Google – by counting how high or low in the Google ranking a given type of source is placed – say climate sceptics – making it possible to say something about the relative prominence of these sources on the Web overall and, arguably, in public discourse (Rogers, 2013). A 'natively digital' approach to method then begins by gauging what methods are already inscribed into digital networked technologies, and then seeks to re-purpose these 'dominant' methods in ways that render them productive for social enquiry (Weltevrede, 2015). As such, the proposition of natively digital methods sets up a more general, methodological opposition: it proposes that social research approaches the digital *from the inside out*, taking up methods that are already embedded in digital infrastructures and practices, and then adapting these to the purposes of social research. This stands in contrast to a methodology that is more common in social research, which does the opposite and approaches the digital *from the outside in*, by taking up social methods like 'ethnography' or 'discourse analysis' and implementing these in digital research.

Research that adopts 'digitization' as its methodological frame-work adopt this latter approach and is primarily concerned with the digital implementation of existing social research methods (Lee et al., 2008). As noted, this type of endeavour tends to focus on particular well-established methods, like ethnography (Hine, 1999; Murthy, 2008), content analysis or survey research. This work certainly does *not* reject the possibility of methodological innovation in digital social research as such, but rather questions the wisdom of striving to invent *new methods*. That is, these approaches tend to locate the innovations enabled by the digital not on the level of method, but more practically, in the research *techniques* that inform the implementation of a method. As the geographer Crampton et al. (2013) put it succinctly: 'New technical implementations of methods need not affect the epistemic qualities of [social] methods' (see also Murthy, 2008; Abbott, 2011). An example of social research broadly in line with the digitization approach can be found in the well-known project 'Reading the Riots' (Proctor et al., 2013) in which social researchers and computer scientists worked together to analyse and visualize Twitter data collected in the wake of the riots that erupted across the UK in the Summer of 2010. This project was among the first social research projects to use Twitter to analyse a societal phenomenon, developing an analysis of the spread of news and rumour during these events. The study also outlined an innovative form of 'real-time' research, as data visualizations produced as part of this study were published while the events associated with the Riots were still unfolding: they were featured in the *Guardian* newspaper shortly after the riots, thus contributing to the public debate about them.[3] However, while this project involved experimentation with various innovative digital techniques, the authors of this study nevertheless did *not* claim to have developed new methods. In a scientific article reporting on their research, Procter, Vis and Voss (2013) defined their methodology as '*a combination of computational tools and more established content analysis methods*'. The principal innovation claimed for this study, then, focused on research techniques, i.e. automated data capture and interactive visualization, or 'real-time' research.

Between the two extremes of the 'natively digital' and 'digitization', there are many in-between positions in the digital methods debate, as well as work that combines elements from both. Sandra Herring's (2009) work on Web content analysis in certain respects qualifies as an example of the digitization of methods, as her works focuses on the transposition of a well-established methodology in social research – content analysis – into digital networked environments. However, her approach explicitly confirms that digital networked content has distinct features – it is dynamic, interactive, and highly formatted – and she makes pointed proposals for how content analysis must be modified to take these into account (in her view, it must be combined with feature analysis). As such, Herring's work can also be read as a contribution to natively digital methods development (for a discussion, see Niederer, 2016). In my own work on digital methods of 'issue mapping' I equally adopt an in-between position: this work relies on online techniques like hyperlink and hashtag analysis to locate, analyse and visualize so-called 'issue-networks' on the Web – networks of organizations, individuals and other agents assembling around a common topic or concern – as in this sustainable living network located with the aid of the Web-based Issuecrawler in 2008 (Figure 3.2). On the one hand, this approach takes advantage of socio-technical features specific to online settings, namely the practices of hyperlinking and tagging that have long been characteristic of the Web (Rogers and Marres, 2000; Marres, 2015). On the other hand, however, the method of 'issue network analysis' is certainly not exclusive to digital research, but rather builds on existing approaches: the term 'issue-network' was coined in the 1970s by Hugh Heclo, which he defined as 'activists and experts [..] forming loose alliances in which they define issues by sharing information about them' (Heclo (1978) cited in Marres, 2006).

Work on the Great British Class survey by Savage and others presents another example of a mixed approach: in this project, sociologists partnered with the BBC to administer an online survey

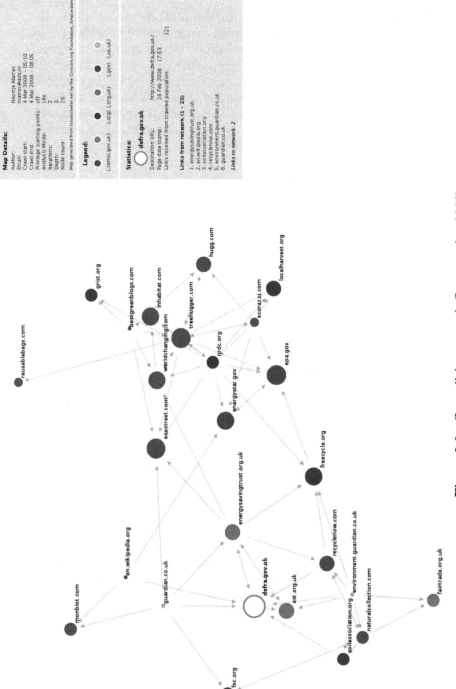

green home experiments

Map Details:

Author:	Noortje Marres
Email:	marres@fds.nl
Crawl start:	4 Mar 2008 – 05:10
Crawl end:	4 Mar 2008 – 08:05
Privilege starting points:	off
Analysis Mode:	site
Iterations:	2
Depth:	2
Node count:	26

Map generated from Issuecrawler.net by the Govcom.org Foundation, Amsterdam.

Legend:

(com) (.gov.uk)   (.org)   (.org.uk)   (.gov)   (.co.uk)

Statistics:

○ **defra.gov.uk**

Destination URL:	http://www.defra.gov.uk/
Page date stamp:	26 Feb 2008 – 17:53
Links received from crawled population:	121

Links from network (1 – 20)

1. energysavingtrust.org.uk
2. en.wikipedia.org
3. soilassociation.org
4. recyclenow.com
5. environment.guardian.co.uk
6. guardian.co.uk

Links to network: 2

Figure 3.2 Green living network (Issuecrawler, 2008)

about the class structure of British society, and generally speaking the project's research design implements a traditional social science research methodology online: sample survey analysis. However, subsequent debates about this study exposed various methodological innovations (Savage et al., 2013), many of which were not unrelated to medium-specific features, such as the fact that respondents were largely self-selected, as is not uncommon in online survey research. Where some sociologists criticized this study for glossing over the resulting biases,[4] Savage et al. (2014) responded to this criticism by questioning the methodological orthodoxy that informed this criticism and offering an alternative: they argued for a culturally informed and 'reflexive' understanding of social categories like class, one that takes seriously how people 'self-identify', thereby highlighting how a medium-specific feature (self-selection) aligns with newer, sociological understandings of a category traditionalists like to consider 'descriptive', like class. They called into question the unthinking reliance on the notion of a 'base population' defined in narrow terms of education, occupation and ethnicity, as the lynch pin of sociological analysis, noting that the very notion of 'population' may need rethinking in view of the relatively open-ended and dynamic collectives that become queryable in online research. Savage's discussion then connected medium-specific and sociological features of his methodology. It also suggests that the debate about 'natively digital' versus digitized methods is *not* just about what methods we choose to adopt, it also opens up a wider range of methodological issues in digital sociology, such as: do we need new – more dynamic, reflexive and culturally aware – concepts to study class in digital societies? The opposition between digitized and digital methods provides a starting point for broader discussions in sociology about the degree to which methodology can and should be adapted in order to adequately take the digital into account.

'The digital' seems to force a choice between innovation or continuity in methods development, as it pitches new methods or techniques versus old ones, but the simplicity of this dramatic opposition between the old and the new is deceptive to a degree. There are wider issues of methodology at stake in digital research, and these issues have troubled social enquiry for a long time, at least since the start of the twentieth century. One of the most important of these is the question of the role of technology in methodology development in social enquiry. *The disagreement about the newness of digital methods signals a much wider disagreement about how sociology advances, and what institutional arrangements make it possible.* To risk a caricature, the advocates of natively digital methods open the door to a technology-led approach in social enquiry. The proposal to work with 'methods-of-the-medium' can be read as proposing that we should take our cues from digital industries in designing our methodology, taking up whatever methods these industries have decided to build into digital platforms. On the face of it, the 'digitization of methods' project advocates a much more minimal role for technology in social enquiry, as here the methodological traditions of social research guide the implementation of method in digital research. However, paradoxically, some proposals for the 'digitization of methods' run a similar risk as 'natively digital' approaches. To speak with Crampton et al. (2013) again, this approach suggests that 'new technical implementations of methods need not affect the epistemic qualities of [these] methods', and as such it can be taken to suggest that whatever is innovative about digital research must be ascribed to technology: if social research methods remain the same and provide the continuity, then it is the technology that is new. By implication whatever is innovative about these studies must be ascribed to the latter as well? This is surely not what is intended by the advocates of digitization, but their arguments also invoke a schema in which technology = new, different, source of change; sociology = old or the same.

Behind the debate about the 'newness' of digital methods lie wider questions about what informs the development of social research. To what extent does technology 'drive' social enquiry and/or should it be allowed to? Does the uptake of digital techniques in social research affect the relation between technology and knowledge in social enquiry? And how does it, in turn, affect the balance of power between academia and industry, between public and private, and between science and society? That is, it also raises the question of whether we should adopt an 'internal' or 'external' approach in advancing social research. That is, should we assume an 'internal' sociological perspective on the digital implementation of social methods and recognize sociological traditions as our primary context? Or should we recognize 'society' as an active agent in directing developments in social research? To put this bluntly: should we be guided by sociology or by the digital? Or should we decline both options, and embrace a more 'interactive' approach in developing social methods by digital means, and approach it as a way of intensifying connections with digital devices and practices proliferating across sociology and social life?

In what follows, I will argue that it is important that we address these wider methodological and political questions, but equally important that we refuse a simple choice either for or against the digital. We must move beyond the opposition between the natively digital and digitization, because both of these projects are far too preoccupied with the supposed newness of digital methods. This preoccupation with the new risks to obscure from view broader possible transformations of social enquiry in digital contexts, which involve changing relations *between* different aspects of social research: between technology and sociology; between data, methods and theory, between the subjects and objects of social enquiry; and between different methodological traditions. Attending to these transformations may enable multiple projects of methodological reconstruction in social research, which I call *interface methods* (Marres and Gerlitz, 2016). But before discussing this general approach, I first want to discuss in some more detail the technical, social and methodological features of digital networked infrastructures, devices and practices that are relevant for the development of social methods.

Digital sources of methodological innovation

Interestingly, while there continues to be widespread debate and disagreement about how technology and methodology come together in social research, there is a growing consensus about what features of digital infrastructures, devices and practices are relevant for social enquiry. The overview that I provide below is far from exhaustive, but cover three broad themes: data and traces, interaction and interactivity, and research design. These three aspects of social enquiry are broadly in line with issues addressed in the previous two chapters, but they are here examined from a more practical, methods perspective.

Networked data, and data capture

As we have seen in the previous chapters, the most prominent and straightforward arguments in support of the digital as a force of methodological innovation in social research focuses on data (Kitchin, 2014; Ruppert, 2013; see also Schwartz, 1979). The relevant characteristics of data generated by digital devices, practices and infrastructures have already been discussed: as a consequence of the widespread uptake of the digital across society, and the enhancement of the data-generating features of digital architectures over the last decade or so, digital data today is abundant, continuous, and highly detailed (granular). Some scholars have questioned this conventional understanding of the digital data deluge (Boellstorf and Mauer, 2015), flagging the patchiness of data coverage in many instances (for example, mostly prove missing in Twitter data sets), and the practical difficulties of accessing digital data (digital data access is generally provisional and temporary, as Web sites may be taken offline and platform settings change). Nevertheless, the claim of data abundance holds in many cases, and I would like to clarify its implications for social enquiry by focusing on one specific social method: network analysis. Let me briefly introduce this method before discussing how it may be transformed by digital data, and data capture.

Network analysis has been around for at least a century (Latour, 2005; Crossley, 2008; Scott, 2012), and can be traced back to the classic work of Jacob Moreno on socio-metrics, which has undergone a revival in recent years (Giessmann, 2009; Mayer, 2012; Rieder, 2012). In the early twentieth century, Moreno developed an experimental method for studying relations of 'affinity' between actors, focusing on small groups such as schools and football teams (Figure 3.3). Significantly, Moreno's aim in plotting social network diagrams was to map out the likes and dislikes among members of social groups, and the visualization of these patterns of like and dislike presented a key aspect of his method: he used these visualizations to elicit feedback about group dynamics from the subjects involved. For Moreno, that is, the aim of network analysis was not only to gain insight into social relations, but also to make these relations available for intervention. His socio-metrics had a reformist aim: 'visualizing the positions of the actors should enable his research subjects to take charge of their own social embedding and initiate changes to optimize their positions' (Mayer, 2011). It was to enable his research participants to become 'participants in and observers of the problems of others as well as their own' (Moreno, 1937, p. 211; quoted in Guggenheim, 2012). Moreno also made attempts to 'scale up' his method, by attempting to extrapolate from his case studies of specific social groupings to 'the nation,' and expanding his methodology into a general theory of society as made up of 'social atoms.' Nevertheless, his method of socio-metrics has become most famous for its application in the study of 'self-contained communities', as in Moreno's famous study analysing the 'likes and dislikes' among pupils and staff in a girls boarding school, which aimed to explain why some of the girls had attempted to escape.[5]

Since these early days of socio-metrics, network analysis has been developed in many different directions, both mathematical (graph

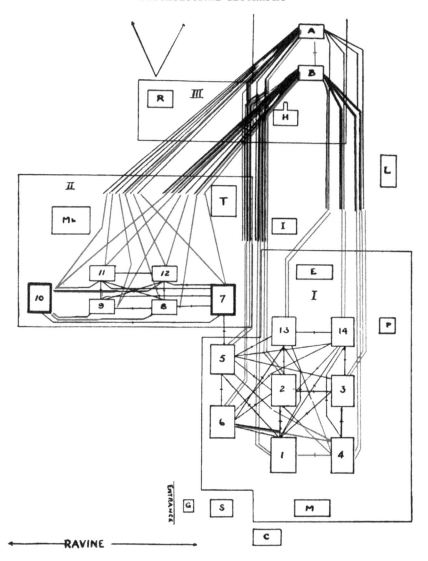

Figure 3.3 Jacob Moreno, Likes and dislikes in the Hudson camp for
girls (Moreno, 1934)

theory), quantitative and qualitative (social network analysis), and radically empiricist (actor-network theory). For most of the twentieth century, the pre-occupation with small scale network formations has nevertheless remained a feature of much of this work (Knox et al., 2006). By contrast, it has been argued that the recent explosion in digital networked data enables a scaling up – or widening 'out' – of network analysis. Bruno Latour and colleagues (2012) have argued that the scope of digital infrastructures make it possible to map actor-networks across a much wider range of sites than was previously feasible (see also Latour 1998). This argument elaborates an earlier ambition of actor-network theory, namely to move beyond the single, contained fieldwork site, and to analyse distributed networks across settings, which ANT did by following actors from site to site, say from the laboratory to the farm (Latour, 1987). Computational social scientists have made a related argument about the 'scaling up' of network analysis: they propose that the digital data deluge makes possible an 'empirical turn' in network theory. Invoking mathematical approaches in network analysis, they stress that previous work tended to have a theoretical focus on modelling networks, whereas the new data abundance makes possible a move 'from modelling networks to the analysis of real-world network dynamics' (Newman et al., 2007; see also Conte et al., 2012). As noted, social network analysis is today undergoing a revival, and some have exchanged small group studies for the study of wider network formations, as researchers turn to social media platforms like Facebook, to collect social network data and study their dynamics on a large scale (Rieder, 2013).

Different approaches to network analysis – social network analysis, actor-network theory, and network science – then offer different methodological frameworks – 'the contained community'; 'following actors' (across sites), network modelling – and these methodologies offer very different starting points from which to proceed in the digital elaboration of this method (Mützel, 2009). This difference in starting point is consequential: while from the standpoint of network theory, the digital signals an empirical turn in methodology development, for actor-network theory, the methodological implication is almost the opposite. ANT is often characterized as a radically empiricist approach, as it proposes that researchers 'follow the actors' wherever these may lead – as the well-known methodological dictum has it (Latour, 2005). This worked pretty well as long as ANT relied on fieldwork methods, but once network analysis is scaled up – or widened out – a new principle must be found: taking up instruments of data analysis to follow networks unfolding in distributed digital infrastructures, the demarcation of relevant and irrelevant entities becomes necessary again – and for that a minimal, empiricist principle like 'follow the actors' won't do. However, while there are thus significant differences in how various methodological approaches incorporate the digital, in some respects they proceed in similar directions: namely, towards a 'widening out' of the networks under investigation, and the uptake of instruments of data analysis to manage this (Crossley, 2010).

This raises the question of whether we will see a wider shift from fieldwork methods to data analysis in social network research. Or is the question rather how these methods can be re-combined in digital research? After all, the pioneering socio-metrics developed by Moreno had both fieldwork and data analytic elements. And there are other methodological re-orientations enabled by the digital, such as a possible return to Moreno's experimental research style: Contemporary work on network analysis has used network visualizations interactively, as in work that deploys visualizations of people's social media networks to solicit responses from users, as I will discuss below (Hogan et al., 2007). However, to understand what digital networked data are 'doing' to social research methods, we must pay close attention not just to the forms of social analysis they enable, but also to more practical aspects of digital research, such as the use of digital instruments of data capture.

Network researchers wishing to analyse Web data, social media content, or data captured by apps and sensors, need to become familiar with computational techniques of data capture, such as Web crawling and the use of APIs (Application Programming Interfaces). While manual data capture ('copy and paste') is certainly not impossible, the uptake of automated forms of data collection have become pretty much de rigeur in digital research, and it is therefore important that sociological research in this area is informed about – and by – these attempts to automate, scale and speed up digital data collection (Murthy et al., 2013; Weltevrede et al., 2014). This involves the use of basic software tools to 'automatically extract structured information such as entities, relationships between entities, and attributes describing entities' from online sources (Sarawagi 2007; see Marres and Weltevrede, 2015). While there are a broad array of user-friendly tools and services that provide researchers with access to digital data, such as Discovery Text for social media, it is nevertheless crucial to understand the broad outlines of how online data capture proceeds: it might seem a largely 'technical' affair, but it has potentially far-reaching methodological consequences for network analysis, as well as other methods.

Significantly, data obtained from online sources by computational means tends to be accompanied by meta-data, sometimes called 'data about data' (Kitchin, 2014). When we automatically capture content from digital platforms, we do not just get access to the 'content' itself, but to a host of related 'data points,' such as account name, geo-location, timestamps, as well as 'social metrics' such as the number of comments, likes, re-tweets, associated URLs (Borra and Rieder, 2014). Much digital social research makes use of this meta-data, for example to analyse and visualize which social media content is shared a lot. Some work directly relies on the formatted, networked quality of digital data, turning it into a source of analytic insight, as in the use of hyperlink analysis to delineate topical networks: links to content or actors can be used as a demarcation criteria, identifying sources that are active and relevant – and thus belong – to a given topical formation, as in the issue-network visualization included above (Marres and Rogers, 2000; Schneider and Foot, 2005). Another example is the study of 'reply chains' on the video platform YouTube: as the YouTube API provides pretty detailed data about user comments, it is possible to analyse the degree to which topics give rise to comments referring to previous comments, forming conversations (Thelwall et al., 2012).[6] To be sure, part of the reason for analysing meta data or formatted content is a practical one: this tends to me more computationally – and analytically – efficient than crunching raw data. But this practical consideration has methodological consequences: *With the analysis of meta-data, the focus of social enquiry shifts from the actors or content itself to consider more formal features of networked activities (uptake, location, and so on)* (on this point, see alsoHerring, 2009).

To suggest that the technical process of data capture informs methodological choices in digital social research goes against established understandings of the role of methods in social research. Textbook accounts of social research methods tend to uphold a strict separation between data collection and data analysis, but the work above mixes these phases: the process of data collection structures data analysis. However, this suggestion also goes against some prevailing contemporary narratives about big data and digital analytics, which promote an attitude sometimes called 'any data'. It is then claimed that digital analytics can be brought to bear on anything from phone records to parking tickets, as long as they are digital (Kitchin, 2014). Similarly, some literatures refer to the 'new' digital data as 'unstructured' – which similarly suggest that digital data is 'hoovered up' pretty much indiscriminately. The perspective I adopt here, by contrast, proposes that digital networked data may be *strange* – insofar as it comes in a form that is in some ways alien to sociology. But this does not mean it has no structure – as discussed, much of it is highly formatted. Indeed, to say that digital data is unstructured, risks to obscure its formatted quality, as well as the source of this formatting: data extracted from digital networked technologies tends to be structured by the infrastructures, devices and practices from which they derive, by way of links, tags, flags and so on (Marres and Weltevrede, 2013). The significant point then is that, in working with digital networked data, social researchers are *not* in full control of the implementation of the data structure, as tends (seems) to be the case with purposefully collected survey or interview data.

Insofar as digital networked data facilitate methodological innovation in social research, this brings distinctive risks and dangers with it. It is to risk a particular, normative form of 'data capture': in taking up digital networked data, sociologists risk to render their research dependent on the platforms and applications from which they derive their social research data (Lewis, 2015). These devices play a formative role in structuring social data, yet at the same time the ways in which they do so are often obscure to social researchers, insofar as these effects derive from technical architectures. The wider uptake of digital networked data across social research may precipitate a 'loss of control' on the part of social researchers over research design (Housley et al., 2014), a point to which I return below. Using a political vocabulary, we could say digital data capture threatens the 'methodological sovereignty' of social research: this is surely a tricky matter, though the challenge is to a degree softened by the fact that this sovereignty had already been 'called out' as problematic many decades ago, by ethnomethodologists among others, and quite independent from the Internet or anything digital.

Interaction and interactivity

A second feature of digital infrastructures, devices and practices that is highly relevant for social research is its 'interactivity'. As we have seen in previous chapters, this term refers to both a technical feature of digital devices and to a social process. This is more than a coincidence. As Christian Licoppe (2004) has noted, the interactive properties of digital media technologies have opened up a potentially vast new realm for the sociological study of social interaction, as they translate into a wealth of new empirical objects for social research.

From social media comments to SMS conversations, and Web analytics that show how long people stay on a Web page, how far down they scroll, to which locations they move their mouse. However, while much about the generation of such interaction traces is technically new, their significance as a source of innovation in social research is still uncertain: much of this data is private, proprietary or practically and technically difficult to access for social research (Langlois and Elmer, 2013). In practice, it means that social studies of networked interaction require the configuration of a dedicated research apparatus or 'dispositif': capturing interactional data using smart phones, for example, may require asking research subjects to take screenshots of their phones at particular moments, or the use of dashboard cameras installed in people's cars, as in Barry Brown's study of people disagreeing with their sat nav systems and their smart phone navigation apps (Brown et al., 2013; see also Laurier et al., 2008). In doing so, the analysis of digital networked interaction builds on important precedents in interaction research, such as conversation analysis.

There are nevertheless some intimate connections between 'new' digital research techniques for the study of interaction and established methodological traditions in social research. The aforementioned study of reply-chains on YouTube, for example, can be seen as analogous to 'pre-digital' studies of 'turn taking' in telephone conversations, and indeed, in face-to-face conversations (Passoth, 2015). The analysis of sat nav disputes evoke social studies of car interactions, which sought to decipher the socio-technical language of honking and blinking between cars (Lynch, 1993). This also means that as we ponder opportunities for 'methodological innovation' in digital social research, we do well to focus our attention not only on the development of new methods 'from scratch', but on gaining a more precise understanding of which social research traditions exactly are rendered newly relevant by the empirical objects generated with the aid of digital infrastructures, devices and practices. The difficulty is, while we would do well to be as specific as possible, the range of social methods that are activated by the digital is impressively wide. In the case of online interaction, for example, we may consider the aforementioned methods of conversation analysis, but equally relevant are many aspects of symbolic interactionism, ethnomethodology, and indeed, the interdisciplinary field called interaction research.

To specify the mutual relevance between social methods and digital interaction takes work, and this is currently undertaken by sociologists across a range of genres, including audiovisual analysis (Knoblauch et al., 2006). Of critical importance is that the 'record-ability' of interaction and interactivity has already been a formative feature of empirical approaches like these: the analysis of audio and video recordings to study interactions goes back decades (Back, 2010; Goodwin, 1994). Indeed, much digital methods research is directly inspired by older methods. For example, Rogers (2013) has suggested that the study of Internet traffic and other digital patterns may draw on so-called unobstrusive methods (Lee, 2000), which are exemplified well by a famous study of the carpets in the Chicago Museum of Industry: in this study, conducted in the 1960s, researchers looked for signs of wear and tear in carpets across exhi-bition spaces as a way to determine which exhibits were especially popular with audiences. Similarly, Internet studies could attempt to re-construct the topography of online content by detecting activity patterns. In this regard, it is important that we specify not only what digital networked infrastructures, devices and practices add, but also what they subtract. A Web page with a scroll bar arguably presents a flatter and less complete surface than the space of the Chicago museum with its broad halls and hidden stair cases. As noted, we may need to complement digital techniques with other methods such as fieldwork to determine the relevant contexts in which the topogra-phy of interaction takes shape.

Another important consideration is that digital infrastructures themselves are informed by social methods, and exemplify sociologi-cal understandings of interaction and interactivity. Take for example Robert K. Merton's famous contribution (1968) to citation analysis discussing the so-called Matthew effect in the formation of reputations in science. Merton noted how 'the allocation of rewards to scientists for their contributions affects the flow of ideas and findings through the communication networks of science'. Search engines and social media offer especially clear examples of this dynamic, as pages are ranked higher in search engine returns when they receive more links and mentions, which only further increases their ranking, received links and visitor numbers, and so on (Rieder, 2012). These dynamics of interactivity have repercussions well beyond digital infrastructures themselves: when the hashtag #Ferguson was used on Twitter so often that it trended, news media reporting on Ferguson increased, and this now 'national' protest event subsequently attracted more protestors from outside the region (Tufecki, 2014b). Furthermore, it is not only the case that sociological dynamics of interactivity can be clearly detected in digital settings; these environments add another layer to sociological interactivity: the algorithms on which search engines like Google rely, like Pagerank, build directly on citation analysis, the method to which Robert Merton made important contributions including his work on the Matthew effect. This effect is actively studied by search engine companies like Google, and their evaluation criteria are designed to take it into account. In conducting sociological studies of reputation in digital environments, we then do well to consider the role of concepts and methods in the configuration of sociological phenomena in digital settings.

Research design: experiments and experimentation

This brings us to a third and last relevant feature of digital arrangements which could be called by different names, but the best label is probably 'research design'. It refers to a broad circumstance: the digital is making possible potentially new ways of configuring the empirical apparatus of social enquiry, with consequences for methods and methodology. There are many possibilities, but some are exemplified by studies I have already discussed, such as the development of real-time research approaches and the re-invention of unobtrusive methods in digital research, as well as the participatory approaches to social media research, briefly discussed in Chapter 1 (see also Chapter 5). However, here I want to focus on the uptake of experimental research designs in digital sociology. On the one hand, experimentalism is a general feature of sociological work that takes up digital methods. As Adrian Mackenzie and colleagues (2015) have highlighted, this work is by necessity experimental – in the sense of being committed to trying out new methods and techniques, and making use of new digital 'skills and tools, borrowed and copied from domains of statistics, software development, hacking, graphic design, audio, video, and photographic recording and predictive modelling – that is, from the media-textual environments of contemporary culture themselves' (Mackenzie et al., 2015, p. 367). On the other hand, much interesting work in digital sociology can be called experimental in a much more specific sense: while sociological research tends to rely on descriptive and observational data, recent work in digital sociology stands out for its interventionist approach. As noted, one of the most striking features of digital arrangements for social enquiry is the opportunities they provide for feedback and active engagement with research participants, audiences and research sites.

Important in this respect is that digital sociology introduces a different type of experimental methodology than is customary in computational social science. Indeed, sociologists are critical of many social scientific experiments conducted in online environments. Take www.youarewhatyoulike.com, an experimental research project initiated by the Psychometrics Centre at Cambridge University, this project invited users to install an app on their phones which analyses their Facebook likes and predicts personality features on this basis, and produced the claim that anything from sexual preference to future income can be predicted on the basis on an aggregative analysis of social media data (Kosinski et al., 2013). This experiment can be criticized on ethical grounds, among others because it does not communicate its research purposes very clearly to participants.[7] The project interface played up the ludic aspect of the research, which was described as a project that 'looks at the things you like on Facebook and then tell you who you are'.[8] However, from a sociological perspective, such an experiment is also problematic methodologically speaking: it seems to presume that individual attributes like 'sexual preference' can be decided from interactive data and content, that is content that is explicitly produced to address other social actors and audiences. However, sociological research is rich in alternative traditions, and this notably includes fieldwork approaches which frame existing social environments themselves as 'laboratories', which were championed by the Chicago School.

Drawing loosely on classic work in urban sociology by Robert Park, who studied his city Chicago as a 'social laboratory' in the 1920s (Gieryn, 2006), sociologists are developing methodologies that adapt digital experiments that are already ongoing in society to the purposes of social enquiry. Noting how experiments have gained special salience in digital societies, in the form of self-monitoring experiments (quantified self) and living labs (such as those initiated by digital industries), sociologists have taken up these ongoing experiments as occasions for sociological investigation (Marres, 2012b; Gabrys, 2014). For example, Ana Gross (2015) has studied data leaks as 'experiments on society'. Her study focuses on a particular data leak, namely the release of the large data set of Yahoo search engine query records mentioned in Chapter 1. This event received much attention in the press, among others because the data set allowed the re-identification of persons using search engine data. In her study, Gross investigates the experimental methods on which journalists as well as data scientists relied to produce such person identifications. However, the aim in her study is not simply to describe these practices, her objective is to determine emergent capacities of 'personal data' in digital societies by doing so. Her aim is to answer the question: what counts as personal data in our 'societies of the query'? And what counts as a person in these societies? Gross then re-configures the data leak as a sociological experiment, deploying it to bring into focus the changing social ontology of personhood in our increasingly data-intensive, networked societies.

Other work in digital sociology is experimental in the more generic, but no less important sense noted above: this work explores how digital methods that at first sight appear alien to sociological enquiry, like data science methods, may nevertheless be used for sociological ends. Take the study by Birkbak and Carlsen (2015) which investigates the visions of social order that are being implemented in social media platforms and digital infrastructures. Their study is inspired by the work of Laurent Thevenot and Luc Boltanksi on social 'orders of worth', the logics, principles and discourses that are typical of different social worlds, like the market, civic culture, or celebrity, and takes up the question how such 'orders of worth' are today envisioned and implemented by way of the algorithms running digital platforms. To answer it, Birkbak and Carlsen could of course have conducted a discourse analysis of documents produced by digital industries and their commentators, or used interviews. But instead they opted to conduct an experiment in online data analysis: they selected a data set of scientific articles, and analysed this data set with algorithms modelled on those implemented by social media industries: a 'friending' algorithm, a 'trending' algorithm, and an 'authority' algorithm. Producing source rankings on this basis, their analysis shows how different sources 'end up on top' depending on what algorithm is applied, and by implication, which order of social media worth is upheld. We can certainly ask whether and how this 'finding' tells us something about social orders or more about technical architectures, and I will take up this question in the next chapter. But in taking up this experimental method to address a sociological question, this work also makes an important methodological contribution: It explores how a critical awareness of the limits of computational social science can inspire an alternative approach to digital methods, an alternative way of taking advantage of the experimental affordances of digital settings in social enquiry.

Finally, sociologists are experimenting with the 'interactive' deployment of digital methods, in order to gauge the affordances of digital settings for more responsive, engaged or creative styles of social enquiry. Some of this work experiments with the interactive features of digital data visualization, as in studies that deploy such visualizations as an instrument for eliciting responses from research participants. Barry Hogan and colleagues (2007) use Facebook network visualizations as a 'narrative device' to guide respondents to narrate their social media networks: network visualizations no longer feature as an 'empirical result' but as an elicitation device (Lezaun and Soneryd, 2007), or interview heuristic.[9] Indeed, there is an ever-widening range of options for interacting with research subjects, as sociologists consider the use of Twitter and SMS to contact research participants. To be sure, such channels can be used in any research project, as a way of 'maintaining good relations' with research participants, and audiences. In other cases, however, such interactive devices are used to radically reenvision the relations between methods and data, between research site and project, as in the work by Michael, Wilkie and Plummer-Fernandez (2014), in which they programmed Twitter bots to produce random statements about their research topic – energy demand reduction – as a way to solicit responses from Twitter users and generate research materials. An outstanding feature of this type of experimental use of digital techniques in social enquiry is the willingness of researchers to deviate from the more conventional 'empirical cycle' of social research: for example, active engagement with audiences is supposed to happen at the end of the research cycle, but in the interactive research style it becomes as an instrument for data collection.

Given these possibilities to reconfigure the empirical cycle in digital social research, it has been proposed that the digital makes possible a distinctive style of 'real-time' or 'live' research, in which responsiveness and interaction between the research process and the research setting become continuous in ways that seemed extremely challenging to implement before (Back, 2012; Lury, 2012). While some of these 'real-time' or live approaches in digital social research focus on curating more responsive or engaged relations with audiences and settings, they may also focus on enabling different ways of organizing a data set or corpus. For example, in our work on mapping issue networks online, we found ourselves experimenting with 'dynamic data sets' as the composition of the hyperlink networks that we located online was constantly changing (Marres, 2012b). Digital networked settings make feasible methods of 'dynamic sampling' (Rogers, 2013), whereby data sets will consist of any set of entities that satisfy particular criteria at a give point in time: whether they use a specific set of key-words, or reference a particular collection of URLs? Holding this referent – a key word(s) or a source set of URLs – stable, we may then decide to include in our data set all contributions or actors associated with these starting points. Not only would the composition of our sample change continuously, these changes could be made monitorable, and may constitute 'findings' in themselves. Indeed, in a 'society of the query' (Lovink, 2008), where users keep an eye on changing rankings as part of their everyday routines, the use of such 'real-time methods' have become pretty routine in and as social life. Will social research follow suit?

Digital techniques are then taken up to develop experimental forms of sociological enquiry, which must be distinguished from the use of experimental methods in computational social science. The aim of digital sociology is *not* to mimick methodologies derived from scientific disciplines and to conduct the 'controlled experiments' that laboratory science is known for. Digital sociology is first and foremost committed to testing the *partly unknown* methodological capacities of digital infrastructures, devices and practices to inform and advance social research. From this perspective, the most relevant feature of digital settings is not that they enable us to exchange 'passive' methods of description for the 'active' manipulation of behaviour. The project is rather to determine whether and how digital settings may help to 'experimentalize' research methodology in ways that advance social enquiry. To be sure, the notion of 'medium-specificity' captures some of this attentiveness to the distinctive features of a given digital apparatus and its affordances for social research. However, the experimental sensibility I invoke here is equally attentive to resonances with existing social research traditions. For example, when we say that digital infrastructures, devices and practices enable more dynamic ways of assembling empirical formations (Marres, 2012a), we are not just celebrating digital networks, we are equally drawing on a long-standing commitment to to the study of social process.

Sociologists already observed *many decades ago* that social enquiry is limited by the structure of data-bases, as they organize data in rather static, domain-specific ways. Newspaper data-bases archive editions of selected news publications; science citation data-bases track references between scientific publications only, and this limits our ability to trace heterogeneous formations across these domains (Callon, 2006). In contrast to this, current practices of online networking like hyperlinking and following occur more informally *across the domains* of journalism, science, policy, art and commerce, and partly for this reason they enable the analysis of 'heterogeneous networks', that is, networks that are composed not just by human relations, but by relations with non-human entities as well, which include medium-specific entities like URLs and substantive phenomena like issues. Methods for the location of heterogeneous formations were first proposed by actor-network theorists in the 1980s in the social study of innovation, but today they have become much more common as digital platforms serve to 'connect users and objects' (Keegan et al., 2010), and infrastructures from GPS to RFID and sensors are increasingly used to trace material and non-human entities from trash to the air and forests through space and time (Gabrys, 2014).

The digital methods debate reconsidered

The 'digital' then opens up a wide array of avenues for methodological innovation and indeed exploration, but it is possible to draw some specific conclusions from this broad overview for the digital methods debate. As we have seen, at the heart of this debate is the issue of the supposed 'newness' of digital methods, and disagreement about this is not just limited to sociology, but extends across media studies, computer science, geography and anthropology. It is now possible to qualify further the main issues at stake in this debate, and also, to clarify why the time may be ripe to reject the opposition between old and new methods, between the natively digital and the digitization of social research. There are at least three important problems with the opposition that I would like to sum up here. Firstly, the idea that 'natively digital' methods are 'medium-specific' leaves room for misunderstanding. It risks obscuring the extend to which the 'methods-of-the-medium'– the methods that are inscribed into digital infrastructures and devices – themselves build on long-standing methodological traditions in social research. As we have seen, digital platforms invoke some well-known sociological approaches, including Georg Simmel's relational sociology and Robert Merton's study of reputational dynamics. But these continuities between digital methods and social research traditions – as in the case of network analysis and interaction analysis above – remain out of view when Internet methods are said to be 'born digital'. The idea of 'natively digital' methods, then, does not really allow us to appreciate methodological continuities between medium-specific and sociological practices, and indeed the extend to which the very idea of 'medium-specificity' builds on sociological perspectives too (as in the study of cars blinking).

The opposition between the natively digital and digitization is also limiting for another reason: it suggests an opposition between a sociological framework and a computational framework for the development of social research methods. This opposition is hard to avoid and commonly invoked, as when Deborah Lupton (2014) proposes that methods of digital data analysis derive 'primarily from computer science'.[10] The opposition also occurs in the well-known article by Mike Savage and Roger Burrows (2007) on the coming crisis in empirical sociology. This article contrasts important sociological methods such as 'surveys and interviews' with the emerging computational methods of 'data mining and geo-locative data analysis', suggesting that the former are under threat of being supplanted by the latter. This warning is not in general mistaken, but this account wrongly suggests that digital methods impinge on sociology *from the outside*, as if they derive from computing, data science, and so on. To be sure, computing and data science frameworks are without doubt the dominant methodological frames of data analysis today, but there is no reason why sociologists should accept this framing wholesale. It namely creates a notable blind spot: Sociologists have for many decades analysed networks, content and interactions using computational means. Indeed, these methods have in many ways been central to the development of post-war sociology, through work on relational sociology, ethnomethodology, actor-network theory and discourse analysis (Mützel, 2009). From this standpoint, digital methods do not look 'alien' to sociology at all (Halford et al., 2013), even if their implementation certainly remains challenging in technological and other ways. But surely sociologists should not just hand over the empirical objects that digital infrastructures, devices and practices make available – networks, content, interaction – to other disciplines?

That is also to say, the opposition between 'natively digital' and digitized methods risks reducing the digital methods debate to a choice for or against particular methodological traditions, pitching (supposedly digital) methods of network and content analysis against (supposedly digitized) surveys and interviews, and this surely is something we should resist. The reality is that many of the methods and methodologies that are relevant to digital social research have interdisciplinary origins – they are used across fields and qualify as 'mixed' methods in the sense that they combine sociological and computational elements. Conversation analysis is an interpretative method but it also contains computational elements as it works with recorded materials which have since its very inception been transcribed using formal codes and software. As already noted, network analysis has been developed across sociology, anthropology, mathematics and computing (Venturini et al., 2014). Salient about the digital is not only that it inspires methods debates across these fields, it also raises anew the question of how different methodological traditions relate. This is the challenge that Carolin Gerlitz and I have proposed to call 'interface methods' (Marres and Gerlitz, 2015).

Before introducing this proposal I want to mention one last problem with the opposition between 'natively digital' methods and the digitization of methods and this is the backlash against it. David Lazer, one of the leading computational social scientists, has recently rejected the idea of 'natively digital methods'. In a rather remarkable turn around, Lazer and colleagues (2014) argued that the famous Google Correlate study overstates the innovativeness of online data analysis as compared to more traditional approaches in data science. In his view, the study relied on the unjustified 'assumption that big data are a substitute for, rather than supplement to, traditional data collection and analysis' (Lazer et al., 2014). This climb down on claims for methodological innovation in digital research is problematic in my view, though *not* because it calls for more appreciation of continuities between social research methods and digital methods. The problem is that appreciation of these continuities here becomes an argument for a return to familiar methodological frameworks. For Lazer et al., insight into methodological continuity becomes a justification for toning down the ambition to develop new forms of digital social research. To put this more strongly, it becomes an argument in favour of suspending projects of methodological reconstruction in digital social research, and I don't think this follows at all.

We are now in a better position to understand the methodological problems as well as opportunities of digital sociology. The challenge for digital sociology is not simply that it requires active engagement with the technological dimension of social enquiry, something that our methodological training has taught us to put between brackets, at least when it comes to how we account for our research, as I discussed in Chapter 1. The digitization of social life and social research opens up anew long-standing questions about the relations between different methodological traditions in social enquiry: what are the defining methods of sociological research? Are some methods better attuned to digital environments, devices and practices than others? Do interpretative and quantitative methods present distinct methodological frameworks, or can these be combined? Which is to say, the question 'Do we need new methods?' is only the tip of the iceberg. To answer it, we need a better idea of our broader objectives in social research. I will therefore conclude this chapter by introducing a methodological principle that can provide some guidance in this respect.

Interface methods[11]

While much of the debate about digital methods has focused on the opposition between new and old methods, we may also adopt a different starting point. We can begin with the observation that digital methods and social research share *methodological affinities* of various kinds (Beer, 2012; Latour, Jensen et al., 2012; Marres and Gerlitz, 2015). At least some of the methods that are built into instruments of digital analytics are not unlike the methods of network and textual analysis on which sociologists have long relied (Beer, 2012; Marres, 2012a). Take a prominent tool of Twitter analytics like Mentionmapp, which allows users to map so-called follower networks on Twitter, displaying relations between users as well as hashtags. These networks are not unlike the heterogeneous networks that actor-network theorists have documented by 'following actors', as in Michel Callon's (1984) famous study of the fishermen of St Brieuc bay, which showed how researchers, fishermen, scientific colleagues as well as scallops, were brought into relation by the problem of how to get the scallop population to grow. If we start from the question not of the newness of method, but of affinity, a particular challenge for the development of digital sociology comes into view: should we affirm the similarities between popular online tools and sociological forms of analysis, or should we insist on the differences?

Faced with apparent affinities, some sociologists insist on the *divergences* between the aims and objectives of digital analytics and the methodological aims of sociology. For example, tools of digital analytics tend to enable the analysis of current information, and the detection of the current popularity of actors and terms, but sociologists are interested in the analysis of phenomena over time (Uprichard, 2012). But we may also take a different approach: we may decline to fixate on the question of difference and similarity between digital and social methods, and recognize instead the *unstable identity* of digital social research techniques. It is not always clear what methodologies they help to advance, and we do not quite know what these tools are capable of. While it is certainly *possible* to identify similarities and differences between data tools and social research techniques, this does not tell us everything: digital methods are programmable and configurable to a degree, and what is more, their usefulness for social research surely depends on context. To activate our methodological imagination, it is then important to consider that digital analytics present social research with a *methodological uncanny*: the tools mentioned above closely resemble the techniques and methods deployed in social research, but at the same time we can not call them 'our own'. Indeed, digital infrastructures are notoriously unstable also in a practical sense: devices and platforms constantly come in and fall out of use, settings and features are revised on an ongoing basis, and data formations and user communities themselves are always in flux (Weltevrede et al., 2014; Harvey, Reeves, Ruppert, 2013).[12]

To be sure, this dynamism of digital infrastructures, devices and practices poses serious challenges to the quality and robustness of knowledge acquired by these means: they pose a threat to the reliability and validity of findings. Nevertheless, some sociologists have proposed that social enquiry is *not* well served by efforts to contain, restrict and neutralize the dynamism of the digital, as this encourages social researchers to ignore or even negate the changeability that is central to digital social life, narrowing the empirical scope of social research as the result. Rather than seeing the instability of digital data, instruments and practices primarily as a methodological deficiency, i.e. as a threat to the robustness of sociological data, methods and findings, the dynamic nature of digital social life may also be understood as an enabling condition for social enquiry, as processes of change help to articulate phenomena and problems (Back and Puwar, 2012). It is this broader sensibility on which the notion of 'interface methods' draws. It begins by recognizing the methodological ambivalence or multi-valence of digital research: digital analytics resonate with our own research interests but they also invoke alien methodological traditions.[13] But, rather than seeking to resolve this methodological ambivalence, we may also affirm it, and take it as an invitation to test the methodological capacities of digital devices. To conclude this section, I would like to give an example of such a test by describing a digital research project in which we engaged critically and creatively with a specific 'interface method,' namely co-occurrence analysis.

Pilot study: the liveliness of climate change on Twitter

Co-occurrence analysis is a basic measure of data analysis, which detects which entities (such as words) occur together in a given text. It has in recent years been implemented in online data tools, such as the aforementioned Mentionmapp, but also in the Twitter Streamgraph. The latter tool uses co-occurrence analysis to analyse what are 'happening issues' on Twitter. Enter 'climate change' and the Streamgraph will provide a curve of the activity associated with that word on this platform over a specific period of time, visualized as the rise and fall of words based on their frequency of co-occurrence (see Figure 3.4). The Streamgraph then depicts endurance and variation of word relations over time. When more words are significantly connected, the stream widens, and as such, this tool is not dissimilar to a method championed in the sociology of innovation, namely *co-word analysis*.

This method was developed in the 1980s by the sociologist of science and technology Michel Callon and colleagues to detect emerging or innovative topics in the scientific literature (Callon et al., 1983; see also Danowski, 2009; Marres, 2012a). Co-word analysis draws on co-occurrence, but adds a further operation, as it identifies word pairs based on proximity, assigning a value to word distances of say 3, 4 or 5 words. Co-word analysis weighs these word relations in terms of both the quantity of connections and the proximity of co-occurrence (Callon et al., 1983; Danowski, 2009). The method was advocated by Callon and colleagues as a way of detecting the emergence of topics – or so-called 'pockets of innovation' or, as the more sociological terminology had it, 'areas of problematization' – in a corpus of texts. Co-word analysis, the argument went, makes it possible to detect changes in thematic associations over time *without having to rely on previously defined categories, and their implied criteria of relevance*, by rendering text amendable to network analysis.

Steamgraph does something similar to co-word analysis, but there are also relevant differences: the online data tools measure only the frequency of words co-occurring as opposed to the strength of their connection based on their spatial proximity.[14] It is thus possible to put popular data tools 'in their place', and say that they are less sophisticated than sociological method for the study of innovation dynamics. However, the resonances between sociological methods and digital analytic techniques also opens up a space of exploration for social enquiry, allowing us to interrogate the capacities of social methods anew. In doing so, we should also take into consideration the context of application of these measures: tools like Steamgraph are part of the continuously evolving infrastructure known as the real-time Web which is focused on 'what is happening right now'. Online data tools are thus closely implicated in the valorization of live content or 'currency' (Marres and Weltevrede, 2013): which word appears most often in Tweets? Which news article gets the most links or retweets? Which actor is mentioned most often? By contrast, co-word analysis as developed in the sociology of innovation in the 1980s was designed to address a very different kind of question: the

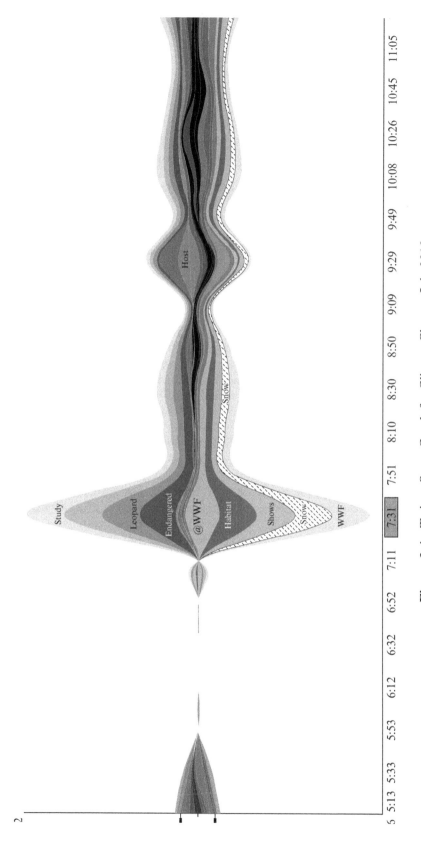

Figure 3.4 Twitter SteamGraph for Climate Change, July 2010

aim then was to detect the emergence of 'happening' problems and topics *at the intersection of categories* and fields – articulations that went undetected in then predominant forms of content analysis (Callon, 1983). To be sure this methodological project is somewhat dated today: among others, it does not address the promotional quality of digital networked content, which confers on the making of connections a much more instrumental quality (accessing new audiences). We can nevertheless ask: Can we today envision a digital apparatus for the analysis of 'happening content' which furthers other agendas than those of currency-centric data analytics: an analysis focused not on popularity of content (liveness) but changes in patterns of *relevance* (liveliness)?

In asking this question, we approach digital methods like co-occurrence as sites of critical and creative engagement with a wider analytical apparatus in-the-making and *treat methods as interfaces.* Designating co-word analysis an interface method, we may treat the implementation of this computational social method as an *opportunity to engage critically and creatively not only with methods that are prominent in todays digital culture but equally with relevant methodological traditions in social research.* To test the capacity of co-occurrence analysis to detect liveliness (rather than liveness), we conducted a pilot study, performing co-occurrence analysis of Twitter data relating to climate change. Our data set included all Tweets using the term 'climate change' for a period of almost three months – from 1 March 2012 to 15 June 2012, adding up to a total of 204,795 tweets, a workably large data set at that time. During workshops in London and Amsterdam,[15] we conducted pilot studies with various keywords (including sustainable living or climate action), performing co-occurrence analysis on hashtags, detecting which hashtags occur together, and analysing whether and how these hashtag relations endure and vary over time (see Figure 3.5) and the online tool of Twitter analysis that we used in our own study, the Associational Profiler.[16]

For example, with which hashtags is our focus word (#drought) connected in each interval? How do these associations change from interval to interval? Together with programmers and designers, we devised an automated technique to produce 'hashtag profiles' which, for a given focus word, presents us with the hashtags associated with it per interval. The resulting visualization shows the variation of these associations overtime, depicting the incoming (appearing) and outgoing (disappearing) hashtags per interval. The lines and blocks indicate endurance and change: lighter lines show stable connections, while darker lines towards the end of the interval indicate ending

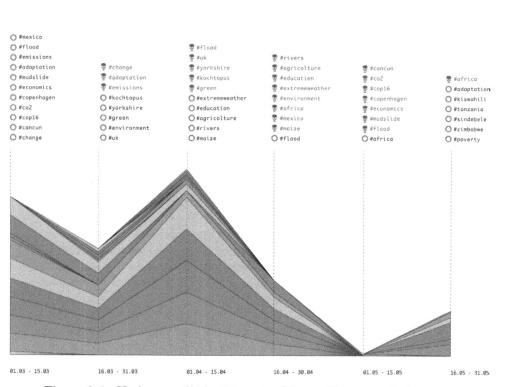

Figure 3.5 Hashtag profile for #drought, Climate Change on Twitter, 2012 (figure designed by Alessandro Brunetti)

connections. These initial visualizations thus display not only a rise and fall but also changes in word associations, and we speculated that altering connections might indicate topical shifts and drifts. Could such analysis help to narrate the 'life' or 'liveliness' of an issue term? The hashtag profile of #drought indicates a number of issue-related events, such as the rise to prominence of the Yorkshire floods in the first interval. This had initially seemed an anomaly to us, but during a presentation John Bloomfield of the British Geological Survey pointed out its significance: in the Summer of 2012, the occurrence of floods during what had been defined as a period of drought posed institutional challenges in the UK, in terms of the public communication of these seemingly contradictory 'weather events' but also with regards to engrained assumptions in drought modelling. Finally, we noted a moment of near-total issue re-composition in the #drought profile, as in the last interval un-summit-related language is almost completely replaced by Africa-specific terms. Had #drought become a different issue?

To be sure, this particular visualization makes it clear that doing co-word analysis with Twitter data comes with particular challenges: the word connections in our Twitter data set were highly ephemeral, jumping from one topic to the next in ways that go against the presumption of thematic coherence in earlier work in the sociology of innovation. Furthermore, Twitter data themselves are highly marked by effects of volume, as it turns out that the preoccupation with currency (trends) is not just a feature of popular tools of social media analytics, but is pursued by 'the actors' and indeed the platforms 'themselves'. In this regard, our case study also taught us about the importance to accept a degree of *maladjustment* between method and medium, and the need to make a number of well-chosen adjustments in order to enable maladjustment at the interface between social method and digital settings. This sense of the need for mutual adjustment and maladjustment between research techniques, method and digital settings seems to us one of the key features of interface methods. We began by recognizing the *relative open-endedness* of digital tools and measures, but if we are to develop forms of analysis at the interface between social methods and digital instruments, it is equally important to recognize that digital instruments come with *methodological biases* built in, such as towards currency. These may require *sociologists to 'work against' digital devices*, to insist on necessary *mal-adjustments* between different components of our research practices, between the analytic measures and dynamics built into digital infrastructures, and those sociologists may wish to pursue.

Conclusion

This is arguably the biggest problem with the claim that 'the digital' drives methodological innovation in social research: it presents technology as a principal enabling condition of methods development in social enquiry, and thereby challenges our ability to impose sociological methodologies in digital research. To go against this troubling tendency – to avoid adopting methods and techniques *simply because they are easy to use* – it is good practice to justify methodological choices on substantive grounds, i.e. to make sure that a chosen method is appropriate in view of the research question, hypothesis or objective. However, it would surely be naïve to deny technology a role in advances in social research. As I proposed in Chapter 1, to affirm that the digital informs social enquiry is not to endorse techno-logical determinism. It is to appreciate that technology – among other elements – is co-constitutive of social research, and social life for that matter (Latour et al., 2012). Yes, digital devices and infrastructures actively inform social research, but *the apparatus of social research must still be actively configured.*

The more specific problem with the idea of digital technology as driver of methodological innovation is this: in privileging technology as the 'cause' or 'engine' of methods development, it risks to render unquestionable the *direction* of processes of methodological innova-tion, limiting our imagination of possible transformations (Suchman, 2007b). This is not just an abstract problem but a concrete one: for example, much work in digital methods has concentrated on network analysis, and this makes sense from a technical, practical, and indeed, commercial perspective: however, the fact that digital media tech-nologies render social networks available for study is of course *not* a sufficient reason for sociologists to start describing the social world as network. As such, the call to develop 'interface methods' is an argu-ment against *laissez-faire* methodology in digital social enquiry (see Chapter 6). The fact that a given method is technologically feasible is not a good enough reason to use it. We should not become over-reliant on digital infrastructures and devices in developing methods and research design. To be sure, the idea of the 'natively digital' is useful in proposing that social research may find its starting point in digital devices, and work with methods inscribed in them. But we still need to assemble our research designs from many different elements, including social theory, sociological research traditions, methodology, and empirical studies of the sociological phenomena in question. The questions of social research methodology cannot be resolved by delegating them to technology, and they require from us that we continuously make choices that, in theory (and perhaps indeed in practice), the technology could make for us: should we assume community is made up of human actors or should we include other types of entities as well? Is the network a relevant heuristic for understanding what is happening among these actors?

Interface methods require that we as researchers are alert to the 'configurability' of digital social research methods: how can we adjust our measures, tools, data set and so on, to serve our research design and methodological ambitions better? Interface methodology resists understanding methods as 'ready-mades', as packages: digital methods must be actively configured to serve the ends of social enquiry, we should not assume, at least not as a matter of course, that they can simply be implemented. In this regard, the principle of 'interface methods' also deviates from the project of the 'digitization of methods'. The latter approach tempts us to minimize or indeed bracket the role of technology in research and methodology design, but this may equally limit our capacity to advance in digital social enquiry. As it proposes that changes in the technological 'base' of social research need not affect its epistemic – and methodological – qualities, this approach leaves us ill-equipped to grasp the epistemic and methodological potentials opened up by the digital. In contrast, I have argued that digital social research operates in a space *between* technology and methodology. We must design our research and methodology both *with and against* the digital: with and against the data formats, measures and features inscribed into the devices and infrastructures with which we conduct our enquiry. Rather than conceiving of technology and methodology as operating on separate levels, interface methods invites us to approach digital research design and methodology *as a relational task*, one which requires us to establish relevant and generative connections between specific methods, instruments, techniques, research questions, sociological concepts, and so on. To acknowledge the role of technology in the methodological configuration of social research does *not* imply that we allow technology to drive knowledge. Device-aware research is different from device-driven research: while the latter is attentive to formatting effects and may seek to deploy them for purposes of social enquiry, it is equally willing to take counter-measures on the grounds of research design.

So, do we need new methods? I have answered this question with 'a firm yes and no', or more precisely, no and yes. No, we do not need new methods, because it is far more important that we recognize the ways in which 'old' methods such as network analysis, ethnomethodology and interaction research are inscribed into supposedly 'new' digital infrastructures, devices and practices. We do not need new methods, because a preoccupation with the new distracts us from the question of how we can productively *combine* existing and evolving sociological and computational methods, techniques and concepts in social enquiry. However, at the same time, we do need new methods very much, as digital forms of enquiry bring together concepts, methods, techniques and practices in ways that challenge certain predominant, limited understandings of what methods are, namely procedures that we (researchers) implement to gain knowledge of a social phenomenon out there. This is the story but not the practice. In digital research, the relations between research, method and technical implementation are all too often reversed: digital media technologies end up deciding for the researcher what methods (h) she will adopt: we want to work with Facebook data, hence we study networks. For this reason, digital research requires an at once critical and creative approach to method. We need to develop methods and methodologies that are better at acknowledging the need for mutual coordination between research design, technical infrastructures, analytic categories, as well as social practices 'out there' in society.[17]

4
Are we researching society or technology?

'You call it Facebook stalking, I call it participant observation... to each his own.'

If you search for this meme, you'll see that the blue-saturated picture which the text accompanies shows a man in the foreground hunched in front of his computer screen, and a woman (his wife/partner?) in the background behind a half-closed door looking dejected. This meme raises, and reflects, a range of issues, perhaps most notably that of 'digital intimacy': what are digital media technologies doing to our relations with our close ones? Tellingly, one website credits this meme to an author called 'Internet husband'. However, I myself first saw the meme on an academic blog, one that accompanied a MA course on Social Media Networking offered by the Centre for Culture and Social Media Technologies at New York University.[1] In this context, the figure also highlights issues in digital sociology, issues having to do with the relations between digital social research and digital social life: how different, really, are the methods of social research from those commonly taken up by social media users? And how social – or rather anti-social – are social researchers as they go about their research, online as well as offline? Should they interact directly with other Internet users? The meme, finally, points towards the precarity of social media research, a sense of the fragility or tenuousness of the methods, objects and objectives (Lury and Marres, 2015) of platform-based research (Gillespie, 2010). This precarity is also highlighted by the question in this chapter's title. Social media research, and digital social research more widely, is marked by a particular ambiguity: when social researchers turn to digital platforms like Twitter or YouTube, they tend to do so with the aim of studying a social phenomenon, like people's experiences of Multiple Sclerosis on Tumblr (Gonzalez-Polledo, 2016), or controversies about new road infrastructures on Facebook (Birkbak, 2013). However, once we start analysing online materials and data, researchers may easily find themselves studying *not* the social phenomenon they set out to investigate, but rather the peculiarities of digital platforms and digital practices themselves.

To be sure, this problem of the ambiguity of the object of study is not exclusive to social media research. Scholars in fields from sociology, Internet studies, science and technology studies, media studies, to anthropology have long insisted on the ambiguity of digital social research. One of the key challenges in doing social research with digital media technologies, they have argued, is to come to terms with the 'reflexivity' of digital social life: in online settings, social life is not only conducted *by digital means*, it is also often explicitly concerned with things digital (Slater, 2002; Kelty, 2005; Lupton, 2014). Take the #gamergate scandal and the related campaigns which unfolded on social media platforms like Twitter, and which raised widespread concern about misogynism in digital industries; or think of the mobilization around Facebook's dubious or illegal practice of scanning private messages (#scan) on Twitter (Jackson et al., 2014). In these cases, *the digital presents both an object and a resource of social life*, to use a classic sociological phrase (Garfinkel, 1984 [1967]). However, while there has been no lack of attention to the ambiguity of digital media technologies in social and media studies, it seems fair to say that much recent work in social media analysis has tended to bracket the problem. Much of this work expresses (and thereby feeds) confidence that digital media tools make it possible to capture 'conversations', public opinion or even 'human behaviour' (Hochman et al., 2013), even if it is increasingly recognized that this will require the sophisticated expertise of specialized data scientists.

In this chapter, I want to present some of the strategies that sociologists and scholars in related fields have developed to address, and render tractable, the problem of ambiguity in digital social research. Each of these approaches offers a different answer to the question in this chapter's title: some sociologists insist that we should study society and *not* technology. Others however argue that we should actively affirm the 'hybridity' of digital social phenomena, recognizing that technology and sociality are inextricably entangled in our societies: in their view we must study technology *and* society. A third approach, finally, looks for a middle way between the first two answers, proposing that we must study society, but with technology. This last approach argues that, while digital social life is inherently hybrid, there is much variation in how this is so: while some practices or phenomena first and foremost engage with technologies, others are primarily concerned with social phenomena. However, while we may be able to use this three-fold distinction to sort out our social research objectives in specific cases, there are also wider issues at stake here. What fields of study are we contributing to by studying digital social life: is it our project to configure a digital apparatus for the study of social life, or for the study of digital societies? Must we answer this question always and once and for all, or can it be suspended at times?

To clarify the methodological issues at stake here, this chapter will *not* focus on the general, theoretical solutions proposed by sociologists and scholars in related fields. Instead I will discuss some examples taken from the *practice* of digital social research:[2] I will discuss a recent social media research pilot project in which I together with others studied debates about 'privacy' and 'surveillance' on Twitter in June 2013 with the aid of online tools of network and textual analysis and visualization. My discussion of this project will serve to identify three different strategies for making the problem of ambiguity tractable in social research: one that privileges the instrumental capacities of digital media technologies (the digital as means of research), a second that foregrounds the medium-specificity of social phenomena that unfold in digital settings (the digital as object and method), and a last approach which aims to 'empiricize' the question of 'what' is the object of social media research: social communities, media-technological dynamics, or processes of issue formation? But before introducing these strategies, I want to discuss a more basic but no less important methodological problem, which is related to the problem of ambiguity: the problem of digital bias.

Problems of digital bias

Any study that makes use of digital methods or data must somehow face the problem of digital bias, which is both tenacious and multi-faceted. As noted in Chapter 1, digital environments are often partial to particular locations, populations and topics (Tufekci, 2014a). For this reason, many continue to be sceptical about digital research as such, arguing that most online data is simply not robust enough to serve as a basis for sound research, as in a recent article in *Science Magazine* which characterized social media analysis as 'Fast and cheap, but fraught with biases and distortion' (Ruths and Pfeffer, 2014). Others, however, have argued that problems of bias in digital social research are only to be expected, insofar as it makes use of embedded infrastructures of information and communication (Rogers, 2013; see also Introna and Nissenbaum, 2000). Social studies of media, information and knowledge technologies have long drawn attention to issues of partiality in public reporting and communication (Cohen, 2002 (1972); Innes, 1951; Nelkin, 1992), and as long as media and communications are biased, it should not surprise us that their analysis must grapple with this problem. This is arguably even more true for digital systems: as we have seen in Chapter 2, the selective disclosure of content is one of the principal dynamics in online environments, and in this respect digital media technologies should simply not be assumed to be neutral. Devices likes search engine query return lists, news feeds, and trend lists are all *designed* to introduce bias into online environments, in the sense that they privilege some sources over others, via their selection and ranking algorithms. They tend to favour popular, fresh and institutionally accredited sources (Introna and Nissenbaum, 2000). However, growing awareness of this means that problems of bias are now more acutely felt in digital research, and the dangers of overreliance on digital networked data and methods are increasingly recognized across the disciplines of sociology, computing, media studies and data science as well. There is also a growing sense that digital media technologies pose a distinctive set of challenges in this regard.

The geographer Crampton and colleagues (2013) have summed up the problem of digital bias well: 'There is little that can be said definitively about society-at-large using only these kinds of user-generated data, as such data generally skews towards a more wealthy, more educated, more Western, more white and more male demographic' (Crampton, 2013, p. 132). While many would support this claim, others have challenged it: they have shown how specific 'subaltern' identities are precisely strengthened and not weakened through the use of digital media technologies, as in Murthy's example of the use of social media as part of anti-arrest tactics by Chicago youth, who in street encounters with police would pull out their phones declaring 'I will put you on Twitter' (Murthy, 2013). However, such debates also make it clear that sociologists must identify specific uses, settings and groups in order to develop claims about the role of the digital in social life (Sharma, 2013). By contrast, critiques of bias typically focus on the 'whole platform': they evaluate the representativeness of the total platform population (people on Twitter), and compare these – either implicitly or explicitly – with another total population (such as the nation). This raises the question of what methodological framework should guide the development of techniques and strategies for addressing problems of data bias: the 'whole platform' critique of bias tends to point towards methods of statistical analysis, outlining measures for the delineation of data sets that may ensure its representativenes, as compared to a base line population. But sociologists have also developed proposals for addressing bias that draw on other methodological traditions, for example by turning the partiality of online data – what specific contexts does it express? – into a *question* for sociological investigation (Snee et al., 2015). Rather than assuming a known population as a point of reference to which to compare online populations, this work foregrounds that social contexts – including transnational, local and cross-boundary ones – are actively configured through digital circulation and exchange.

A second important problem of digital bias has to do with the empirical apparatus of digital social research itself – and could be called, machine bias. dana boyd and Kate Crawford (2012) sounded the alarm about the methodological and normative biases implicit in the socio-technical architectures of online data capture and analysis, pointing out that these arrangements are opaque, unstable as well as highly partial in terms of what phenomena they render accessible for social research. As discussed in Chapter 3, to access and analyse data generated with online platforms like Twitter, researchers today often rely on online interfaces, and they may also rely on online tools for data analysis and visualization, like the Twitter Streamgraph. Reliance on online interfaces, however, has significant implications for what data sets are queried by these means as well as for eventual findings. In a test of different techniques for collecting Twitter data, Driscoll and Walker (2014) demonstrated how consequential the chosen method of online data collection is for empirical analysis. Collecting Twitter data containing the hashtags #debate and #debates around the time of a Presidential election debate between Barack Obama and Mitt Romney, they showed how different collection methods produced vastly different data sets: the Search API produced a much larger data set than the Streaming API (Figure 4.1). However, while Driscoll and Walker shows a clear difference in volume of data collected, it may be difficult to determine exactly how the two data sets differ, as digital platforms are far from transparent about the inclusion criteria built into APIs.[3] While, being good researchers, we can seek to offer precise accounts of our chosen approach to online data capture – what query terms we used, what date range, what technique for capturing tweets (search API versus

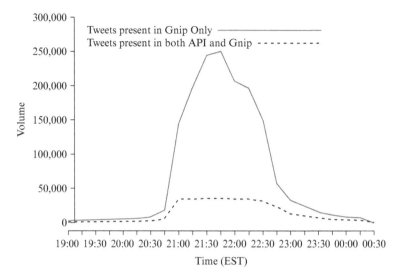

Figure 4.1 Comparison of tweets with the hashtags #debate and #debates collected via Gnip PowerTrack and Twitter's Streaming API (Driscoll and Walker, 2014)

streaming API), it remains often difficult to establish following what criteria exactly the actual data set was produced. As such, it can seem practically inevitable that the technological arrangements of online research leave their mark on digital data (Weltevrede, 2015).

While we gain access to more data, and a wider range of empirical settings, when taking up online techniques for data capture, reliance on these techniques diminishes the influence that social researchers can exert on research design (Marres and Weltevrede, 2013). Platform architectures, then, do not just affect the robustness or transparency of data sets and data analysis, they also influence the very structure of research projects. Much online research relies on 'the methods of the medium' (Rogers, 2013): they rely on the very methods of network and textual analysis and visualizations that are also built into digital platforms themselves, in the form of the network algorithms suggesting who to follow or friend, or textual analyses producing lists of trending terms. For this reason, we can say that digital social research also suffers from a third problem of *methodological bias*. We can observe the operation of this type of bias on a general level, when we consider what type of social media research is prominent today, in scientific and public circles: we then notice that distinctive measures and values (such as 'influence') structure both social media activity and social media analysis, creating a feedback loop in which social research on influence does not speak from the position of an 'external observer,' but rather figures as a participant in an evolving methodological configuration: that of the valuation of influence through its measurement and analysis.

Methodological biases are also at work in studies focusing on the analysis of *topical networks* on Twitter (Burgess et al., 2015; Marres and Gerlitz, 2016). Indeed, the predominance of topical analysis of Twitter data can partly be explained as an artefact of Twitter APIs: the interfaces for Twitter data capture follow a query-based model, inviting the generation of Tweet collections containing particular terms. In other words, they favour key-word-driven research. Importantly, the problem is not that it is *impossible* to use other methods – there is, for example, the option to analyse the 1 per cent sample of Twitter data that the API also makes available (Gerlitz and Rieder, 2013). But the query-based approach is one of the easiest ways of producing an empirically coherent data set. But the price to pay for this coherence is partiality: for example, actor relations in key-word-based data sets are mediated by these words, as users are present in the data analysed by virtue of the words they use (Vis, 2013). It also invites researchers to adopt the perspective of the 'whole platform': topically defined data sets include contributions of any user *of the platform* using the term (at least in principle). *Query-led online data collection then introduces a bias towards platform studies*, towards research that seeks to answer the question 'how did this topic fare on platform 'X' (Twitter)? This problem of 'viewing the world' through the platforms eyes is a returning issue in online data analysis. As Thellwall, Vis et al. (2012) put it in their paper on You Tube data analysis: 'the factors analysed are those that happen to be reported by YouTube (e.g. commentator age, gender and location), ignoring any factors that were not reported but which are nevertheless important (e.g. reason for joining YouTube)'.[4]

These forms of platform bias are problematic but not easy to avoid in social media research. Indeed, the expectation that we can impose our own preferred methodological frameworks in online research often results in misunderstandings of the very opportunities and constraints opened up by this type of research. A colleague once recounted to me the criticisms she had received of her blog analysis of working-class men: the study was rejected for publication in a scientific journal, among others on the grounds that the study failed to satisfy methodological standards of representativeness: it did not include an independent verification of the occupational categories of the bloggers in question (what their professions were). To be sure, such a suggestion makes sense from the standpoint of, say, survey analysis, but from the perspective of blog analysis, it is not quite relevant or even inappropriate: blogs participate in public discourse, and surely 'verified identity' is not a prerequisite for participation in public discourse, nor does discourse analysis require this. Indeed, what are called 'problems of bias' in digital research are not always problems of bias, but something else, namely the inability of some social scientists to appreciate that there are different possible ways of configuring the empirical apparatus of social enquiry.

There are then at least three problems of digital bias that deserve the attention of digital sociologists: (1) biased data and content, (2) biases built into research instruments, and (3) methodological bias. Importantly, the pervasiveness of these problems has led some social researchers to turn digital bias into a topic of empirical investigation. For example, Wikipedia research has demonstrated content biases in Wikipedia reporting on specific issues like climate change and nuclear energy, showing that the sources cited on this platform in relation to these issues lean towards industry and scientific sources (Niederer, 2013; Borra et al., 2015; Moats, 2015). Others however, have sought to devise social research strategies that render problems of digital bias tractable. These strategies can broadly be divided in two categories: those seeking to correct for digital bias, and those aiming to expose or deploy it.

Two methodological strategies for dealing with digital bias

Recent work in digital sociology, media studies and computing has developed a variety of methodological strategies to address problems of digitial bias. Most of these approaches frame the problem of digital bias in negative terms, treating it as a source of noise, exclusion and asymmetry that poses a serious threat to the quality of digital social research: insofar as online information is partial, sociological studies that rely primarily on this type of information will suffer from the very same problem (Venturini et Guido, 2012). To militate against it, sociologists have suggested the use of data from mixed sources (both online and offline), and this indeed seems one of the most effective ways of addressing digtial bias (Hine, 2015). Another proposed solution is to 'correct' online data sets for biases, and to remove from the data obvious artefacts of media-technological effects. In this vein, Thelwall, Vann and Fairclough (2006) recommend that in conducting issue analysis with the Web, it is advisable to 'remove from the data wherever possible all occurrence of Web phenomena that serve to obscure [the issue]' (see also Rogers, 2013). From this standpoint, whenever the process of online data capture results in some sources figuring more prominently than others in the data set, (e.g. because some sources receive comparatively more hyperlinks than others) this effect has to be neutralized by removing duplicates (see also Pearce et al., 2014).

Others, however, have asked whether this 'precautionary' approach to digital bias is always the most suitable (Rogers, 2009). Scholars in media and technology studies have proposed that insofar as digital media technologies actively inform and inflect social life, it is necessary to develop a more affirmative understanding of their role in the mediation of social phenomena. These scholars, that is, advance an 'affirmative' approach to digital bias, proposing that the media-technological dynamics that precautionary approaches like the above define negatively – as sources of noise or corruption of data – may also indicate a constitutive aspect of the enactment of social life by digital means (Boullier, 2016; Marres, 2015). The use of hyperlink analysis to locate networks on the Web can help to make this clear. On the one hand, hyperlinking presents a socio-technical phenomenon that is specific to online settings, and accordingly hyperlink analysis can be used to demonstrate biases that are specific to these settings. We can ask, for instance, whether overall hyperlink patterns are relatively centralized or de-centralized (Kelly, 2010), or whether and how innovations in hyperlinking, such as the introduction of Twitter or Facebook buttons, influence which type of sources feature prominently online (Gerlitz and Helmond, 2013). However, hyperlink analysis may also be used as a method for investigating substantive phenomena, for example to detect how actors come together in topical formations online, as discussed in Chapter 3.

Take the example of the WCIT issue-network. Similar to the Green living network in Chapter 3, this network was located with the aid of the IssueCrawler, a Web-based tool that was specifically developed to capture, analyse, and visualize hyperlink networks on the Web. This particular formation brings together sources dealing with the World Conference on International Telecommunications (WCIT), an international summit that took place in Dubai in December 2012, and which became the focus of public debates about Internet governance during this time, in part because civil society organizations who usually participate in these types of conferences weren't invited to this one. To locate the event network on the Web, we asked NGOs working in the area of Internet governance to suggest URLs relevant to the issue at hand, and accordingly, we expected to find an advocacy network. Strikingly, however, the social media platform Twitter is the central node in this network. This could, however, be due to a variety of effects: it could be because Twitter buttons and feeds have become increasingly common on the Web, or because Twitter presents a key site of mobilization in the controversy around the WCIT conference. That hyperlink analysis suggests Twitter as a relevant source may then be due either to media-technological dynamics of 'digital bias' or, more positively, to the substantive dynamics of issue network formation, or both. As hyperlinking is an instruments for the organization of social, organizational and public life online, they are not just sources of biases, but may equally carry a substantive or even social 'charge'.

There are, then, two different ways to treat the methodological problem of bias in digital social research: the precautionary approach treats digital media technologies as a source of noise or corruption that must be neutralized, while the affirmative approach treats digital devices as an empirical resource for social enquiry. The former proposes that digital content must be dis-embedded from online settings in order to secure the validity of our analysis (Guido and Venturini, 2012). The latter seeks to bring publicity devices that are specific to digital culture within the empirical frame of social and cultural research (Rogers, 2009; Marres, 2012a).[5] Both approaches recognize that digital devices like hyperlinks may result in the privileging of some sources over others in online settings: hyperlinks do not offer 'neutral' tools for delineating data sets, they are instruments for the organization of networked information, and as such they participate in the valuation of digital content. Where the two approaches differ is on the methodological question of whether digital methodologies must militate against these effects of bias, or must find ways to affirm their role in processes like issue formation (for a discussion of this issue, see Madsen, 2009).[6] For the affirmative approach, digital devices are in part *formative and therefore potentially indicative* of substantive dynamics of social, political and public life: they organize sources in ways that bring relevant socio-technical formations to the fore (Gillespie, 2010).

The Janus face of the digital in social research: object and resource

Problems of digital bias then raise wider issues about what constitutes the object of digital social research, which can be summed up in the question: are we researching society or technology? This is a big question, but it makes itself felt in the minutiae of online research. Let me give an example from a recent project undertaken by a masters student. This student was interested in issues of electronic waste and turned to digital platforms to document social engagement with this matter of concern. Taking up tools of online data capture, he scraped the platform Flickr, collecting all photos related to the hashtag #ewaste on this platform. As some of the Flickr content was geo-tagged, the student proceeded to map the locations associated with #ewaste photos on Flickr, surmising that this could provide insight in the geographic distribution of engagement with the issue (see Figure 4.2). This figure, however, raises the question of digital bias: to what extent does this distribution tell us something about Flickr (where it is used), rather than about the issue of #ewaste? Does this map present locations from which Flickr images are regularly uploaded, or does it show us in which places e-waste is a relevant issue?[7] This is an important question,[8] but there is also a further, and more general, methodological issue raised by this example: in taking of digital methods like geo-visualization of online content, how should we define our topic of analysis: should we approach platform features – in this case Flickr's – and practices as external to the social phenomenon under investigation (engagement with e-waste), or are these 'architectures of participation' somehow part of the phenomenon under study?

Importantly, these kinds of questions have been asked for many decades in fields like media sociology, technology studies and Internet research. Stanley Cohen's classic work on 'moral panics' (2002 (1972)) argued that news reports about rising crime told us more about the influence of news media on society, than about the phenomenon of crime, and McRobbie and Thornton (1995) have shown that a more recent 'participatory' turn in media culture only intensifies the role of biased media in the mediation of social and political tensions. Sociological studies of knowledge technologies such as scientific research instruments have long insisted on their double-sided role: devices like telescopes and survey questionnaires both make phenomena available for observation but at one and the same time they 'inflect' or even 'shape' the phenomena they render

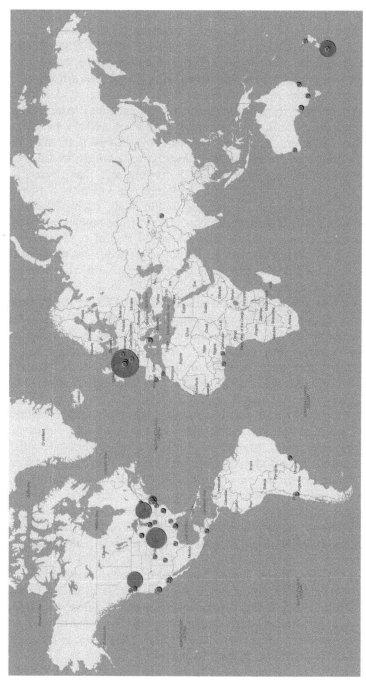

Figure 4.2 Locations of e-waste according to Flickr (Goran Becirevic, 2014)

visible in distinctive ways (Latour and Woolgar, 2013 [1979]); Osborne and Rose, 1999). This phenomenon has also been extensively discussed in Internet research. Don Slater (2002) defined the Internet as both 'a tool and a communication space' and in her work on virtual ethnography, Christine Hine (2000) has emphasized the 'hybridity' of online practices, as both technology and human activities participate in producing the documents and interactions that we encounter online.[9] Schneider and Foot (2005) helpfully identify two different kinds of research objectives that may be pursued in online research: in 'analysing patterns within and across Web materials', our aim may be 'to document and make sense of Web-based phenomena', or 'to understand relationships between these patterns and factors exogenous to the Web' (Schneider and Foot, 2005, p. 157). Online research then confronts us with a basic methodological choice: do we wish to study digital practices and processes, or is it our ambition to deploy digital devices *instrumentally*, in order to gain insight into social phenomena that extend beyond online settings?

However, this long-standing question of how to frame the empirical object of digital social research has become newly relevant, and arguably more acute, with the rise of digital platforms, mobile devices and smart systems. For one, these technologies are, to a much greater extent than early Web technologies, designed to facilitate analysis, and indeed, we can say they are increasingly *configured* to serve as instruments of social research. As discussed, social media platforms such as Twitter and Facebook present researchers with a range of measures that render online activities analysable: they do not just present text to analyse and links to follow, but also offer share, mention, like, follower, re-tweet counts. As discussed in Chapter 2, digital platforms significantly broaden the 'grammars' of online interaction beyond those scripted into the Web (Rieder, 2013): they continuously make new 'action formats' available to users – Facebook recently announced it will shortly introduce the option to 'dis-like'[10] – *as well as to analysts*. Platforms make available inform-actional formats (Marres, 2015) which facilitate practical and analytic operations at the same time. These analytic operations of platforms inform which information is made visible to which users, as in the case of the Facebook newsfeed (Carlsen & Birkbak, 2015), but platforms also make these analytic capacities available to third parties, who among others may deploy them for purposes of social research, such as mapping follower-networks.

However, as the 'grammars' written into digital network technologies continue to evolve, they confront digital social researchers with a further set of methodological questions that take us beyond the choice that previously faced Internet research. In framing the Web as a site of research, Schneider and Foot (2005) proposed that we could either define online environments as *sui generis*, or as *expressive* of social realities beyond them. Because platforms are far more explicitly designed to serve as research instruments, social media research is, on the one hand, confronted with a more narrow choice: either we go along with the research programmes that are built into the analytic interfaces of platforms (*social media as research instrument*), or we conduct social studies of platform technologies and practices (*social media as topic*). On the other hand, there is also a third option: we may refuse this methodological choice, on the ground that the distinction between the platform as instrument and the platform as object is far more unstable than the above formulation of these two options recognizes. We then say that social media platforms present social enquiry with an inherently *ambiguous phenomenon*. To use the classic vocabulary of ethnomethodology (Garfinkel, 1984 [1967]): social media platforms can be qualified as 'both topic and resource' for social analysis. Indeed, this description is not only applicable to social media research but also to digital social life (Burgess et al., 2015; Thielmann, 2012). Inform-actional formats like shares, mentions, likes, followers, tags, retweets are designed to fulfil *a double role*: they organize activities online, and at the same time they make these activities available for analysis and interpretation.

Today's digital social infrastructures and devices are then both more clearly configured as *instruments* of social research, and they add more layers of potential bias.[11] On the one hand, the structuration of interaction and content in digital platforms allows social researchers to ask many more questions (who follows who? who mentions who?), but it also gives rise to platform artefacts (are these followers bots? do these mentions indicate relations between actors (accounts) or do they signal attempts to gain an audience (publicity)?) A study by Rieder and Gerlitz (2013) helps to clarify this multiplication of the sources of bias in social media research: analysing a random sample of Twitter data, they compared the composition of Tweets sent from different sources (see Figure 4.3), and found that messages sent from desktop machines tend to be differently composed than messages sent from smart phones or Twitter applications like Tweet deck: messages from mobile devices are more likely to address other users (they contain relatively more mentions), and those sent from desktops

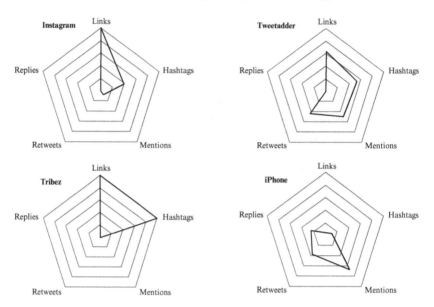

Figure 4.3   Tweet composition by source (Rieder and Gerlitz, 2013)

include more links (URLS). This finding raises a set of challenging questions for research design: For example, if we decide to analysis which URLs are referenced in a given debate on social media, does this mean we are privileging desktop users, or even adopt a desktop perspective on the issue in question?[12] The multiplication of digital devices in todays societies then seems to aggravate the problem of the ambiguity of the empirical object of digital research.

How (not) to deal with it? Affirming the problem of ambiguity

How do social media researchers deal with the problem of ambiguity? The problem certainly does not go unrecognized, and leading researchers in this developing field are careful not to overstate the empirical reach of their studies. Rieder (2013) distinguishes several categories of empirical Facebook research, including user research and identity studies, suggesting that the primary focus of Facebook research is Facebook practices themselves.[13] In discussing their large-scale comparative study of Twitter data, Axel Bruns and Stefan Stieglitz (2012) equally emphasize that their findings first and foremost pertain to Twitter use. But they do express the ambition to generalize from Twitter studies to wider phenomena, but in doing so firmly keep media technologies in view: 'Current work on Twitter will be able to be combined with studies of other (social) media platforms in order to develop a more comprehensive and detailed picture of *information and communication flows in society*' (Bruns and Stieglitz, 2012; italics mine).[14] In defining the object of social media research in this way, these Twitter studies follow traditions in media and communications studies that affirm the mutual imbrication of content and form, of discourse and technology (Wajcman and Jones, 2012). The object of social media research, they propose, is not either society or technology, but rather 'media technology in society'.

This framing of the empirical object as a hybrid – part society, part media technologies – makes good sense in my view, but there are nevertheless methodological dangers associated with it: it may create a blind spot for problems of digital bias. Take for example the Twitter study by Smith and colleagues, 'Mapping Twitter topic networks: from polarized crowds to community clusters':[15] the stated object of this large scale analysis of Twitter data is 'social media networks', and one of the study's main contributions is the identification of so-called 'conversation types' on Twitter. Offering a taxonomy of six types, the authors identify distinct forms of twitter interaction including 'polarized crowds' and 'broadcast networks', and claim that conversational structures differ, 'depending on the subject and the people driving the conversation' (e.g. news stories versus political conversation). The trouble is, such an account does not have very much to say about the role of Twitter in the structuration of conversation, something which nevertheless seems to play a significant role. If we examine the conversation types in more detail, it turns out that 'polarized crowds' contain especially frequent 'replies' and 'mentions' between users, while the broadcast network contains many more re-tweets. So, while it seems clear that platform settings participate in the structuration of these 'conversation types', this study does not shed light on this. Because of its focus on substantive questions (what type of conversations about what topics?), it is ill-equipped to investigate the role of platform settings. As the analysis focuses on detecting patterns in the behaviour of 'topical networks', it is not able to shed light on relations between the social and the technical. The declared object of study – 'social media networks' – here entails a *conflation of platform features, content and activity* into the category of 'conversation type'. As such, it risks rendering the role of digital media technologies in the organization of sociality un-questionable.

A different approach to social media research is opened up

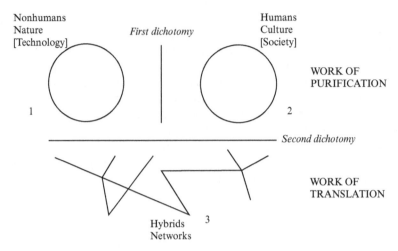

Figure 4.4   Latour's constitution, from *We Have Never Been Modern* (1993, p. 11; additions in square brackets). Copyright © 1993 by Harvester Wheatsheaf and the President and Fellows of Harvard College

by empiricist studies of technology and society. The diagram in Figure 4.4, taken from Bruno Latour's (1993) book *We Have Never Been Modern*, can clarify this approach. It begins with the recognition that digital platforms present us with sprawling, heterogeneous entanglements of users, algorithms, data, servers, work flows, business plans, communications protocols and trackers and so forth, or in other words: hybrid assemblages. However, in researching such hybrid assemblages, we must at some point address the question: are we researching society or technology? That is, the diagram highlights that *we must do work* in order for the object of research to emerge. If our aim is the study of society, or as the case may be, technology, we must perform operations upon these heterogeneous assemblages. Latour called this the work of purification, to emphasize that the configuration of empirical objects tends to strip them of heterogeneity, but in digital social media research, it seems more appropriate to describe this work as the configuration of the empirical apparatus. This latter term highlights the practical, socio-technical work involved in implementing research design: what is our question, what is our platform, what our methods, data tools, audiences? However, in configuring our research apparatus to address these questions, we must at the same time remain capable of being surprised by our findings. After all, while we may set out to study society, we may end up studying technology, and the other way around. Empiricism dictates that we cannot assume to 'know' our object of enquiry independent of our empirical studies, at least not conclusively.

To be sure, it is possible to address the problems of bias and ambiguity in a piecemeal fashion in digital social research. In many cases, these are specific problems that can be alleviated through specific measures. For example, in conducting hyperlink analysis on the Web, it is often a good idea to block links to 'purely technical' addressees (e.g. Firefox, Adobe Acrobat). However, in other cases, the problem is a more open-ended one. In social media research, the chosen research setting (digital platform X and/or Y) and the chosen methods (say hashtag analysis or friend-networks) may conspire to render impossible any neat distinction between the object and method of social research (Cicourel, 1964). What here belongs to the 'empirical object' and what belongs to the socio-technical apparatus of research? In social media research, this is not only a methodological but also a practical problem. Take the example of the researcher who encountered the hashtag #FF – which it turns out stands for #FollowFriday – in his Twitter data set. His project was to analyse social media debates about Hinkley Point, a nuclear power plant that may or may not be built in the UK (Moats, 2015). The problem, in his case, was not the meaning of the hashtag itself, which was clear enough: it's an invitation to select new users to follow every Friday. But the question remained: does the presence of this tag in the Twitter data set about Hinkley Point indicate noise, a telltale symptom of bad research design, and thus requiring exclusion, or does it present a positive contribution to the issue formation in question? To effectively deal with such questions we need a research strategy. To conclude this chapter, I will therefore discuss three methodological tactics that digital social researchers have developed to render the problem of ambiguity tractable in practice.

Three tactics for dealing with ambiguity: critical extraction, performative deployment, radical empiricism

No doubt the most familiar research strategy for dealing with the influence of digital technologies on social life is to adopt a critical approach to 'digital bias'. As discussed, such an approach assumes a largely negative understanding of the contribution of digital devices to the organization of the social phenomenon under study, and has as its overriding aim to secure the substantive focus of digital social research: to make sure that we study society, and not (media) technology. A clear example of this approach can be found in the treatment of 'bots' in social media research: as discussed in Chapter 2, there is an abundance of automated accounts active on platforms like Twitter and the often commercial content spread by them tends to present itself like spam or noise to social media researchers. For example, when we set out to map debates about 'privacy' on Twitter in the wake of the leak of NSA files by Edward Snowden in 2013, we were struck by the predominance of generic content associated with the hashtag #privacy on this platform. Among the tags used most often in combination with #privacy, we found astrological signs (#pisces, #aquarius etc.) and generic media terms like '#blog' and '#email', something that was probably due to marketing bots hijacking the trending topic of privacy on Twitter.[16] Indeed, it is common practice for commercial entities or even activist groups to hi-jack trending hashtags to promote their (unrelated) messages, a phenomenon that has been called 'hashtag jumping' (Christensen, 2013).

To secure the substantive focus of our study, our instinctive response was thus to 'remove the bots', and to delete from our data set all tweets using the above, non-issue-specific generic hashtags. This methodological tactic can be called 'critical extraction' insofar as it aims to secure the independence of the empirical analysis from media-technological dynamics (Driscoll and Walker, 2014). Building on the precautionary understanding of digital bias discussed above, it applies specific measures to clean the data and exclude 'platform artefacts' to ward off undue influence of digital devices. Some of these measures build directly on existing approaches in social research. Another example of critical extraction is the move in Twitter analysis to remove all re-tweets, and this operation draws directly on content analysis, where the correction for duplicate content is a fairly common way to ensure the neutral application of content classifications to code content (Herring, 2009). However, efforts at critical extraction in social media research may also require medium-specific measures, such as the blacklisting of software-related links from hyperlink analysis. Importantly, 'critical extraction' is a widely endorsed approach across methodological traditions in social research, and does not necessarily entail a particular epistemology (i.e. realist, constructivist, and so on), although generally speaking it does entail a commitment to a substantive focus in digital research.

But purging digital data of extraneous content also serves a practical purpose: data reduction is a practical necessity in online

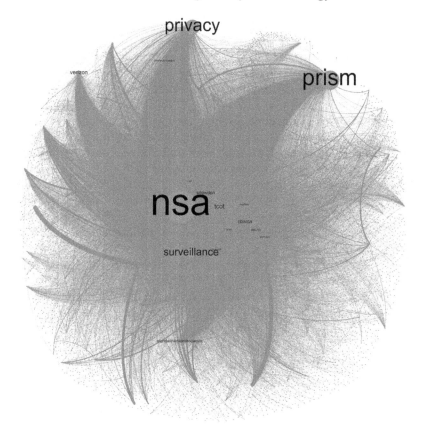

Figure 4.5   Privacy on Twitter after Snowden, Bi-partite User-Hashtag
        Network, Visualized with Gephi (Marres and Moats, 2015)

data analysis, especially for those coming to this practice with an interpretative mind-set, looking for coherence and patterns in data visualizations in order to generate insight. One popular tool used by social media researchers to start this process and gain a visual overview of the data is Gephi, the open source software for network analysis and visualization (Bastian et al., 2009). In another study of privacy debates on Twitter after the Snowden data leak, we began by extracting from our total Twitter data set a network of hashtags and users and produced the visualization in Figure 4.5 using this tool.[17] In this bi-partite network, users are connected to the hashtags they use; the more times they use them the stronger the connection (thicker lines). While such a figure offers a first rough sense of the data set's composition, the problem of noise remains: this visualization is still far too cluttered to be interpretable. To translate this mess or 'hairball' into a legible network, we therefore proceded to delete from it any data that did not directly pertain to our topic, privacy.[18] For example, we removed the top end of the graph – the terms #privacy and #surveillance were part of our query, so their presence in the graph does not tell us much. However, these operations raise a tricky question: how far can we go in erasing elements from the data? In minimizing the marks left by digital platforms on the data captured by their means, are we not in our own way contributing to the *distortion* of our empirical object?

A precautionary approach is difficult to sustain in social media research, because the exclusion of social media dynamics from analysis reduces the empirical scope of the research, and indeed, risks to create an empirical artefact. Take an intervention such as 'removing duplicates' – for example re-tweets: this may seem an appropriate way of ensuring that the analysis covers a broader range of contributions (Pearce et al., 2014). But it arguably also renders illegible particular social processes facilitated by digital platforms: isn't re-tweeting, the passing on of other people's messages, a relevant social act? In other words, are not medium-specific activities like re-tweeting in part constitutive of digital social phenomena? In some cases, applying a measures like 'removing all duplicates' would mean distorting the empirical object. One of the limitations of critical abstraction, then, is that it assumes a largely negative understanding of the role of digital media technologies and its attendant devices in social life. A second, 'performative' research strategy, is designed to replace this with a more positive appreciation of the role of digital devices in social life.

To adopt a 'performative' perspective on media technologies is to emphasize that digital devices do not only render social life traceable and analysable, they actively participate in its enactment. From this vantage point, digital social phenomena like a Facebook friend or a Twitter trend are in and of themselves heterogeneously composed: they are part media technology, part social, and much else besides (Lievrouw, 2014). As discussed above, this idea of the 'hybridity' of the social and the (media-)technical derives from social studies of technology, but in social media research it translates into a specific empirical strategy: if digital devices participate in the doing of social life, then they may be deployed as resources for researching social life (Rogers, 2009; Marres, 2012a). Freely after Marx, such a performative research strategy says that 'sociologists have long *described* the role of media technologies in the performance of social life; the question is how we can deploy them to analyse its enactment'. Examples of such performative deployment of digital devices in social research can be found in the hyperlink analysis already discussed above. Another example is the study of social media genres and re-tweet patterns.

In the wake of the NSA leak, a variety of more or less 'platform-specific' tactics were pursued on Twitter: wry commentary including tags and mentions, circulating news through re-tweets, linking to online how-to-guides for anonymous browsing. This is also to say that engagement on a platform like Twitter does not just involve conversation and debate, but relies on a wide variety of specific information formats (replies, tags, retweets) that operate across communicative registers (news reporting, informal talk (banter), advocacy campaigning, knowledge diffusion). Adopting a performative approach to Twitter analysis, these specific registers of communication become an important focus for investigating the *forms* that the issue of privacy takes on in this social media setting. To this end, we may, for instance, trace the circulation of URLs on this platform. Using a prototype tool called the 'URL sequencer' developed by Erik Borra and David Moats, we visualized the trajectories of privacy-related URLs being re-tweeted on Twitter.[19] Especially interesting, we found, are the modifications of a tweet containing the URL (the addition of RT (for re-tweet), an @reply, comment, and so on), which indicates active involvement of users in the sharing of content online, and arguably, a more 'social' way of sharing (see also Murthy, 2013).

However, the performative analysis of digital media bias, too, has its limits: it only works as long as the ambiguity of social media objects does not raise any issues. From a performative perspective, namely, the question in this chapter's title is the wrong question to ask. Indeed, *not* asking this question seems a necessary condition for this approach be successful. It proposes that we study society *and* technology, or 'socio-technical formations'. However, this becomes difficult to sustain when critical issues arise in social media research: what exactly are we analysing when mapping 'privacy' debates on Twitter? Are we investigating public concern with privacy, or rather, the use of Twitter in advocacy campaigns? Affirming the hybridity of online phenomena makes it difficult to answer this question, as such an approach is precisely predicated on the assumption that medialogical and substantive dynamics are mutually imbricated in digital social life. To address this problem, David Moats and myself (2015) have proposed a third, empiricist approach to conducting social research with digital platforms.

This third, empiricist, approach places the problem of the ambiguity of digital social phenomena centre stage, and turns this chapter's question into an *empirical* question. Rather than defining the object of digital social research once and for all – as social phenomena, or socio-technical formations – it proposes that we *keep asking* this question as part of digital social enquiry: are we studying media-technological or social processes? We then affirm the (constitutive) 'hybridity' of digital social phenomena, but add to this an awareness of the variability of empirical phenomena: *While we may set out to do social research with digital platforms, we may easily end up studying media-technological dynamics, and the other way around.* From this vantage point, 'platform capture' is an important *problem* in digital social research, as it is in social life: when taking up digital instruments, social research puts itself at risk of losing sight of its formative concerns, as happens to other social actors who take up social media. We must therefore *not* give up on the critical task of specifying, and re-specifying, our objects of enquiry, whether they be social, technological or other substantive aspects of the digital. One of the best ways to ensure this is to be flexible in our empirical approach (Jacomy, 2015), and to be prepared to adjust the definition of our empirical object in view of our findings, to allow 'the empirical object to emerge' from the analysis.

This approach is still under development, but to illustrate its possible contribution I would like to give one last example from the analysis of privacy with Twitter. One of the striking features of this issue space in June 2013 was the broad range and variation of expressions associated with this term. The two diagrams in Figure 4.6 depict hashtags used in Tweets containing the phrase 'my privacy' on Twitter before and after Snowden leaked the NSA files.[20] They suggest that the hashtag profile of 'privacy' – and perhaps indeed, the composition of this issue space – on Twitter changed significantly during this period. Perhaps counter-intuitively, privacy on Twitter became a *more generic* issue in the wake of the NSA leak: before the leak, privacy was associated with the 'jailbreaking' of smartphones, popular phrases such as 'I have a gun' and 'you don't know me' as well as regulatory issues such as the EU data protection act. After the leak, such specific terms were largely crowded out by familiar front-page key-words such as 'NSA' and 'President Obama, even though, on Twitter, the latter were also associated with more specific campaign terms like 'stopwatchingus' and 'bigbrother'. As such, these figures suggest that social media can help to render visible complex processes in digital media societies, such as shifts in the

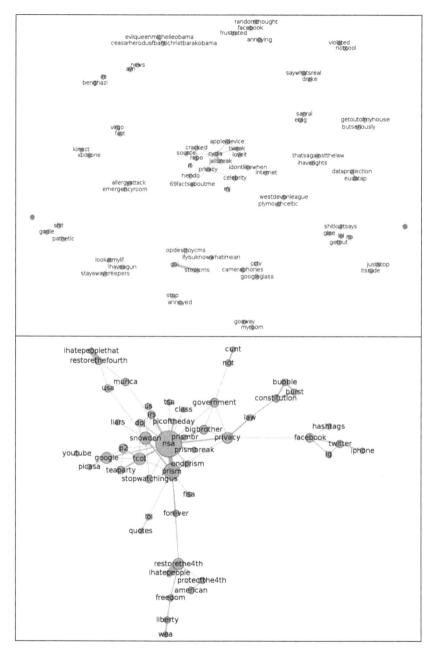

Figure 4.6   'My privacy' on Twitter, co-hashtag networks, before and after Snowden (June 2013), by Hjalmar Bang Carlsen

registers of social communication and issue articulation in the wake of public events – such as the shift from everyday expression to political engagement. It may render analysable sudden transitions but also mixtures and exchanges between such different registers of engagement, a phenomenon which has become such a powerful feature of our contemporary public culture.

Conclusion

In this chapter, I have shown how a tricky methodological question arises in digital social research practice: what are we studying when we take up online data tools to do social research? It is widely recognized that digital settings raise problems of bias: digital content is partial to particular locations, populations, topics and forms of expression. Indeed, social studies of media technologies have long insisted on the hybridity of socio-technical phenomena, but there has been less appreciation in digital social research of the fact that this circumstance raises important methodological issues. Its empirical object is ambiguous. While we set out to study digital practices, we may find ourselves considering substantive social issues, and vice versa. I have argued that this fundamental issue of how we frame the object of digital social enquiry should not be treated as a mere 'distraction' from empirical and technical engagement with the digital, and that it cannot be settled through 'mere' definitional work (what is your domain of study?). Instead it goes to the core of what digital sociology is and can be: a research practice that affirms and tests the configurability of digital infrastructures, devices and practices for social enquiry. In other words, it is the task of digital sociology to put in place research designs that 'can let the [sociological] object emerge' (Goodwin, 1994; see also Suchman, 2007b). To do this, we must be *flexible enough* to adjust our empirical framings in the face of ongoing reconfigurations of digital infrastructures, devices, as well as practices (Jacomy, 2015).

To be clear, this argument is related to but goes beyond basic constructivism – the idea that the objects of social enquiry are not given but that social research always participates in its organization or to use a more contemporary term – 'curation.' To be sure, to insist that digital social research involves configuration work draws on this broad sensibility. However, my claim about the ambiguity of digital sociology's object is different insofar as this does not stem from a general philosophical condition, such as the fact that we apprehend social phenomena with 'human minds'. Rather, this ambiguity arises on the socio-technico-material level of the infrastructures, devices and practices that enable digital social enquiry (as well as digital social life). This ambiguity is of a constitutive order ('hybridity'), but it is equally marked by variability and instability, which is why it takes the form of a *methodological issue*, one that has ongoing relevance and sometimes acquires urgency in social research practices, requiring resolution and forcing a methodological choice: 'Is it your objective to deploy digital platforms as empirical resources for the study of society, or should we include media-technological dynamics in our enquiry, and consider technologies as participants in social life?' The answer will be different depending on the case and the project.

Our answer will also partly depend on the stage in the research process we are at. I proposed that a precautionary approach is especially helpful in the early phases of research: it works for data reduction. An affirmative approach to the role of digital devices is useful during data analysis, as it sensitizes us to specific features and dynamics in digital data, whereas an empiricist approach is suited to the evaluative phase in which we (re-)consider the main focus and findings of our study. To adopt an empiricist approach means that we should be prepared to adjust the very definition of our empirical object in the light of our findings. If bots turn out to be important contributors to 'conversations' on Twitter, we may then have to include these among the range of protagonists in our study. This happened in our study of privacy on Twitter, as it turned out that notwithstanding the significant presence of spam bots, there were also bots that made relevant contributions to the conversation, as in the case of @KRfront (the Keyword Revolution Front) which represents a website that automatically generates blog posts composed of a mix of trending social media words and 'red flag' keywords that feature on government anti-terrorism lists' ('bomb, jihad, shoe, etc.'), with the stated purpose of confounding or jamming surveillance systems like those of the NSA. *This account is clearly a bot, but one whose purposes are explicitly political and specific to the issue.* It is therefore *not* in the best interest of social media research to decide on the inclusion or exclusion of bots once and for all.

Recognizing the complementarity of different research strategies turns digital research into a complex affair, but one of the advantages is that it enables us to approach digital social research as an interdisciplinary undertaking. Of course, the question of how to frame the empirical object – are we studying society or (media) technology? – *is* partly a question of which (sub-)discipline one seeks to contribute to, and of loyalty to distinctive subjects and their attendant problematics.

But, crucially, the problem of the ambiguous object of digital social research is *not resolved* by reformulating it as a question of disciplinary allegiance. While different disciplines have developed different methodological strategies for dealing with ambiguity in social research, the problem has a stubborn way of surfacing in digital research when we do not expect – or indeed desire – it. Rather than carving up digital social research along disciplinary boundaries – dividing it up between those who study society and those who take (media) technology as their primary focus – digital sociology offers opportunities for engaging with the entanglement of the social and the (media) technological in potentially new ways. It offers opportunities for a more *variable treatment* of heterogeneous formations. To affirm that digital social formations are hybrid in a fundamental way, does not absolve us from having to answer this chapter's question: are we researching society or technology? It only means we must *not* answer it too soon. Instead of assuming a stable object of analysis, the qualification of the empirical object must become part of the objective of research.

While this methodology is in many ways still to be developed – and we need to learn how it has *already* been developed across fields – it is clear that to practise flexibility in this way is to invite a re-negotiation of relations between (sub-)fields like the sociology of technology, media sociology, computing and digital media studies. Given the technical, methodological and empirical complexities involved, it seems that collaboration between diverse competences will become only more and not less important to digital social research. For this reason, it is also critical that we do not withdraw into theoretical or inward-looking debates about what constitutes the 'proper object' of digital social research. However, worries about this are only partly justified in my view, because the problem of ambiguity has broad relevance: it does not just affect digital knowledge practices, but affects digital societies in equal measure. It also seems to me that recent failures and refusals to take seriously the ambiguity of digital social research are connected to what Andrejevic (2014) calls the great 'power differentials' in digital research. In my view, today we do not ask detailed, methodological questions like 'what exactly are we (or they) analysing when we (or they) apply their algorithms to these data?' enough, and this may be partly due to a perceived lack of access, or relevance, of social research to the big data-sets, instruments and machines of computational social science. But it is critical that we ask such methodological questions if we are to contribute to the development of more responsive forms of digital social enquiry.

5
Who are digital sociology's publics?

'Is everyone a sociologist now?'

This question is raised today by sociologists, cultural commentators and others who are struck by the ways in which digital technology enables everyday people to document, research and analyse social life. However, we should not forget that this question is an old one. Sociologists associate this question first and foremost with ethnomethodology, the approach developed in the 1960s by Harold Garfinkel and others and which started from the claim that 'social actors produce methodical accounts of social life as part of social life' (Lynch, 1991). As discussed in Chapter 2, there are intriguing similarities and differences between the general statements that ethnomethodologists made in the 1960s and the specific, socio-technical practices proliferating in digital societies today (Thielmann, 2012; Beer and Burrows, 2013). In digital societies, the 'production of methodical accounts of social life as part of social life' can serve as a pretty apt description of digital infrastructures and devices, such as the visualization of social networks, or the automatic reporting and alerting tools that proliferate across the worlds of journalism, activism, celebrity culture and everyday life. But there are also differences. For the ethnomethodologists, to draw attention to the 'methodical character' of social life was a way of re-describing social life, but in digital societies the proliferation of 'methodical accounts of social life' involves concrete, socio-technical modifications of social practices, arrangements and processes. As we click a button to report an incident, or keep an eye on a feed to monitor the situation, or 'map' our own networks, it is clear that methodical practices are directly informed and inflected by specific instruments and techniques designed into digital infrastructures and devices.

The question is, what does this proliferation of methodical tools and practices in digital societies mean for social research? This situation raises difficult questions, of which an important one concerns its implications for sociology as a form of knowledge. Back in the 1960s, some ethnomethodologists offered the diagnosis that social research was and should be 'democratized'. They argued there was no longer much point in defining sociology as a separate discipline: who needs sociology if everyone is already doing it (Lynch, 1991)? However, one could say that today's situation couldn't be more different: in our societies, the wide uptake of instruments for researching social life as part of social life is accompanied by a consolidation of hierarchies in social knowledge: whereas computational social science is celebrated as a new form of 'universal' knowledge, everyday data practices are derided as unrigorous, biased and superficial (Kennedy and Moss, 2015; Couldry and Powell, 2014). This paradoxical state of affairs can also be observed in the growing field of participatory research. With the rise of citizen science, the participation of lay actors in scientific research is clearly increasing, but at the same time, concern is growing that the diversity of our knowledge cultures is decreasing, as only a select set of institutions have access to the analytic equipment and data required to produce authoritative knowledge about society. This circumstance, at least, suggests that there is still very much a need for sociological reflection in digital societies: What do we make of this apparent paradox of the simultaneous democratization and technocratization of social research in digital societies?

In this chapter, I will argue that we need to adopt a 'non-innocent' perspective on the democratization of social research if we want to make sense of these paradoxes. It also requires wider investigation of the role and status of participation in digital societies. Generally speaking, it is hard to overstate its importance as a social, cultural and indeed economic phenomenon today. Participation has been one of the principal key-words, slogan or tropes, perhaps *the* principal trope that is invoked to distinguish digital societies (Kelty, 2012). Many believe that 'participation' is what sets contemporary societies apart from what went before, arguing that digital media technologies enable ordinary people to become active contributors to social, cultural and political life, no longer being limited to the role of the audience (Shirky, 2009; Jenkins, 2012). In this view, that the rise of digital platforms 'has led to a new collaborative, participatory or open culture, where anyone can get involved, and everyone has the potential to be seen or heard (Beer and Burrows, 2007)'.

When considering this investment in participation as an ideal in digital societies, we should also take into account that it is part of a broader family of legitimatory ideals that have been deployed to cultivate support for digital transformations of society. This includes ideals of collaboration and the idea that the digital facilitates an 'open culture' in which 'everyone can participate', which has become a common trope and indeed a cliché. As Nathaniel Tkacz (2014) has discussed, the trope of openness in digital culture is the result of a complex set of 'double' translations of political ideals into technological and cultural slogans and back again. The idea of the 'open society' derives from liberal philosophy, where the ideal was formulated of *a democratic society modelled on science*, with critical debate among competent colleagues serving as the template for civic life and public politics (Ezrahi, 1990). The idea of openness was subsequently taken up in the world of computing, to designate a distinctive – egalitarian and anti-proprietary – approach to software development (open source), which in the late twentieth century in turn inspired the labelling of cultural and political practices as 'open', as in the Spanish open architecture movement (Kelty, 2008; Jimenez, 2014), and the online magazine 'Open Democracy'. The ideal of participation can then be regarded as one element in a wider constellation of politico-scientific ideals that have been taken up across society, culture and politics to give 'normative' direction to processes of digital transformation.

Participation is in many ways the default language for making sense of the societal uptake of digital technology, and their capacity to 'transform society', which has been taken up by governments, business, cultural organizations and so on (Powell, 2014): to make a given practice or arrangement more 'digital' is to make it more participatory. As I will discuss in this chapter, the promotional deployment of the ideal of participation in digital societies poses significant, further challenges for our understanding of the role of social research in digital societies, and the contribution digital sociology can make in this context. To better understand these challenges, I will in this chapter offer a critical discussion of the thesis that digital societies can be defined in terms of a shift from 'audience to participation'. I will show how sociologists and scholars in related fields have *for many decades already* questioned the accuracy of the idea of the 'audience' to describe what people do when they engage with media and technological culture. I then discuss a number of alternative concepts that sociologists have offered to make sense of media-technological transformations of society, such as the idea of the 'representation of society to society'. One of the benefits of this concept is that it can clarify the contributions of sociology to society, and this remains very much the case in the digital society. Digital transformations today are changing the existing machinery for representing society to society (Boullier, 2015), and this process of re-configuration requires critical and creative engagement from sociologists.

'From the audience to participation': for and against digital exceptionalism

Narratives about openness, inclusion and collaboration take many forms in digital societies, but the spirit of these ideas has been force-fully captured by the claim that these societies are undergoing a shift 'from the audience to participation'. This general idea is perhaps first and foremost associated with popular books like 'Here comes everybody' (Shirky, 2009), but social and cultural researchers and theorists have developed this broader argument during the last decades. Writing in the late 1990s and early 2000s, at the time of the rise of the Web as a cultural, intellectual and political force, some spoke of the emergence of 'networked publics' (boyd, 2010; Langlois et al., 2009; Marres, 2006). We argued that in online settings like the Web, publics do not so much feature as the collective, external 'addressee' of public discourses, but rather take the form of actors actively assembling and organizing in distributed formations. Efforts to understand how public formations in digital societies challenge established definitions of the public continue today, as for example in empirical research on the Anonymous hacker movement and the ludic mode of spectacular intervention that networked forms of organization enable (Coleman, 2014). After the rise of large, com-mercial social media platforms from the mid 2000s onwards, the idea of a shift 'from audience to participation' has been elaborated to take into account the *economic* aspects of participation in media and technological societies (Couldry, 2012). Social, cultural and media researchers have described the emergence of an economy of 'prod-users' (Bruns, 2008) and 'pro-sumers' (Ritzer et al., 2010) – forms of organization in which everyday subjects figure not as the passive recipients of ready-made content or goods, but as active participants in their generation.

Sociologists have then offered comprehensive analyses of the shift from audience to participation. This shift captures – and sums up – wider transformations of the cultural political economy, changes which are accompanied by increasing criticisms of their normative effects. Thus, Terranova (2011) has highlighted the growing tensions between individual self-assertion and the exploitation of 'free labour' in the digital economy (Terranova, 2011; Arvidsson et al., 2012). Participation here signals at once the democratization of cultural expression and the rise of exploitative regimes centred on value extraction from people's everyday activities. Digital participation has also become an increasingly *contested* proposition in digital societies: notwithstanding its uptake as a (*the?*) core proposition of the digital economy, the ideal has deep roots in digital culture and can be traced back to grassroots, 'bottom-up' social and cultural movements that emerged in the 1990s. This includes the 'tactical media' movement, which celebrated the radical opportunities that media technologies offered for DYI practices of cultural and public expression, the creative appropriation of content, and the re-purposing of mainstream media culture as in re-mix music practices (Garcia and Lovink, 1997; Lasen et al., 2011; Garcia, 2014). These movements also advocate a deliberately broad understanding of media technologies – as not limited to the computational, but including writing, video, the arts and crafts. Challenging the narrow techno-centrism of consumer culture, they found in the emerging culture of the Web an inspiration to organize spaces for participatory culture, with the aim of offering an alternative to the passive and conformist 'audience culture' that they associated with broadcast media like TV, also known as MSM, for mainstream media.

While digital participation has itself become mainstream today, many traces of the earlier progressive aspirations remain in digital culture today, whether in the form of large not-for-profit platforms like Wikipedia, the 'counter-cultural' image of digital companies, or ongoing experimentation in the digital arts as a form of anti-institutional culture. These associations between the digital and experimental culture and politics have been given various labels by practitioners and intellectuals, as in the case of 'net.art' or 'hacker culture' but a more technical term is 'digital exceptionalism'. This denotes the belief that digital culture is somehow different from other, older media regimes such as the age of television, because the digital makes possible more democratic or experimental media practices, re-awakening ideals and realizing forms of participation on which the mass societies of the twentieth century seemed to have given up, and which are generally considered non-viable from a societal perspective (Turner, 2013; see also Morozov, 2013). Importantly, the practices of digital sociology are connected with this cultural trope of 'digital exceptionalism': these research practices draw on the early commitment to the experimental quality of digital culture, and the progressive belief that it may activate experiments in knowledge-making and change relations between publics, disciplines and creative practices in 'knowing societies'.

But we should also consider the specific contributions of sociologists to wider debates about the digital society and culture. While many social researchers and theorists endorse the ideal of digital participation, they have also criticized the very idea of a fundamental shift 'from audience to participation' in digital societies. To start with, sociologists have questioned the empirical usefulness of a strict distinction between the (passive) audience and (active) participants. This distinction does not really help us to describe everyday media and technological practices. This is because many if not most practices across media, politics, science and culture tend to contain elements of both these modes of engagement. Digital participation tends to combine forms of more passive audience-ing with active engagement, and indeed this is written into the very architectures of digital participation: viewing and commenting, posting and following. From this vantage point, audience and participation don't present a strict opposition but a continuum, something that is also captured by the 'power law', the popular figure in online data analysis discussed in Chapter 2. In relation to *any* issue or event, there is likely to be a relatively small set of active participants, and a comparatively much larger set of more passive audiences (lurkers). To capture such hybrid forms of 'audience participation', media researchers have proposed concepts like 'gatewatching', which describe how classic 'gatekeeping models' in journalism and publishing – according to which editors decide what gets published when and where – are today not replaced by, *but combined with* more distributed and egalitarian models of content validation (Bruns et al., 2013; Moats, 2015).

The general idea of a shift 'from audience to participation' is then of only limited use as an empirical description of digital transformations of society and culture. This has led scholars to disassemble the phenomenon of digital participation and to produce more fine-grained accounts, as in the classification produced by Chris Kelty and colleagues (2015), which orders digital platforms by their features, mapping the degree to which they facilitate audience response, user commenting, ranking, flagging, and so on, of content. Such an account presents the 'audience' and 'participation' as two ends of a spectrum of engagement forms, and this also challenges claims about

the radical newness of digital media practices. Assymetric distributions of passive audience-ing and active participation (as in the Power
law) have long been observed in public life, as at least from the early
twentieth century onwards public intellectuals have debated the
'bi-furcation' of the public in mass societies: the splitting of the public
into a smaller group of active, involved participants and a wider,
more uncertainly positioned collective called audience (Lippmann,
2002 [1927]; Pateman, 1989; Marres, 2012c). And media sociologists had already problematized the opposition between audience and
participation in the study of 'pre-digital' media, like tv: in empirical
studies of everyday media use, they showed that practices commonly
referred to as instances of the 'audience', such as television watching,
are in many ways highly participatory, as in Livingstone and Lunt's
(1994) study of television talk. They describe the active sociability
involved in people gathering around the television, both in the actual
space of the living room and through wider, mediated conversations.
Social studies of technology have advanced similar claims about
the participatory qualities of technological cultures, for example in
Endre Dányi's (2006) study of Xerox as a political technology taken
up in the 1980s in Hungary by dissident movements, who used pho-
tocopiers as instruments for dissemination and public mobilization.
Such studies remind us that some of the participatory capacities that
are attributed to digital technology today are better understood as
features of everyday technological and media practices much more
broadly defined.[1]

Long before the 'invention' of social media technologies as devices
of participation, sociologists have insisted that practices of media
technology-in-use involve participation (Gillespie et al., 2014).[2]
From the 1980s onwards, social, cultural and media studies have
shown that everyday media and technological practices rely on the
active contributions of everyday people far more than conventional
notions of 'consumption' and 'use' allow us to recognize (Oudshoorn
and Pinch, 2003; Morley and Chen, 1996). Sociologists and anthropologists of technology have directed attention to the 'invisible
labour' that users perform in order to to make technology 'work'
in society (Leigh Star and Strauss, 1999; Wajcman, 1991). For
many sociologists and media scholars, then, there has never been
an 'audience' society, if by audience we mean a mass of passive by-
standers. From this perspective, the slogan of a shift 'from audience
to participation' in digital societies is deceptive on a whole number
of levels. The people 'formerly known as the audience' were already
participants in media and technological societies, also when they were

still known as the audience. Consequently, it is wrong to attribute the capacity to turn people into 'participants' solely to digital technology, and the slogan advanced by digital entrepreneurs and commentators that society has just entered a new area of participation must be qualified. Society was already participatory. Participatory media and technological cultures are not new phenomena, let alone invented by geeks. What is more, the grand idea of a move from audience to participation obscures a series of *other* important transformations of participation enabled by the digital. I will discuss these in the next section, before returning to the question of whether and how the ideal of participation can still be of use for digital sociology.

Three features of digital participation: valuable, technological, metricized

One of the problems with the idea of a shift from audience to participation is that it diverts attention away from other transformations occurring under the umbrella of the digital. When a given practice or organization is made 'digital', whether it is local government services, or the organization of a social event, this is likely not only to give everyday actors a more clearly recognized role in these activities, it is equally likely to be accompanied by broader changes in the relations between actors, such as the displacement of responsibility from public to private agencies, from everyday people to employees and customers, and vice versa, as discussed in Chapter 1. From a sociological standpoint, 'digitization' is therefore best understood as an occasion for a much wider, multi-faceted set of societal transformations, including privatization, experimentalization, commercialization, deregulation and/or responsibilization. In this context, the ideal of participation becomes ambivalent, as it may now serve as a cover for under-the-radar processes with significant normative implications, and obscure their problematic aspects and implications for society, culture and politics (Wynne, 2008). This is not only because of the positive connotations of participation with democracy, agency and control, but also because of another feature of this ideal, namely the engrained tendency to imagine participation as an autonomous activity: Western democratic theory has long conceptualized participation as happening in 'a world onto its own', an autonomous sphere into which other – economic, logistical, etc. – considerations shouldn't really penetrate (Marres and Lezaun, 2011). This assumption has a complex history that I will touch on below, but first we should consider in more detail the transformations of participation in digital societies.

Becoming valuable

The first of these transformations I have already touched upon above: in digital societies, participation has become a valuable good, economically, politically and morally speaking. The mainstreaming of digital participation, its uptake as an organizational form across industry, government and civil society has coincided with a move towards the *valuation* of participation. As noted, digital participation has been historically associated with the worlds of social movements, protest culture and creative practice – and indeed, participation in general is historically associated with the public and the voluntary sector. However, with the re-branding of digital technology as an 'architecture of participation', participation came to be framed, much more expressly than before, as a distinctive, ideal procedure for engaging with users, consumers and citizens and for the 'intelligent' management of populations and publics. This change in status was not simply a consequence of digitization, but is also connected with wider political processes, such as attempts to 'shrink the state', and delegate governmental tasks to business and social organizations. But it has deeply affected the very status and/or logic of social and public engagement in our societies. As Chris Kelty (2012) puts it: 'Participation is no longer simply an opening up, an expansion, a liberation, it is now also a principle of improvement, an instrument of change, a creative force. It no longer threatens, but *has become a resource: participation has been made valuable*' (p. 24, italics mine). This valuation of participation takes specific forms in digital arrangements, and includes the production of data – with X users signed up, we gain access to X number of profiles – and metrics about participation – so many unique visitors, so many comments – and the development of communicative strategies for market-, audience- and brand-making – the website as community; the identification of targetable influencers.

Importantly, the valuation of participation is not unique to digital environments, and neither is it strictly speaking new. Javier Lezaun and Linda Soneryd (2007) have shown how other, older methods of participation, such as focus groups and citizen consultations, have come to serve a similar purpose in recent decades: while these instruments are often introduced as a way to take into account consumer preferences and citizen opinions and views, participation techniques like focus groups, too, tend to generate significant amounts of data not to mention opportunities for publicity. Participatory events, Soneryd and Lezaun show, in practice serve as occasions for rendering publics knowable for and by government, business and organizations, and this knowledge is valuable and deployable by them and others towards a variety of purposes including the legitimation of their own actions: demonstrating opinions makes it possible to act on those opinions and when positive offer a rhetorical resource in support of political or commercial propositions (see also Soneryd, 2016). However, while the deployability of participation can thus be observed across domains, it is even more notable in the case of digital participation: here, participation data and metrics are not only taken up by experts, but are made available to a variety of third-parties and users themselves, thus intensifying their deployability (Gerlitz and Lury, 2014). Partly for this reason, the ideal of participation is problematized to a greater degree in digital settings.

As noted, part of the problem with participation as an ideal is that it risks obscuring certain formative features of digital participation as a social, economic and political proposition. But a good understanding of digital participation precisely requires that we come to terms with its practical implementation in socio-technical architectures. Chris Kelty (2012) makes a second relevant observation on this point. Digital participation is a *layered* phenomenon: in digital settings, one doesn't just participate in 'digital culture' or 'life online'; one also participates in a specific conversation, an event or a community, and one adopts the role of 'user' of platform X or subscriber of service Y. This means on a practical level that to participate by digital means is to be enrolled in an organizational infrastructure. However, our ideals and theories of participation do not equip us very well to come to terms with this latter circumstance. Early ideals of digital participation, such as those that were part of digital culture from the mid 1990s onwards, tended to imagine spaces of participation as autonomous, but today's digital technologies of participation materialize the very opposite circumstance: here participation becomes deeply entangled with the conduct of everyday life and processes of economic, political and social organization. Indeed, an outstanding feature of digital participation is its insertability into other practices and settings (see also Marres, 2012c): as digital devices render participation ever more 'easy' – providing the option of a click here and the insertion of a 'Duh' comment there – acts of participation become ever more integrated into ongoing practices and arrangements. However, as digital environments help to make participation insertable into social life, they encourage the opposite of autonomous participation. They enable its instrumentalization: participation comes to serve social, economic and political ends and objectives that are not those of participation itself. While this is a highly problematic – and in many cases harmful – development, we should also recognize that ideals of autonomous participation *themselves* become problematic in digital societies. We should not only decry instrumentalization, but also develop positive accounts of the inter-articulation of participation with other modes of actions (work, everyday life, innovation): when does this work? (Marres and Lezaun, 2011).

The coming out of the technology of participation

A second relevant shift concerns the role not just of the digital but of technology in participation: as participation is increasingly mediated by digital infrastructures, devices and practices, technology comes to play an increasingly prominent role in its framing, organization and practice. Of course, we did not have to wait for the Internet, social media or smart phones for media technologies to start playing a significant role in participation and the organization of publics (Gillespie et al., 2014). They always did. However, as digital media technologies proliferate across social, political and public life, they have become *ever more visible and notable* elements in the doing and staging of participation. Take the paper by Monique Girard and David Stark (2007), in which they discuss a citizen consultation that took place in New York in 2006 to facilitate discussion of the regeneration of Ground Zero, where the Twin Towers used to stand. Their article includes photos of people sitting around tables and discussing architectural designs, and on the table between them sit some rather large and colourful laptops, as well as digital recorders. Partly because these machines are now somewhat dated – the consultation in question took place in the mid 2000s – the prominent role of the digital in this participation event is striking. Elsewhere I have referred to this circumstance as the 'coming out' of the technologies of participation (Marres, 2012c), meaning that technology today plays an increasingly noticeable and explicit role in public engagement. This also means that participation in our societies becomes ascribed to practices that were not defined in those terms before. Take 'smart' energy technologies, such as digitally enhanced electricity meters, which are described in policy literatures and on environmentalist blogs as enabling citizen participation in sustainable transitions and climate change. Such accounts invest technology with special 'powers of participation': the configuration of experimental systems for making energy 'visible' as part of everyday life here becomes a way of endowing everyday people with the ability to participate in current affairs (energy and environment).

Today, technologies of participation are then introduced across sectors, but the digital nevertheless plays a critical role in transforming the opportunities for everyday engagement. Take the role that digital mapping technologies have recently acquired as technologies of participation, as described by Petersen (2014) and Plantin (2015). They have studied the use of applications like Google maps in the 2007 San Diego wildfires and the Fukushima Daiichi nuclear disaster in 2011 respectively, showing how non-experts came together in these events to collect and upload monitored data concerning the spread of forest fires and levels of radiation to public platforms. While the robustness of these forms of public knowledge were called into question during these events, they nevertheless produced a powerful examplar: digital knowledge technologies can be re-configured as instruments of participation in collective enquiry. In taking up online cartographic tools to assemble data, to document the facts and raise awareness, these San Diego and Fukushima collectives then brought into view potentially new ways of organizing publics through data practices. This also has implications for social research itself: the very online mapping tools described by Petersen and Plantin can also be used by social researchers themselves, to produce accounts of everyday participation in the production of knowledge about disasters. The uptake of digital technologies – and their data- and metric-generating capacities – for purposes of participation, then presents digital sociology not only with an important topic, but also a potential resource for social research.[3]

There is an important difference between the experimental use of technologies of participation, as in the examples above, and wider, socio-technical architectures that support institutional forms of participation, such as elections. In the latter case, too, the production of data, metrics and technical expertise about participation, in the form of voting machines and opinion polls for example, is an important part of the process. But the machinery of participation here nevertheless tends to sit in the background: ultimately elections are not about the technologies that facilitate them. In the case of digital participation, this is *not* self-evident: the use of technology in the enactment of engagement – a smart electricity meter, a clever new phone app – is often part of the point of digital participation. It raises the question: are we witnessing a broader approximation between technology and participation in our societies? This very much remains to be seen, but to pose the question is to consider a possible further development in the transformation of media societies, which was described by John Thompson (2011) as the 'dis-embedding' of participation. Thompson noted that what is distinctive about media societies is that participation here can no longer be modelled on the face-to-face conversation, because of the prominent role that media technologies play in the staging, curation and organization of participation. For Thompson (2011) this move 'beyond the face-to-face' entailed the re-location of participation into the mediated spaces of technologically enabled participation, which he referred to as 'spheres of information and symbolic content that are largely detached from physical locales' (p. 49). By contrast, the forms of digital participation that I have described here situate participation in specific contexts, such as energy use in the home, or natural disasters. Digital participation highlights mundane settings as the notable locations in which engagement takes place, and as such, it involves attempts at the re-embedding of participation.

Metric-ization

The localization – or even materialization – of digital participation in specific practices should not be mistaken for the un-doing of its abstractness. On the contrary. One last critical feature of digital participation I want to highlight here is what we may call its 'metric-ization'. Anderson (2011) provided a helpful account of this process in an early paper on algorithmic publics, which notes that we increasingly encounter the public in the shape of numbers, and more specifically usage statistics, now that actions like reading, viewing, commenting, approving, flagging and so on, are increasingly mediated by digital infrastructures (see also McKelvey, 2014). As Christin's (2015) study of the use of dashboards in newsrooms also makes clear, the mediation of digital publics through the display of (live) measures, has important implications for the worlds of journalism, policy, marketing and their attitudes towards the public.[4] But digital participation operates equally on the relations between social domains. Platforms for participation – such as social media, but also digital forms of organization like the 'data lab' – brings a variety of agencies into relation, which include representatives of the professions listed above (journalism, policy, marketing) but also a range of less determinate agents, such as third-party advertisers, data brokers. As Gerlitz and Lury describe in their (2014) study of the social scoring site Klout, the very figure of the reputation score – Justin Bieber has seventy, your friend has ten – produces an interface with the capacity to draw users themselves and a variety of agencies into changing relations (see also Gillespie, 2010). For example, individuals with a high Klout score may accede to the category of 'influencer', and enter into direct contact with marketing services, while a platform's emerging partnership with an insurance company may result in the presentation of health monitoring services to specific user groupings.

Digital media technologies specifically enable the monitoring, measurement and analysis of participation, and these capacities are critical to their transformative effects on society. The traceability and analysability of the actions of large populations is *not* an accidental by-product of digital architectures, but one of the strategic objectives associated with digital platforms and the wider development of the platformization of the Internet (Gerlitz and Helmond, 2013). A critical element of this strategy is to bring diverse audiences and constituencies into relation by way of the digital – users, journalists, advertisers, software developers, campaigners – and the *adaptability* of digital platforms to these diverse constituencies is key to their success. This can partly explain the spread and success of info-action formats such as 'liking', 'sharing', 'fav-ing' and 'mentioning': these formats are highly countable and thus determinate, but at the same time they are open-ended enough to keep the register of action in suspension. In liking or sharing or mentioning things on Facebook, are we practising sociality, participating in a public, or organizing into a market (Kelty, 2012)? *'Each of the above' is the answer that digital architectures actively seek to ensure*, as the multi-interpretability of action is critical to platforms' capacity to connect – their ability to engage heterogeneous actors. But this multi-sidedness of digital platforms has sometimes dramatic political implications. A famous and forceful example are the Arab Spring revolutions: as the demonstrations on Cairo's Tahir Square brought large numbers of people out onto the streets, social media platforms like Twitter and YouTube saw concurrent explosions in user traffic, making these among the most successful days in their history, in view of audience reach (Figure 5.1) (Abdel-Rahman, 2015).[5] On digital platforms, the Arab Spring events then unfolded in at least two dimensions at once: that of politics (revolution) and commerce (traffic boom). While less dramatic, this double-sidedness of digital participation can also be observed on a more mundane level: on the one hand, social media use is an ordinary practice that is part of the everyday lives of many people; on the other hand, social media make available a new

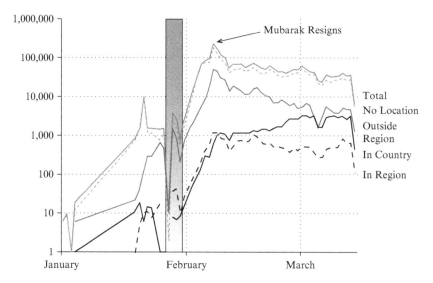

Figure 5.1 Project on Information Technology and Political Islam (Howard et al., 2011): Logged number of tweets on #egypt, by location

Note: 'Outside Region' refers to Twitter profiles that had locations outside both the country and the region, and 'No Location' refers to profiles that either had no location data or have been deleted or suspended since archiving began. The central bar indicates the period in which journalists began reporting that protests had reached the level of 'thousands' of participants.

numerical infrastructure with the capacity to transform economic, cultural and political relations across society. Digital platforms open up 'spaces of multi-valence' (Marres, 2012c): in these spaces, action is measured, structured – and valued – according to multiple logics at once: everyday life, commerce, politics, knowledge, and so on.

To sum up, participation is a key feature of digital infrastructures, devices and practices, but to understand digital participation we must view it in relation to other projects. The enactment of digital participation strengthens – or even creates – relations between different forms of action, across sociality, economy, politics and culture, and it has the capacity to intensify and transform relations between social domains. The adjustability of digital infrastructures is a critical factor in all this: to provide one last example, some large banks are now considering to accept social media accounts as a alternative to bank account numbers in national and international bank transfers,

and this would entail not only a significant transformation of inter-
bank arrangements,[6] it is equally likely to involve modifications in the
practices and architectures of social media exchange: both economic
and social logics – as well as legal and political – are at stake in the
reconfiguration of digital architectures of participation, a point I will
return to in the last chapter. But we can now see more clearly what
the problem is with viewing digital participation through the prism
of a shift 'from audience to participation': it does not help us to
understand how digital architectures of participation help to render
action tracable, curatable, valuable and deployable across social
domains.[7] However, even if the sloganeering around participation is
problematic; it certainly does not follow that the ideal of participation
ceases to be relevant to progressive efforts to transform digital societies. Yes, the ideal of digital participation needs to be re-constructed,
but I want to argue that it remains both empirically plausible and
normatively important for digital sociology. But we must first consider the changing relations between participation, intervention
and knowledge in more detail. Added to the social, economic and
political aspects of digital participation, it is key that we recognize its
epistemic dimension.

Digital participation as a device of social research

Building on the observations above, we can begin to re-specify the
phenomenon of digital participation. What in popular discourses has
been presented as a dramatic shift from passive spectatorship (the
audience) to active contribution (participation) in practice entails
a more gradual expansion in the trace-ability, analyse-ability and
manipul-ability of engagement. Rather than only realizing a cultural
or political ideal, digital participation more boringly involves the
configuration of an administrative infrastructure, a vast, empirical
apparatus for rendering populations and publics researchable and
influencable (Ruppert et al., 2013). This is not the whole story of
digital participation, but in some respects *the difference between audience and participation must be understood as a difference in the degree to
which engagement is traceable*: we refer to users of media technologies
as 'audiences' when their engagement is difficult to detect and doesn't
seem to leave a trace, whereas participation occurs when contributions are captured, rendered visible and actionable. Furthermore,
from this standpoint the point of participation is not just participation. It is rather that the record-ability of participation generates

opportunities for feedback. (Digital platforms facilitate participation, the analysis of participation, and its curation *in one and the same go*, which is why one could say that social media are platforms for social research before they are platforms for social life.) As we have seen, digital industries also market this research-ability of publics and populations back towards their users, as popular online tools for digital analytics allow them to track who visits their pages, checked their profile, and so on. The approximation of social research and participation then does not just happen at the back-end, but equally at the front-end, at the user interface, as users take advantage of the researche-ability of social life enabled by digital platforms: 'data production, as well as benefit from data analytics, occur[s] consistently and [is] directed to a variety of recipients' (Powell, 2014).

That participation is rendered researchable in digital settings has distinct implications for sociology, as distinct from, for example, journalism. From the standpoint of journalism, the introduction of participation metrics into journalistic practices – as in the newsroom – has been described as a new thing, as journalists previously worked with an image of the public that was 'rather hazy' (Anderson, 2011). However, from the standpoint of social research, the metrical representation of user activities is not exceptional at all: for many decades social research has produced quantitative representations of publics and populations, with the aid of surveys, opinion polls and focus group methods, and these research instruments have long been central to understandings of the role of social research in society, as envisioned in classic work by Paul Lazarsfeld and Robert Merton on focus groups and opinions research (Simonson and Weimann, 2003). From the standpoint of social research, that is, participation metrics fit into particular methodological traditions of knowing society. *Digital architectures of participation simply present one more step in a long-standing process of the configuration of participation as an object of social research and intervention.* Furthermore, social research methods like focus groups were expressly designed to enable sociology to make a contribution to society (Lezaun, 2007; Osborne and Rose, 1999). The sociologist Robert Merton initially developed his focus group research methods in order to evaluate the efficacy of anti-Nazi propaganda films during the second world war: did they convince audiences? This method then presents one of sociology's contributions to the war effort in those days (for a discussion of other anti-fascist social research methods, see Turner, 2013). By developing methods for public opinion research, social research emerged as a notable mediator of the public during the twentieth century. As focus groups came to inform election campaigns and opinion polls featured regularly in the news, participation research became the instrument though which society could know itself (Boullier, 2016).

From the perspective of sociology, digital participation cannot be understood in strict opposition to older regimes of media consumption. It rather appears as an extension of social research traditions for knowing and intervening in society that have developed in tandem with media systems during the twentieth century. For sociology, then, the newness of digital participation is still in question: will digital participation metrics acquire capacities that break with twentieth century models for representing society to society? It is probably too early to say. But it is clear that participation metrics, as such, are not new for sociology. This can partly explain why sociology has been 'slow' – as is sometimes said – to appreciate the new phenomenon of digital participation: to sociologists it didn't look that new! Nevertheless, in what follows I will argue that digital participation should be of special interest to sociology precisely insofar as metric-ization is one of its formative features: the intersection of the enactment of participation and its researchability in digital architectures, is a phenomenon sociology can help to elucidate. The contribution of social research to society has historically been defined – as well as contested – in terms of precisely its capacity to transform social and political collectives into 'researchable' populations, and in that way to make them available as engageable 'publics' (Lezaun, 2011).

So why do the participation metrics generated through digital arrangements today have been called a new phenomenon, and what are their distinctive features? It has been argued that digital participation entails the privatization of social research, as the development, management and valuation of digital infrastructures for 'knowing publics' (Kennedy and Moss, 2015) is in the hands of digital industries. By comparing digital participation metrics with focus group and opinion poll methods, we can further specify this critique. The older, more established methods for representing society to society have long been used commercially also, but participation in focus groups and polls is a deliberate act, and their findings are publicly reported. What's different about digital participation? Some have argued that in digital societies social research becomes more like surveillance. It is not only that digital industry research centres are relatively inaccessible to social researchers, the problem is rather that the very relations between social research and social actors is constituted outside the domain of mutual awareness: digital subjects often don't even know they are 'participating' in research (Andrejevic, 2014). On the other hand, digital participation arguably enables more *interactive* forms of knowing society than polls and focus groups. As noted, digital participation metrics are included in the user interface, and this raises the question of what potentially new relations of feedback, modes of response and mutual attunement are possible between social research and publics in digital societies. To investigate this we need to adopt a relational perspective on digital participation, and examine what relations between actors digital participation enables and fails to enable.

Such a perspective is less idealistic than those that equate digitization with democratization, as in the ideal of the shift from the passive audience to active participation, but it is not necessarily any less critical. Once we consider that the project of rendering publics researchable has important precedents in twentieth century social research, sociological critiques of this project can equally come into view. Sociologists have long been critical of the application of social research methods – like focus groups and opinion polls – in economy and society: they have argued that it entails an 'instrumentalization' of social enquiry as well as participation. The project of making both participation and social research serve other purposes than their own goes against not one but two ideals: against the autonomy of participation and against the autonomy of knowledge (see for an influential formulation of this perspective, Habermas (1991 [1962]).[8] Sociologists, like others, have long hoped that digital participation provided a way of addressing these problems of instrumentalism: they conceived of digital participation as the anti-dote to narrow means–end logics, especially in the early days of the Web, when it appeared that the ideal of autonomous participation could be transposed onto the Internet, as online environments were imagined as all-encompassing spaces ('cyberspace'), which could be studied as cultural universes of their own (Slater, 2002). However, as we have seen the re-configuration of digital participation architectures over the last decade or so seems in many ways diametrically opposed to this autonomist framing of participation: mobile, smart and platform applications precisely render participation deployable in relation to other logics and objects (so many shares, likes) and they render it insertable in all sorts of contexts (like us on social media! It will say on the wall of a café, a fence cordoning off a construction site, a theatre ticket, . . .).

There is a clear need for critical studies of the purposes to which digital participation and participation research are put in digital societies, but general critiques of instrumentalism – i.e. criticisms of the *fact* that digital participation is deployed towards ends other than its own – is only of limited use to digital sociology. This critique does not enable us to move beyond the ideal assumption of the autonomy of participation: when digital platforms are criticized for their colonization or exploitation of the ideal of participation, the ideal of autonomous participation is not re-examined, it just gets inverted. The absence of autonomy is deplored and while this may make moral sense, it does not help our understanding of the changing roles of participation in digital society, economy, politics and culture very much. Recent concepts developed for the study of the digital cultural economy and public politics like 'pro-ducers' or 'networked publics' do not suffer from this short-coming, but they have other limitations, insofar as they do not bring technology itself within the frame of social enquiry. These concepts highlight changing models of social, political and economic organization but technology itself does not figure as a participant in them, and neither does knowledge. They do not really help us to grasp the re-formatting of participation as a traceable, analysable and curatable phenomenon: in some respects, these models retain the useful fiction that participation presents a world-unto-itself. How to include technology into the study of participation then remains a challenge in social research, but a useful step in addressing this shortcoming is to 'expand the frame' on participation (Suchman, 2007b; Marres, 2012c; Chilvers and Kearnes, 2015): rather than conceiving of participation as 'world-unto-itself', we then explore how participation enables the establishment of relations between diverse actors, forms and sites of social, economic and political life, or what I call above inter-articulation and Gerlitz and Lury (2014) called 'commensuration' drawing on Espeland.

Re-qualifying digital participation: a machine for knowing society with society

Participation is not only a topic for social enquiry, however; for sociology it is also an instrument and a normative ideal. It is not an exaggeration to say that supporting participation and the development of public ways of knowing society have long – perhaps always – been an important project for sociology. It goes back at least to the claim that the pragmatist John Dewey made at the beginning of the twentieth century: that the best format in which to publish social research is the newspaper (Jones, 1998). Such a historical anecdote also serves (again) the pernicious effect of 'audience to participation' ideas about digital transformations. They wrongly suggest that digital technology is the harbinger of participation, as what makes possible new ways of enabling, organization and knowing publics. From a sociological perspective, it is far more correct to say that digital technologies provide new opportunities to pursue long-standing objectives of social enquiry, i.e. to develop more participatory ways of knowing society. To appreciate what difference sociology could make to digital participation, and vice versa, it is then not enough to consider the formative features of digital participation itself: we need to consider historical relations between publics and sociology in a much broader frame. To do this properly requires at least a book of its own (Didier, 2009), and I will limit myself here to only a few observations; but it should be clear that the development of innovative techniques, methods and methodologies that could enable more responsive and responsible ways of knowing society has been a defining objective of twentieth-century sociological research.

Going back to the early twentieth century, we can already find critiques of unidirectional and 'un-interactive' ways of knowing society, critiques that are quite similar to todays criticisms of digital social research becoming methodologically indistinguishable from surveillance. When John Dewey called for the development of new forms of social enquiry that would take 'the form of a newspaper', he decried 'static' and 'un-responsive' understanding of the public. He proposed that in technological societies, publics are becoming ever more *dynamic, changeable and un-containable* and as a consequence the slow production of knowledge makes it ever more challenging to ensure its public relevance (Dewey, 1927; Marres, 2012c). Sociologists of the early twentieth century did not only develop ideas but also outlined alternative methodologies, methods and instruments to enable more responsive, dynamic and interactive ways of knowing societies: Tonnies developed the methodology of the socio-graphic observatory, which was designed as participatory space for examining social contexts with social actors (Burke, 2012).[9] Jacob Moreno envisioned his socio-metrics as an interactive method that served a clear reformist objective: 'Visualizing the positions of the actors should enable [these actors] to take charge of their own social embedding and initiate changes to optimize their positions' (Mayer, 2012). As discussed in Chapters 2 and 3, the methodological frameworks that have been built into social media architectures draw extensively on these classic social methodologies. The question for sociologists is how they may re-appropriate their own histories in the development of more responsive ways of knowing society with the digital.

These historical perspectives also suggest an alternative approach to the project and aspiration to move 'beyond the audience'. Behind this normative project lies hidden an intellectual challenge: how can we – as a society, with its discourses, its established ways of talking, and institutional arrangements – move beyond *the assumption* that publics are essentially static, passive and containable in the settings in which they become observable? Digital participation opens up anew an old promise that social researchers and theorists had already formulated by the early twentieth century: if we can become better at tracing distributed, dynamic and uncontainable publics, it may become possible to make knowledge more responsive to these publics, to orientate social, political and public action and intervention less towards static ideals and more towards changing formations of the public. *Can we know society in more responsive ways? Can we develop styles of social enquiry that take advantage of the expanded interactivity between technology, people and non-human entities that is enabled by the digital?* When it is said that digital sociology enables new ways of engaging sociology's publics, this is not only a practical but also an intellectual proposition: how can long-standing projects in social theory and research of 'contesting the audience' – of contesting the *understanding* of publics in passive terms – inform sociological engagement with digital participation today? On this point, too, the significance of digital architectures of participation resides in their ambivalence. On the one hand, these architectures open up opportunities for moving beyond the long outdated model of the external, static, containable, public (as many sociologists have argued we should since the early twentieth century). On the other hand, from a sociological perspective, digital architectures for researching publics present a regression to outdated anti-interactive and anti-public ways of knowing society. In too many cases they configure social science as a form of surveillance, meaning that it is not possible for the subjects of social research to assume the role of participant in social research.

Once we take sociological history into account, we can give an alternative account of the promise and problems of digital participation. The sociological contributions above point towards a different way of understanding the ideal implied in the shift from audience to participation. It should not simply be understood as pushing for ever more active, engaged, committed actors and populations, but also expresses a different aspiration, namely that of a move towards more responsive, attuned and interactive ways of *representing society to society, of researching publics with publics* (Boullier, 2015). It suggests a particular answer to the question of what the problem is with digital arrangements for 'knowing publics' as currently configured. They may be interactive, but they often are not responsive – in the sense that they do not really enable mutual adjustment between the concerns of users, researchers, technologists and other actors in the development of new forms of knowing publics (Kennedy and Moss, 2014). As one computational scientist put it bluntly during a workshop: 'we prefer passive data', such as credit card records or GPS trace data (meaning data produced without any direct participation of data subjects). Media scholars have shown that prevailing methodologies of digital participation tend to favour highly asymmetrical regimes of social enquiry (Pasquale, 2015; Andrejevic, 2014): while users, consumers and citizens are enticed to participate, the infrastructures, methods and experts of 'knowing publics' more often than not withdraw into specialist knowledge, and on a general level exhibit high levels of non- and un-responsiveness to social, political and ethical concerns about the directions into which digital societies and research are developing. From the standpoint of an expanded, sociological understanding of interactivity, there is then notoriously little feedback in digital knowledge infrastructures, or at least, too little feedback of the important kind, that of knowing the public with publics.

The interactive features of digital platforms open up possibilities for participatory social enquiry: as we have seen in previous chapters, they enable ongoing involvement of research participants in the research process, and they position users as both the subjects and addressees of research, and sometimes its agents (Gerlitz and Lury, 2014). However, many platforms operate in a highly individualized register, taking the single user, consumer or company as its object and addressee. For this reason, digital architectures actually risk to be *less interactive* than older empirical mechanisms for representing society to society. Established research methods like opinion polls have traditionally been used in explicit reference to wider contexts such as public affairs, and the publication of results was generally orientated towards a set calendar of centralized news production (the morning papers, the 8 o'clock news). In these ways, these methods enabled explicit attunement between members of a public and collective contexts. By contrast, digital equivalents like trend analytics, which show which keywords were most used on a given day, or what people searched tend to presume a far more fluid context. As McKelvey (2014) points out, digital participation is organized in *continuous, always-on, dispersed and personalized* forms, and this makes for a rather amorphous context and fuzzy spatio-temporal frame of expression. We know that participation metrics offer an aggregate view, and as such they can make visible latent expressions of shared interests, but can they be said to express a collective context? I'm not sure. This uncertainty further limits the opportunities digital participation provides for mutual attunement between actors. While digital societies are becoming ever more 'participatory', regimes of knowing society are at risk of becoming less so. But wait, isn't digital research precisely known for its embrace of participatory forms of knowledge, in the form of *citizen science, open science, crowd science, and so on*?

Are digital ways of knowing society participatory? A typology

Isn't the digital the harbinger of participatory knowledge, does it not enable the implementation of knowledge democracy? Digitization is associated with the proliferation of new organizational forms and informational formats, and public knowledge is a key marker of many of these: from open data to crowd research, and participatory research events called hackatons (Irani, 2015). Sociologists themselves have taken up digital media technologies with the express aim of practising 'public sociology' and of developing more engaged approaches to knowing society using social media like Facebook (Carrigan, 2016; Healy, forthcoming). For many sociologists, the digital has re-awakened older commitments to participation as both a method of social research and a mode of address (Back, 2012). However, whether and how commitments to digital participation in social research will translate into viable approaches to advancing social enquiry remains to be seen, and indeed, this has been called into question. As noted, digital infrastructures have facilitated highly asymmetrical forms of social enquiry, of 'knowing' society and publics (Kennedy and Moss, 2015). It is not self-evident that research projects that are framed and presented as furthering ideals of participatory knowledge live up to these ideals in practice. While research may proceed under the banner that 'knowledge is for everyone!' – to use a slogan of the UK-based Open Data Institute – this does not necessarily mean that the methods, forms of models of knowledge implemented under this label enable more diverse ways of knowing society.[10] Commitments to participation should not be taken at face-value, and the methods, models and forms of digital research that are today advertised as furthering openness and participation require detailed investigation (Dickel, forthcoming). To indicate what form such an investigation might take, I would here like to propose a typology that situates digital forms of knowing society along a spectrum that goes from weak to strong participation.[11]

At the lower end of the spectrum are arrangements for digital social research that configure society as a resource and audience of research. An example of this model can be found in the Administrative Data Research Network, which has been tasked by the UK government with coordinating access to governmental data for social research. The data managed by this organization includes data pertaining to vulnerable groups (criminal records, job centre data) and citing the moral duty to protect personal data, the network only accepts data requests from registered scientists employed by a recognized research institution. The network does engage with publics, with the stated aim of educating them about administrative data research.[12] As such, this arrangement does not enable participation in social enquiry. It also upholds a strict separation between a population of research subjects and a public defined as an external addressee of social research findings, and not its agent. This model goes against prevailing ideals of openness, but the policy implemented by the Administrative Data Research Network is less exceptional than we might think. As noted, many computational social scientists prefer to work with data that have been produced without knowing participation of research subjects. As the definition of transactional data has it, they prefer 'by-product data', which computational scientists praise precisely because these forms of data minimize active participation of research subjects in the research process, which they consider a source of bias (Marres, 2012a). Notwithstanding recent sloganeering around participatory research, the ideal indicates a pretty common position today. Much computational social science de facto proceeds under a different slogan: 'in the age of participation, against participation', and we could refer to this model as 'digital paternalism'.

A second prominent model for digital participation in social research is contained in propositions for open social science, citizen social science and crowd social science. These proposals open up key elements of research infrastructures and the research process to non-experts: open data movements render data widely accessible; citizen or crowd social science open up specific research tasks to non-experts, such as data collection or coding content. These models move beyond the assumption of the public or society as passive addressee of knowledge and recast social actors in the role of potential participants. Crucially, however, while these models change the distribution of research tasks and ownership, they do so without re-distributing epistemic authority or agency. Frameworks for citizen science tend to adopt a resource-model of participation: they frequently model practices of data collection and analysis on technical arrangements like distributed computing, making the allocation of tasks and resources a key question. Indeed, citizen social science is frequently promoted by an appeal to efficiency-savings and resource optimization. As participants are expected to execute pre-defined knowledge tasks, they may be defined as knowing subjects, but they are not expected to make any active epistemic contributions to the advancement of knowledge (Haklay, 2013). As such, projects of citizen social science remain hampered in important respects: users are treated as participants in the research when it comes to the contribution of labour (data capture, application of coding schemes), but not when it comes to the authorship of knowledge. It seems fair to say that citizen social science tends to frame participation not in epistemic or methodological but first and foremost in organizational or economic terms, and this model can be called 'logistical participation'. One advantage of this is that citizen science can operate on a different, larger scale than participatory social research was traditionally restricted to, as in the case of action research developed from the 1940s onwards. But the flipside is that open science models do not really address the golden question: is it possible to render processes of enquiry – knowing itself – more participatory? Can we envision distributions of epistemic agency and authority that do not uniquely depend on the accreditation of experts?

This limitation can also be observed in the particular case of open data, which is in some ways the mirror image of citizen science, as here it is not the tasks but the objects of social science that are rendered more widely accessible. Notably, in open data projects the methodological apparatus of research is held stable – mostly taking the form of statistical data analysis – and this has a similar outcome as in citizen science. The widening of participation in research is not really expected to translate into a redistribution of epistemic capacities. While more people may have access to data, they are expected to have the same expert skills that are expected of the experts, if they wish to qualify as legitimate participants in the process of enquiry. As Alison Powell (2014) has astutely observed:

> The promise of openness is hard to fulfil unless one can gain access to these capabilities: government agencies can open up their data stores to public use through open data projects like the UK's data.

gov.uk, but the re-use of this data may be limited by access to facilities and expertise. [..] Openness thus retains a promise of legitimacy and accountability while precluding the kinds of access and representation that democratic citizenship might require.

On a more general level, it is becoming increasingly clear that epistemic and democratic ideals are not as combinable in digital societies as some had hoped: digital technology may not make it possible, after all, to align the epistemic ideal of the advancement of knowledge and political ideals of public engagement in the ways that philosophers of science and political theorists of an earlier era had proposed (Ezrahi, 1990). To many sociologists, this does not come as a surprise, as sociologists of knowledge have for many decades pointed out flaws in these ideals. They have demonstrated, for example, that ideals of knowledge democracy implicitly model the role of the citizen on that of the scientist, while under-acknowledging the parochial origins of scientific culture in white male ways of doing things (Haraway, 1997). But we are still faced with the popularity in these ideals.

This is where a last form of digital participation in social research comes in: these are projects that take as their starting point that we do *not*, in fact, already know how to simultaneously advance the aims of knowledge and participation in digital social research, and I will refer to them as 'experiments in participation' (Lezaun, Marres and Tironi, 2016). In recent years, digital sociologists and researchers in related fields have undertaken methodological experiments that seek to test the capacities of digital practices of data collection, interpretation and communication for developing knowledge collaboratively. Many of these experiments engage with and draw on everyday, 'non-expert' practices of digital research. Take the research by Dawn Nafus and Gina Neff (2016) on the practices and methods of self-tracking developed by the 'quantified self' movement in California and elsewhere. They show how these practices do not just increase participation, in the sense of granting non-experts a more active role in research, but articulate alternative ways of configuring enquiry: for example, rather than seeking to collect comprehensive data, practices of self-tracking may seek to determine a relevant minimum: for example, to determine the link between well-being and nutrition, it is probably not necessary to record the calories that you eat every day of the week, it may be enough to indicate how you feel once a day, after lunch, with a number between 1 and 5. Importantly, for Nafus and Neff these practices of self-tracking present both a topic and a possible method for social enquiry: in more recent work, Nafus has started using smart watches as a method for researching community engagement with issues of environmental pollution.

In experiments in participation, digital technologies are not only deployed to re-configure not only the distribution of tasks in social research (who collects the data, who codes the content?), but are used towards a more open-ended, methodological objective: to test alternative ways of configuring relations between researchers and researched, and between data, methods and contexts. Another example is Christian Nold's (2015) research on Heathrow air pollution with local residents, which initially made use of smart phone apps for recording noise pollution, but later came to include a wider range of material prototypes for detecting pollution levels in a participatory way. The work finds its starting point in recent UK controversies about noise pollution measurement, in which policy measures for determining levels of noise pollution levels were called into question by environmental organizations. Together with residents living in the vicinity of Heathrow, Nold developed creative prototypes to exemplify and/or inspire alternative kinds of knowledge about noise pollution, including a measurement device called 'I speak your feelings' which invites residents to record experienced levels of noise pollution around Heathrow (Figure 5.2). To be sure, these experimental forms of measurements do not seek to 'compete' directly with administrative methodologies of noise pollution measurement in terms of reliability or robustness. Rather, they re-introduce effective forms of measurement as relevant to public knowledge culture and examine ways in which research subjects may be involved as research participants. An experiment like this explores, to paraphrase Aaron Cicourel (1964), *ways of achieving better interaction between subjects, objects, settings and contexts of social research.*

Conclusion

How can we deploy digital architectures, devices and practices to render research more participatory? This question is asked across disciplines and fields today, but this chapter has argued that sociology can make a distinctive contribution to our understanding of this ideal and efforts to advance it. Not only have sociologists reflected for many decades on the participation of social actors in culture, economy, science, innovation and politics, the very ideal of digital participation re-activates older visions of how relations between knowledge and society may be transformed in the age of technology

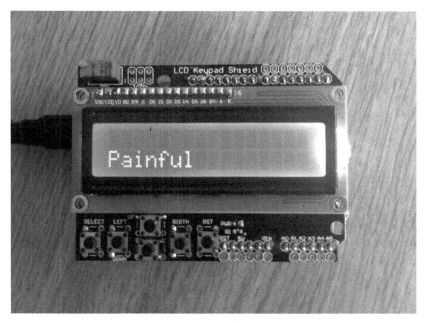

Figure 5.2 'I speak your feelings', Christian Nold, Prototyping Heathrow Noise Pollution (2015)

and media, and over the course of the twentieth century, sociologists have developed concepts that can help to assess these ambitions. Sociology, in other words, can make a contribution to the evaluation of digital participation, and to the respecification of this ideal. There is however one further challenge that sociology faces in this respect and that I would like to flag by way of conclusion. While sociology can help us to understand why participation has become such a prominent ideal in technological and media societies, its own efforts to increase participation in knowledge making are running into difficulties in digital societies. There appears to be a mismatch between the participatory methodologies that sociologists have developed over the last decades, and the methods, techniques and forms of digital social research. Sociologists tend to conceive of participatory enquiry *in dialogic terms*, as involving deliberation, discussion and debate with and between non-experts and experts. However, as discussed in Chapter 2, digital forms of analysis tends to focus on activities and events, on 'what people do' and on 'what's happening', and not only on what they say (Newman et al., 2007).

As we have seen, this (trans-)actional quality of digital data has been used as an argument to dispense with participation in social enquiry altogether, an ambition which many sociologists would dismiss as foolish, given the central role that actor's understandings and awareness of social life play in social life. But the prevalence of this type of data nevertheless presents interpretative styles of social enquiry with an important problem: while sociologists may know how to democratize research in the register of talk (by promoting dialogic forms of knowledge), they are much less equipped to contribute towards this aim in the registers of action (what people do) and events (what's happening). I think it is important that we openly recognize this lacuna, rather than limiting our contribution to the implementation of dialogic models in digital research. While ideals of 'knowledge democracy' have become ubiquitous, we are surprisingly ignorant as to how this ideal may be implemented on the level of the empirical apparatus that enables social research. Contrary to popular wisdom, I think we do not yet know the answer to these questions: how to combine diverse ways of knowing? How to practise social enquiry in more responsive ways and still advance knowledge? How to configure the interactivity of digital participation in ways that serve the ends of both knowledge and democracy well? Participation is endlessly debated as a political, economic, cultural challenge and opportunity, but it is still too rarely taken seriously as a challenge of political epistemology. We are very good at imagining participatory knowledge in an idealistic register but much less so in an empirical one.

What we do know, however, is that the strict separation between the population as research subject and the public as an addressee of social research is not sustainable in digital societies. As knowledge is deployed interactively in digital societies – as it is rendered actionable to further the ends of politics, culture, commerce and government – this type of methodological purism will cease to be viable (Schick and Winthereik, 2013). We should therefore not only criticize the anti-interactive methodologies that are pursued in computational social science, but point out the problems with it. Another knowledge culture is possible. But we do not necessarily know what form it will take. This is also why the ideal of 'digital exceptionalism', which has been a defining feature of digital culture for so long, remains relevant. In order to determine the epistemic capacities of the changing empirical apparatuses of digital societies – what forms of knowledge do they enable? – we need spaces to experiment with alternative methodologies for data capture, interpretation and interactive research. As I hope this chapter has made clear, these experiments have much to gain from an engagement with sociological traditions. But they must also be interdisciplinary. Indeed, given the competencies required, it seems fair to say that digital sociology as a form of knowledge can only be participatory. To succeed it must bring together diverse constituencies: sociologists and computer scientists, designers and software developers, users and social theorists. As participants in such knowledge collectives, sociologists must add a third role to their intellectual repertoire: sociologists are used to perform the role of a *critic* of digital participation and over previous years they have also learnt to adopt the role of a *user* of digital technology (Lupton, 2014). But sociologists must equally take on the role of a *participant* in the configuration of empirical architectures for social enquiry. Which is to say, the collective task of re-configuring the relations between social research and participation is likely to involve a fair amount of experimentation on sociology itself.

6
Does digital sociology have problems?

Over the last decade, digital regimes for knowing society have been critically examined not just by sociologists but by a variety of social actors. While organizations as diverse as National Bureaus of Statistics, social movements and the car industry have conducted their own inquiries into digital transformations of knowledge infra-structures, a series of recent public controversies have brought some of the issues at stake in stark relief. Take the case of the Facebook 'real-name controversy'. In 2014, the social media platform introduced an identification system that required users to register under their official names, in an effort to combat 'fake accounts', which at the time were thought to amount to twenty per cent of all registered Facebook users. While not the first of its kind, the scheme soon became subject to widespread criticism, among others because of its discriminatory effects and implications. The real-name policy challenged long established practices of anonymity in digital culture, including those of LGBT communities, whose characteristic forms of stranger sociality were now apparently excluded from this online platform. The system also rejected the registrations of various ethnic groups including Native American on the grounds that their names were not 'real'. (These and other notable problems of discrimination against specific social groups by the Facebook real-name system, at least in its initial release, are dutifully catalogued on the Wikipedia site dedicated to the controversy.)[1] In addition to these important issues, there are also a number of problems to do with this public controversy itself. Christian Sandvig (2014) has argued that the public upheaval about the Facebook real-name system itself was constrained by a rather restrictive 'identification policy': the mainstream press, like the *New York Times*, only began reporting on the problems with the authentication requirements put in place by the online platform once they could be connected to clearly identifiable social groups, with clear political representation, like Native Americans and the LGBT community.

The Facebook real-name controversy then raises a question about our collective capacities for problem definition in digital societies: was it not enough of a problem that the real-name system disregards long-term commitments in digital culture to anonymity? Did this violation in itself not constitute a newsworthy event? As Sandvig (2014) emphasizes, anonymity presents a formative feature of digital culture, one that goes back to the early days of the Internet, but 'the media' do not seem capable of taking this seriously as a political and cultural value. Instead, the identification of recognized 'vulnerable groups' appeared a necessary condition for news reporting on what could now be much more easily framed as a 'rights issue'. Could we say that the media went along with Facebook in imposing on digital culture the requirement of 'identification' of known and authenticated actors, thereby raising wider questions about the political culture of the Internet and its chances for survival after the mainstreaming of digital technologies? In pondering this, however, we should also pause to consider the fact that Wikipedia is 'there for us' to address this very issue. On this platform, a page dedicated to the controversy described the disagreement in rather technical but generous terms, acknowledging a broad range of actors among the 'potentially affected', and going well beyond the range of well-recognized political subject positions covered by the *New York Times*. This is how Wikipedia sums up the problem with the real-name system:

> The system penalize[es] users who are in fact using their real names, which Facebook has nevertheless deemed to be 'fake', while simultaneously allowing anyone to create fake yet plausible-sounding names, as well as obviously implausible-sounding names comprising word combinations that Facebook's software fails to recognize as unlikely to be real. Facebook furthermore prohibits users from accurately representing names which according to the site have 'too many words' and prohibits initializing first names, preventing users who do so in real life from formatting their own names as they see fit.[2]

In this chapter, I will investigate this and other controversies about digital architectures for knowing and intervening in society, and the issues they raise for social life as well as for social research. In line with Sandvigs concerns about the restrictive understandings of what

counts as a moral or political problem in digital societies, I will argue
that the issues raised by digital ways of knowing and intervening in
society are often framed too narrowly: much attention has gone, in
recent years, to the ethical and political issues they raise, but digital
research, broadly defined, generates a much wider range of problems,
including important methodological and epistemic issues. To be sure,
there has been no lack of public attention to digital forms of knowledge in recent years, from critiques of online surveillance to outrage
about the ever growing lists of services and apps that discriminate
against some segments of the population and various allegations of
ethical violation. Strikingly, however, questions of epistemology tend
to remain under-explored in these controversies about digital ways of
knowing society: the question of whether digital devices allow us (or
them) to know society in the way they claim to tends to be overshad-
owed by more urgent ethical, legal and social issues, otherwise known
as ELSI. I will argue in this chapter that investigating the knowledge
dimension of digital social enquiry is useful, because it brings into
focus a much wider potential transformation of digital social life and
social research: in these societies, interactivity between social analysis
and social life intensifies to the point that representational assumptions are thrown into crisis, not just intellectually, but publicly. As the
conduct of social enquiry becomes increasingly problematic in digital
societies, we are facing a new crisis of representation.

Proliferating controversies about digital ways of knowing society

It is not just Facebook that has a habit of attracting controversy:
digital ways of knowing society have become subject to widespread
criticism and public debate today. Over the last years there has been
much justified criticism and indeed outrage about a broad range
of ill-conceived digital applications that invade people's privacy,
perpetuate biased views of the world, put particular social groups at
risk by rendering them 'discoverable', and so on. Several examples
have been discussed over the course of this book. Some of these
controversial applications, such as the Samaritan Radar discussed in
Chapter 1, pose a more or less immediate risk to vulnerable groups:
this service risked stigmatizing people deemed in danger of suicide by
notifying their social media contacts about this. Some pose a physical
risk, like the Facebook creepy search graph which renders Facebook
profiles searchable by attributes, including those that indicate vulner-
ability ('likes getting drunk'). Other controversial applications have
been attributed harmful effects on society that are more pernicious,

like the 'Report-a-problem' Iphone app trialled in Boston, which logged a disproportionately high number of problems in more well-to-do neighbourhoods, which have a higher incidence of iPhone users (and, one imagines, time to spare), conjuring up the image of a city in which only the pot-holes in middle-class neighbourhoods get fixed (Crawford, 2013). Then there are controversies that focus specifically on misuse of digital data and services in scientific research: the most famous is probably the Facebook mood manipulation experiment, in which the content of the newsfeeds of a large number of Facebook users were manipulated in order to test the capacity of social media content to influence people's moods. But there is also a range of less well-known controversies, such as those involving Amazon's Mechanical Turk, a casual labour service on which some computational social scientists rely to perform more menial research tasks, like data cleaning and coding content. Not only is Mechanical Turk known for its lack of protections of labour rights, this practice also raises questions about the levels of quality control and general intellectual culture (Irani and Silberman, 2013).

The range of social, political and ethical problems made visible by these digital controversies is impressively broad, including data misuse, data theft, user manipulation, stigmatization, privacy violation, discrimination, flawed quality control and unethical labour arrangements. The proliferation of such controversies can be interpreted in multiple ways. To start with, it can seem surprising that at least some of these issues were not anticipated by the developers of controversial services and applications: these problems are not uncommon and should be familiar to people versed in research ethics and information policy. Did the software developers, researchers, managers, marketing departments, policy makers, et cetera involved in these projects really not expect these ethical, social and legal issues to arise? Steve Jackson and colleagues (2014) offer a relevant interpretation of this situation in their article on 'policy-knots' in digital innovation. Discussing a range of digital controversies, including one about an app called 'Girls Near Me' with functionality similar to the 'creepy Facebook search graph' above, they propose that digital companies today increasingly approach social and political issues in a 'beta-testing' mode. It has become customary to release experimental products and services to users at an early stage in their development, as companies increasingly rely on user trials and field tests to identify not only technical problems with the applications in question, but also ethical problems with their functioning in society (see on this point also Schmidt, forthcoming).

Given the abundance of digital controversies in recent years, we can indeed wonder whether digital industries consider social, ethical and political controversies as simply par for the course, as they generate attention and publicity and possible problems can always be dealt with 'later'.

But another interpretation is also possible: could it be that digital ways of knowing and intervening in society have become *genuinely* problematic today? Many of the issues raised by digital services and applications seem quite simply avoidable, but that doesn't mean that all of them are. Digital controversies may not only indicate the presence of 'known' social problems, towards which digital industries, organizations and actors are somehow insensitive or indifferent, and behave irresponsibly, and/or for which they have not been 'trained' (although this certainly seems to be the case too). These could also indicate a wider problematization of digital ways of knowing and intervening in society. They might signal that digital techniques for the facilitation, analysis and curation of social life are themselves revealed to be problematic; that they generate the type of issues that are sometimes called 'public problems', which in the words of the pragmatist thinker and journalist Walter Lippmann arise 'when no one knows what to do', when unprecedented kinds of consequences make themselves felt, and 'where the facts are most obscure, where precedents are lacking, where novelty and confusion pervade everything' (Lippmann, 1927, p. 121 (cited in Marres, 2012c, p. 49)). In that case, we should take seriously not only the ethical, social and political issues raised by new apps, tools and services, but ask a range of wider questions: are emerging digital infrastructures, arrangements and practices of data capture, analysis and feedback unsettling taken-for-granted relations between social research and social life; between the subjects, agents and audiences of social enquiry; between data, methods, and publics? Whether this is indeed the case – and whether such grand claims are plausible and appropriate – is the subject of ongoing investigations across the social sciences and humanities, but it would compel different assessments of proliferating digital controversies: they would indicate that wider relations between research, technology, society and democracy are today being re-negotiated, contested and put at stake, in ways that force and require public interrogations of changing arrangements for knowing society, and compel a variety of social actors to devise 'Test[s] we can – and should – run on social media' (Crawford, 2014).

In this last chapter, I would then like to examine whether and how proliferating controversies about digital tools, services and research projects across social, cultural and public life signal wider problems with ways of knowing and intervening in digital societies. My hunch is that these controversies cannot be understood as mere 'birth pangs' accompanying the rise to prominence of new regimes of social research and intervention. To be sure, it is possible to question the preoccupation – and privileging – of *knowledge* controversies in the evaluation of the role of digital industries in society. Aren't there other, more serious problems in digital societies, like growing wealth disparity, inequality, corporate dominance and worker exploitation (Dean, 2001)? Critiques of digital transformations of society from the perspective of political economy are certainly *not* besides the point, but they nevertheless tend to leave out of consideration a circumstance of fundamental importance to social research. In digital societies, our very capacities to know social problems are put at stake, as digital regimes for knowing society unsettle existing frameworks of enquiry, including those of critical enquiry. Digital controversies do not simply draw attention to ethical issues, but neither do they only require a political response. They raise problems of knowledge, and critical enquiry is not exempt from these problems, and the need for a viable methodological framework for empirical enquiry, if it is not to be reduced to a type of pure knowledge that always 'already knows' what the problem is. It seems to me that to the extent to which critical theorists dismiss knowledge controversies, they do so at their own peril. Many of the above controversies focus on single issues raised by the implementation of digital ways of knowing societies, but they equally bring into relief wider methodological, epistemic and ontological problems with computational ways of knowing society.

What kinds of problems?
Not only ethics, and politics, but knowledge

Digital controversies often seem to touch on rather ephemeral or sensationalist topics, and as such it may be tempting to dismiss these controversies as expressing digital culture's penchant for the extreme, outrageous and only semi-serious. As David Moats and I (2015) asked in our article on digital controversies: 'Outrage is the dominant mode of engagement with social media, according to the popular online magazine Slate.[3] But what about controversy? Just a glance at the lists of 'trending topics' on popular platforms like Twitter, Instagram, or Facebook reveals a host of scandals, debates, disputes, and polarizing campaigns'. You could say that controversies around 'creepy' searches and apps and risqué allusions to 'girls near me' exemplify a particular genre of publicity, one that expresses a need for distraction and a preoccupation with more or less hilarious titbits. Furthermore, many of these digital controversies can be called reflexive, or 'recursive', in that they involve the use of digital media to make a fuss about digital media (Kelty, 2005). It may therefore seem plausible to interpret digital controversies as first and foremost expressions of digital culture, as staging activity focused on demonstrating what is significant and distinctive about digital ways of living. This interpretation is appropriate and relevant, but I also think a wider analytic framework is called for. Crucially, controversies about digital ways of knowing society do not just unfold in digital settings, they have also spawned a broad range of public, organizational and policy initiatives, including debates, reports and frameworks, art works, governmental committees, hacks and protests, and the development of new ethical frameworks.

Striking about many of these initiatives is their tendency to frame the issues raised by digital ways of knowledge society in two main registers, the economic and the ethical. In the UK, the House of Commons Science and Technology Select Committee recently published a report on the 'Big Data Dilemma', formulating an issue agenda that concentrates on economic growth, education (skills shortages) and ethical and legal problems like personal data protection.[4] Where the report refers to research and knowledge, it tends to be as one side of a coin with ethics or the economy placed on the other, as in this discussion of data use: 'The anonymization and re-use of data is becoming an issue that urgently needs to be addressed as big data becomes increasingly a part of our lives. There are arguments on both sides of this issue: Seeking to balance the potential benefits of processing data (some collected many years before and no longer with a clear consent trail) and people's justified privacy concerns will not be straightforward' (p. 46). To be sure, this report constitutes clear progress as compared with previous UK government positions. In October 2014, the UK Information Commissioner's Office (ICO) was still of the opinion that computational analytics do not pose a serious challenge to established frameworks of research ethics, stating that established mechanisms of anonymization and data protection are sufficient and adequate for the regulation of big data research, concluding that 'big data is not a game played under different rules'. In the intermediate period, social researchers and sociologists have made significant efforts to bring ethical issues with big data analytics to public attention. The Data and Society Institute in New York recently launched a committee for big data ethics which includes sociologists among its members, and a group of UK-based social researchers and theorists have recently published a manifesto on Socializing Big Data (Ruppert et al., 2015). These initiatives have brought to light a proliferation of ethical problems emerging from digital architectures of data analytics: lack of consent, unlawful appropriation, harmful exposure, among others. While these problems are important in and of themselves, they also point towards a wider problematic. There currently exists a notable mismatch between the ethical frameworks of social scientific research and the ethical policies implemented by digital industries.

Compare, for example, the most recent 'Statement on Ethical Principles of Sociological Research' published by the British Sociological Association in 2002 with Twitter's Data Policy.[5] The former, academic ethics guidelines posit, for example, that sociologists 'should explain in appropriate detail, and in terms meaningful to participants, what the research is, who is undertaking and financing it, why it is being undertaken, and how it is to be disseminated and used'. It goes on to state that 'research participants should be made aware of their right to refuse participation whenever and for whatever reasons they wish', and '[. . .] should be able to reject the use of data-gathering devices such as tape recorders and video recorders'. Requirements like these stand in stark contrast not just to practices in digital research, but also to the official information policies of digital industries, including the influential (if increasingly beleaguered) digital platform Twitter, that featured prominently in the empirical sections of this book. Twitter's Policy Statement simply posits that 'we may disclose your non-private, aggregated or otherwise non-personal data, such as "your tweets, and the people you follow or that follow"'. There is consequently no duty to inform users about Twitter-based research, and as such Twitter's requirement are rather more minimal than those stipulated by the British Sociological Association. What is more, it is not evident at all that even the above more minimal requirements are enforceable by Twitter and its platform architectures. The Twitter developer agreement (October 2014), for example, appears to formulate a different set of rules. Addressing the third-party clients that make use of Twitter data, including online social research tools such as the T-CAT platform discussed in Chapter 3, this policy states that 'you may be given access to certain non-public information'.

How do we interpret these divergences and gaps between academic and commercial policies on research and data use? There are different ways of framing the problem and it matters greatly which one we choose. For one, we may want to challenge the supposed leniency of industry frameworks, especially as regards the appropriation of personal data for commercial purposes and the many issues they don't even seem to cover, like the rights of subjects of online experiments, and this has rightly been the focus of public controversies about digital ways of knowing society discussed in this book. But we may also turn our critical attention towards a different disparity, that between the ethical requirements stipulated by an academic body like the BSA, and ongoing research practices in digital social research, inside and outside the university. It is certainly not easy to imagine how the ethical guidelines contained in the BSA ethics statement of 2002 could be implemented in projects of social media research projects like those discussed in Chapters 3 and 4. To highlight one seeming absurdity: should we really try to message all accounts in a given Twitter data set notifying them of our data analysis project and giving them the opportunity to opt out of the data set? And what does the framework make of sensor-based research projects like those using self-tracking technologies and other forms of embedded data capture: is installing data captors in public places forbidden, as research participants here cannot be said to have 'the right to reject the use of data-gathering devices?' It is then also possible to turn our evaluation around: why has the British Sociological Association at the time of writing not yet published an updated version of its 2002 ethics statement?

The issues that arise here are surely not reducible to the usual problem of academic politics, but rather present versions of the dammed-if-you-do-dammed-if-you-don't dilemma, or to put this in less dramatic terms, the slippery slope. On the one hand, social media research has become a common and popular practice across social, organizational and public life, and its relevancy to social enquiry seems obvious. On the other hand, when social researchers take up online instruments of data collection, analysis and visualization they enter into highly troubling relations of dependency with the infrastructures and organizations that make them available. As social researchers take up online tools, we too sign up to the terms of use stipulated by digital industries, whether we are aware of it or not. Indeed, our very research projects may be interpreted as expressions of consent to these terms of use, and even, as implicit endorsements of the many dubious projects they also facilitate. To be sure, we should not overstate the exceptionality of digital research in this respect (Wagner-Pacifici et al., 2015; Geismar, forthcoming). The ethical problem of complicity with the organizations that serve as our sources of information presents a general problem of research ethics, which is certainly not limited to digital research, nor indeed, to social research. Relevant analogies can be found in research that relies on bureaucratic records and statistical information assembled under dubious governmental and corporate regimes. However, it does seem the case that these problems are aggravated in the case of an empirical apparatus that is networked, automatic and participatory. In this case, it is next to impossible to clearly distinguish our own research apparatus from the digital machineries for capture, selection, and interpretation 'out there' that our research relies on (Marres and Weltevrede, 2015).

Faced with such dilemmas, digital social researchers have developed a range of practical strategies to increase the distance and establish separations between their own research practices and those of digital industries. For example, Perng et al. (2012) work on the Norwegian Breivik massacre in 2011 on Twitter presents some of its research materials in the form of hand-drawn copies of tweets sent during the massacre. Their stated reason for doing so is that they 'had to translate the tweets from Norwegian into English anyway' but it also works as a 'distancing act', aesthetically dissociating their study from the platform on which it nevertheless relies. However, the gaps, disagreements and apparent contradictions between different ethical frameworks that become apparent in digital research are various, complex and multi-faceted. Some of the most pernicious have to do with the pre-occupation in prevailing research ethics regimes with the category of the 'human subject'. As the Association of Internet Researchers statement on ethics (2012) notes, the category of 'human subject' is a critical regulatory category – one that helps to determine, among others, which research projects must undergo more substantive ethical review – but it sits oddly in relation to online research.[6] A recent case study by Narayanan and Zevenbergen (2015) clarifies the mismatch between digital research and ethical frameworks in this regard: their study discusses a recent US-based computational research project on Internet censorship which aimed to automatically detect online censorship using browser plug-ins. The project inserted an unsolicited piece of code into the browsers of users visiting the project site, so that these users browsers' would notify the research project if any of their attempts to access other Web sites were intercepted by censorship agencies. This intervention clearly raises questions of consent – should users be asked if they approve of the installation of this browser plug-in, or would this request compromise them further? As Narayanan and Zevenbergen show, however, the project also raises a more profound definitional (ontological) question: does inserting code into a browser qualify as an operation upon a human subject? (see also Gross, 2015 on this issue).

To make sure that such more fundamental questions get the attention they deserve, sociologists have argued that a fundamental review is necessary of the ethical frameworks currently guiding the implementation of computational data analytics across society. In the report cited above, Ruppert et al. (2015) call for a 'reframing [of] conventional debates that typically focus on individual rights and ownership to an ethic that recognizes the connectedness and interdependent relations that make up Big Data'. Such advocacy for ethical frameworks are important not least because the problem of harm to individuals and collectives clearly overrides other kinds of concerns. Ethics, then, should come first, but it is nevertheless the case that the current pre-occupation with ethics also has problematic consequences: it favours the development of approaches to digital research that demonstrate ethical clarity, and risks distracting attention and support away from forms of enquiry that are less clearly 'identifiable.' More generally speaking, the ethical framing of digital research risks directing attention away from questions of their contribution to knowledge. While this makes sense in several respects, not least as a way of protecting research from external influence (the independence of knowledge), it has the consequence that issues raised by digital research are parked outside the space of enquiry, strictly speaking, beyond the realm of research design, the formulation of research objectives, and methodology.[7] I would like to argue, however, that some of the issues raised by digital research precisely have to do with the methodological frameworks implemented in computational social science. *Forms of knowledge* have become the focal point of controversy in digital societies. These equally are in need of critical interrogation.

Computational social science: no problem, or the mother of all problems?

It is possible to offer a different interpretation of recent controversies about digital ways of knowing society: in these public controversies the very methodologies, epistemologies and ontologies of digital research are problematized and put at stake. This is the interpretation that this book aims to contribute towards, and it starts from the realization I briefly flagged above: it is today in question what are the viable epistemic and methodological frameworks for digital social research. To say this is not to trivialize the important ethical problems, about the treatment of research subjects and the societal responsibilities of social scientists that these controversies raise. But *at the same time* these controversies also raise fundamental questions about our capacity to know society in today's technological age. Take the following question: 'who qualifies as a legitimate member of a social collective'? This is at once a political, ontological and methodological question: Does one need to have a name to qualify as a person? Should non-humans, bots, and avatars be recognized as members of society? These type of questions arise in social and public life, as during the Facebook real-name controversy above, and they can be treated as ethical and political issues, for instance as an issue of 'minority rights'. But these very same questions arise equally in social enquiry, as part of debates in social theory – do societies consist of humans, or do they include other agents and actors? – and in the process of social research design. A colleague told me about a disagreement she recently had with her fellow social media researchers: while her collaborators proposed to exclude all non-identifiable accounts from their Twitter data set, she argued they should be included.

Crucial to the issues raised by digital ways of knowing society, I want to argue, is that they affect both social research and social life in equal measure. These issues are located on the interface of digital social research and digital social life. Take the question: How does observation affect the phenomenon under observation? Sociologists have asked this question for many decades already: how does the expectation of being overheard affect what is being said? This interest goes back at least to the work of George Herbert Mead, who defined sociality in terms of the ability of orientating our experience towards others. Yet today's controversies about digital surveillance put this classic sociological question at the heart of public debates about what society we are to live in. Something similar applies to only seemingly arcane methodological questions raised by digital data analysis: can and should activities like data cleaning and data coding be reduced to logistical tasks, or do they inevitably have an epistemic and methodological dimension (Bialski, 2016), meaning that even the simplest task of classification may involve substantive decisions. To be sure, these are specialized questions of the philosophy and methodology of science in some respects, but they also have significant possible implications for the relations between social science and society, including what are and may be realistic and legitimate demands of participants in citizen science projects (or as the case may be, in Mechanical Turk projects).

As Esther Weltevrede and I (2015) have argued, many of the methodological problems of digital social research closely resemble the normative problems of digital societies. Take problems of data-centrism, the problem that social research risk to attach disproportionate and undue attention to phenomena simply because they are present in the data. In digital societies, however, this problem does not only affect research but equally social life, where the more we rely on information technologies, the more we risk becoming 'like the drunk who looks for his keys under the lamp post because that is where the light is brightest'.[8] While these analogies between social research and social life are in some respect elusive, they also suggest that the distance between society and social science may be less wide than sometimes seems, for example when the technical aspects of digital social science are played up. As Weltevrede and I (2015) put it:

> The epistemic troubles generated by [digital social research] are not just problems of social and cultural science, but are relevant to all social practices that involve the collection, management, analysis, and operation of social data by digital means. In this context, the 'best' attitude to the epistemic trouble that arises in digital social research might not be to resolve or contain these issues quickly, and 'to make them disappear', but rather, to render these problems researchable qua problems, and to make their effects visible and reportable for practical purposes.

If the problems of digital social research are not unlike the problems of digital social life, then social researchers have a responsibility not just to deal adequately with these problems in their own research practices, it is also important that they clearly articulate these problems, and develop socially relevant problem definitions.

It is now possible to state more clearly what the problem is with predominant approaches to the ethics and economics of computational social science. The problem is that they do not help us to understand the methodological, epistemological and ontological issues raised by the development of digital ways of knowing society. Taken for granted the methodological frameworks of an un-reconstructed scientific empiricism, far too much work in this area assumes an at best pragmatic and at worst opportunistic attitude towards questions about the scope, validity and relevance of knowledge claims. Indeed, much computational social science projects simply go along with whatever ontology, epistemology or methodology is wired into the platforms, packages or tools they use to capture, analyse and visualize data, without querying whether and how they are appropriate to the research project at hand. This is how it all too often goes, in the practice of digital social research: If the data comes from Twitter, we'll do co-follower networks, if it's Facebook, we go with bi-partite graphs of friends and shares. Work in this field, then, all too often adopts a *laissez-faire* attitude, displaying the troubling tendency to go with whatever ontology or methodology happens to be hard-wired in the apparatus that generates the data. Indeed, this is sometimes even offered as a justification for research design, as when the decision to analyse social networks with social media data is substantiated by pointing out that 'most of this newly available data is already pre-organized into a network form' (Gruzd and Haythornthwaite 2011: 176).[9]

Contesting *laissez-faire* methodologies

To be sure, there are extraneous reasons for the predominance of methodological *laissez-faire*, not least the practical opportunities that digital analytics open up. But of course this is not a sufficient reason to disregard the methodological issues. The 'can do' attitudes in digital social research also express a particular epistemic orientation to the world. Take Duncan Watts' contribution to the *Guardian* newspaper debate section entitled 'Stop Complaining About the Facebook Study',[10] in which he argued that we are living in a 'golden age for social scientific experiments' and that the prospect of significant scientific advances should surely trump the current ethical concerns. A *laissez-faire* attitude is here not only assumed, but also requested from relevant by-standers, including publics and regulatory agencies. To be sure, this request displays a degree of moral insensitivity, and we should not forget it is meant as a contribution to public debate, and thus, to provoke, but it equally expresses epistemic insensitivity. It calls to mind Isabelle Stengers' (1996) insightful analysis of the Milgram experiment – the other one, not Milgram's six degrees experiments of which Duncan Watts produced a famous digital re-run – the one in which he asked people to administer electric shocks to strangers, with the aim of measuring their level of obedience to authority. As in the case of the Milgram experiment, we should not only worry about the effects of the social experiments on experimental subjects, even if this concern comes first – we should equally be concerned with the state of mind of the experimental scientists in question, who, in the case of Milgram, was so clearly indifferent to the possibility that it was *his experiment* that was encouraging problematic tendencies in his research 'subjects'. Was he even measuring what he thought he was measuring? Probably not. The hubris of the experimenter that has been so often commented upon, Stengers' analysis makes clear, does not only translate into moral insensitivity, it is equally likely to entail insensitivity towards more intractable problems of knowledge, and we should include here a lack of interest in the subtler kind of methodological issues. Digital experiments, then, return us to important debates in the methodology of the social sciences about the viability of experiments as a method of knowing society.

This is also why interactivity – of the complex kind that operates across society, knowledge and technology that I have examined in this book – matters. While the promise and value of computational social science is assumed to reside in its capacity to represent social life, this methodology itself plays a role in society that cannot be dismissed. Digital social research is not only a way of knowing society, as if from the outside, it is equally a participant in wider dynamics of mutual adjustment between digital settings, actions and content. I have made the case in this book that such dynamics of interaction assume special importance in digital societies, as opportunities for knowing and intervening in social life proliferate across social domains. Specifically, digital forms of interactivity present not only an important topic for social enquiry, they also require active methodological engagement. Sociological studies of digital methods (Healy, 2015; Lewis, 2015) have made it forcefully clear that we cannot assume that default representational frameworks of social science can be upheld in digital research. The irony is then that what is promoted as a reveil of representational social science – and called 'a new way of discovering the laws of human behaviour', as discussed in Chapter 1 – in practice throws simple representational frameworks into crisis. Due to their interactivity, digital platforms such as Twitter present at once a setting for the recording, expression and influencing of social, cultural and public life. No, digital media technologies do not offer a neutral 'window' on the social world. And the problem here is not a negative one: it is not simply that digital technologies give a 'biased' view of the social world. Such a problem definition upholds the representational point-of-view that are precisely problematized by the interactive features of digital technologies. To be clear, it is certainly possible to conduct digital social research in a representational framework, but work conducted within such a framework leaves out far too much of what is empirically important in the study of digital societies. It produces a blind spot for the very role of digital technologies in the enactment and transformation of sociality.

The most remarkable thing about the predicaments of digital sociology, then, is the ease with which they have been dismissed in recent years. As the data analyst I already quoted put it: 'We prefer to work with passive data.' There is still significant confidence today that interactivity can be contained and digital data can be treated as 'passive' data, but this circumstance alone of course cannot make the position credible. Given that prized interactivity of digital technology, isn't it obvious that digital research operates in the space between representation and intervention? As I have shown in this book, this question, and the disagreement that it masks, is not new at all, and takes us back to key classic debates in sociology, not least to the work of Max Weber and his efforts to come to terms with this basic circumstance: in social life, action is explicitly orientated towards the concepts and methods used to make sense of these actions. But this classic sociological concern acquires fresh relevance in digital research today where the peculiarities of interactivity raise puzzling questions: when we find racist content via Google, should we blame society or digital industries? However, more needs to be done to explicate the sociological frameworks presumed in questions like this. A circumstance that warrants special attention in this respect, I have argued, is the prominence of sociological concepts and methods – like social networks and social network analysis – in the very organization of action in digital settings. Not only do they play a formative role in the organization of digital activity, they should also cure sociologists from a false assumption, the mistaken idea that their discipline is being marginalized in the digital age. The opposite is equally true: sociological concepts and methods are playing an increasingly central role in research across the social, natural sciences and engineering.

Digital societies are marked by expanded dynamics of sociotechnical interactivity: as methods and concept for rendering social life accountable are implemented in interactive architectures, social, technical and epistemic dynamics of interactivity fuse in ways that require further sociological investigation. Indeed, many of the troubling issues brought into focus by digital controversies concern interactivity: What culture are digital industries cultivating as the quest for girls surfaces and resurfaces as a predominant pursuit? How come a UK-based suicide prevention agency feels that it serves the interests of its constituencies by teaming up with a Californian tech giant? These problems certainly have to do with wider political dynamics, including the reduced budgets of Britain's austerity state, but they also indicate that interactions between technology and society present key public concerns today. Social research plays a critical role in these problematic situations: they are concerned with the ways in which the analysis of social life – whether in the form of creepy graphs or textual analysis – intervenes in social life. And this might well mean that the sobering diagnoses about the role of social enquiry in society today must be inverted. In this view, social science will forever lag behind computational science in its ability to represent and intervene in society (Galloway, 2014). I think that the opposite is true: computational scientists may not care very much about the methodological trouble they're in, but social researchers at least have the methodological resources to take on the problem of interactivity, and to render it amenable to empirical enquiry. Yes, computational social science presents a problem, in the good sense, and this problem is as much an intellectual one as anything else: how is social enquiry possible under conditions of interactivity? Computational ways of knowing society put us in methodological trouble, whether we care about it or not.

Expanding the frame on sociological experiments

So what to do? Online experiments exemplify many of the problems with digital ways of knowing society – including indifference to the methodological challenges of researching society with technology, and lack of accountability, as experimental scientists claim the right to interfere in social life while expecting social actors to behave 'as normal' and to remain indifferent to the research conducted on them. However, somewhat paradoxically I have argued in this book that one of the most promising ways of addressing problems with experiments in computational social science is to develop more experimental forms of social enquiry. Because our capacities to combine knowing and intervening are changing in digital societies, in both social research and social life, the viability of experiments as a way of knowing society requires renewed interrogation by sociologists. As I have shown, sociologists have in recent years actively taken up this task, as they investigate the role of experimentation in digital societies, and take up experimental methods themselves. This engagement with experiments has been a distinguishing feature of recent work in digital sociology. Tapping into long-standing socio-logical traditions of experimental enquiry, from the Chicago School to ethnomethodology, this work gives the lie to the idea that the repertoire of empirical sociology is limited to observation.

Work in digital sociology is very much 'under development' and faces many methodological, ethical and political challenges. On the one hand, experimental approaches in sociology must actively disprove scepticism about their capacity to conduct experiments, and the more general assumption that it is impossible to conduct 'experiments on society' (Guggenheim, 2012). Not just scientists, but many sociologists, too, used to agree 'that sociology is limited in its empirical understanding because society does not comply the lab-like conditions of record-ability that empirical research requires' (Carnap, 1995 (1962)). While affirming the need to engage with social experimentation, digital sociology must at same time do the work of distinction and demonstrate that different kinds of experi-ments in society are possible: it must show that, notwithstanding the myriads of problems with digital experiments, it is possible to deploy digital arrangements to develop alternative, more reponsive forms of experimental enquiry. In taking on these mutiple challenges, finally, it is important that digital sociologists keep an open mind: while the interactivity of digital platforms invites creative experimentation, we must at the same time remain critical, and examine to what extent classic critiques of experiments in social enquiry remain valid, and to what extent they must be re-considered.

Not surprisingly, then, recent work in sociology has produced divergent views on the role of experiments in digital societies. Sociological research confirms that we should be very much con-cerned about the role of experiments in society, but it also proposes that it would be a serious mistake to dismiss social experiments altogether. Francisca Grommé (2015) has examined the use of social media analysis in crime prevention by municipal governments, and her study warns about the stereotyping effects of these methods – e.g. identifying deviant youth by the shoes they wear – warning that social media methods risk introducing discriminatory thought styles into the policy lexicon. Barocas et al. (2013) describe the ever more targeted use of social analytics in industries like insurance to human resources, and argue that this threatens to validate antiquated, pejo-rative forms of social assessment (does she have the right friends?).

More generally, sociologists have warned that the uptake of experimental forms of intervention across policy, culture and innovation risk reducing these spheres of activity to promotional endeavours: experimental environments like some smart cities are more akin to marketing demonstrations than critical tests (Schinkel, 2016). While critical studies of digital experiments are thus ongoing, in my view this work needs to engage more explicitly with the methodological frameworks implemented in – and by way of – digital experiments.

As I discussed in Chapters 2 and 3, digital experiments also offer a promising methodology for social enquiry, on condition that they are deployed with an open mind. Experiments provide a way for sociologists to examine the interactivity of digital architectures, devices and practices, as in the study by Birkbak and Carlsen (2015) discussed in Chapter 3, in which they study the socio-logics, or 'orders of worth', enacted by Facebook, Twitter and Google by way of an experiment in online data analysis. Digital sociology then shares an appetite for experimentation with other approaches in digital research. However, these sociological experiments also confer an obligation on us: what type of experiments are OK and which are less so, methodologically and ethically speaking? For example, what do we make of the 'social bots' experiment by Boshmaf et al. (2011) which used automated accounts to contact a large number of Facebook users, to test their likeliness to interact with bots? A distinguishing feature of digital sociology is that it not only undertakes experiments, but equally investigates the role of experiments in digital societies. For example, Ana Gross (2015) research on personal data leaks approached digital transformations as 'experiments in society'. Defining data leaks as experimental occasions, in which social actors are provoked into accounting for wider societal transformations, this study develops a distinctive experimental methodology, one that starts from the assumptions that the capacities and properties of important social and cultural entities – like 'a person', and 'data' – become unsettled in digital societies. How do data come to be 'about' persons? what methods can still enable anonymization? As Gross shows, these questions concern social research, but they are equally gaining wider relevance across society today, and the answers to them are not 'already known', and in many cases they indicate profound problems. What should digital sociologists do? We should develop experimental methods to investigate the ontological and epistemological disputes arising in digital societies, and contribute to making the issues at stake in them available for collective enquiry.

As noted, an important contribution of social studies of digital experiments is that they 'expand the frame' (Suchman, 2007b) on digital experimentation. Investigating the role of experiments in society, they offer a broader perspective than is customary on the unsettling effects that arise from the 'interactivity' of digital technology and social life. In doing so, these studies disrupt the 'smooth' narratives about the opportunities that interactive technologies open up for social life: digital platforms, devices and practices do not just facilitate the 'enhancement' of social relations. They may equally expose and aggravate ongoing social dynamics, such as those of stigmatization, discrimination and polarization, as in the case of applications like auto-suggest, report-a-problem, and flag-a-friend. Significantly, the expanded perspective on digital experiments considers many more actors than only users, platforms, developers, and analysts as relevant participants in digital experimentation. It also includes, say, users with initials by way of first names, or people who live in neighbourhoods with a lower than average incidence of Iphones, or the regulatory body that governs the insurance industry. More precisely, it considers a broader range of relations that may be 'experimentalized' by digital transformations – not just relations between users and industries, clients and services, but equally those between neighbours, the insured and uninsured, between those who consider themselves participants in digital culture, and those who do not. From this perspective, however, the 'interactive' relation between digital technology and sociality – the intensifying movements between representing and intervening in social life – is not just a positive feature of digital arrangements, it brings into relief important societal problems.

From an expansive perspective, many aspects of digital transformations prove to be profoundly problematic, putting social relations at stake. Social researchers cannot just route around the problems of digital societies, as many of these controversies touch on the core concerns of social enquiry, namely, on the role of data, social methods and knowledge technologies in digital societies. These controversies also raise wider questions of the philosophy and methodology of the social sciences. We may be living through a renewed 'crisis of representation' today, as the expanded interactivity between technology, social life and knowledge enabled by the digital calls into question the capacity of science to represent society – both methodologically, ethically and politically. To be sure, the problematization of representational frameworks in digital societies are not quite like the 1980s crisis of representation that was theorized by philosophers like Richard Rorty (1980). Today's crisis is not about the collapse of epistemic ideals – we are today not mourning the loss of belief in universal knowledge, the passing of epistemic ideals. Rather, ways of knowing society have emerged as important, practical topics of contestation in digital societies, and these controversies need to be taken, at least initially, at face value: what should and shouldn't data be used for? who should have access to knowledge technologies? What responsibility does research confer towards the researched? These questions have long been posed in the philosophy and methodology of social science, but digital transformations are unsettling available answers, and today they feature centrally in public and political debates. This signals renewed relevance of these scholarly practices, but it does not mean that academic disciplines can simply reclaim the authority that the philosophers of the 1980s thought they had lost. The issues of digital societies may not be unlike the issues of social enquiry, but they require situational, contextual and responsive engagement.

Notes

1 What is digital sociology?

1 'Samaritans launches Twitter app to help identify vulnerable people.' Samaritans, 29 October, 2014. At the time of writing, it was announced that Facebook launched a next iteration of this service, developed in collaboration with Samaritans, 19 February 2016. http://www.bbc.co.uk/newsbeat/article/35608276/facebook-adds-new-suicide-prevention-tool-in-the-uk

2 McVeigh, K. (2014) Samaritans Twitter app identifying user's moods criticized as invasive, 4 November, http://www.theguardian.com/society/2014/nov/04/samaritans-twitter-app-mental-health-depression. Thanks to Nissa Ramsay for drawing my attention to the Samaritans Radar controversy.

3 Not coincidentally, one the most famous demonstrations of sociology's capacity to produce distinctive knowledge about social problems – by the early twentieth century French sociologist Emile Durkheim – had suicide risk as its topic. However, here I draw on different sociological traditions, those building on interpretative sociology, pragmatism and symbolic interactionism, to explore what a sociological study of 'suicide risk' in digital societies might involve and would need to consider.

4 'Turning knowledge into action' was the phrase used in 2008 by the info-activist organization The Tactical Technology Collective to describe their data visualization toolkit for advocacy organizations.

5 Anonymous, 'Good bye Samaritans Radar..Hello Facebook Report Button', Purple Persuasion blog, 11 March 2015 https://purplepersuasion.wordpress.com/2015/03/11/goodbye-samaritans-radar-hello-facebook-report-button/

6 One of the first written occurrences is in the title of an article by Wynn (2009) in *Sociological Forum*, which deals with the question of how sociologists can use digital formats like blogging in their teaching.

7 Lanchester made this point in a commentary on the GCHQ files leaked

by Edward Snowden, and 'the kind of intelligence gathering that sucks in data from everyone, everywhere: from phones, internet use from email to website visits, social networking, instant messaging and video calls, and even areas such as video gaming; in short, everything digital'. Lanchester, J. (2013) Why the British Public Should Be Worried about GCHQ', *Guardian*, 3 October, *https://www.theguardian.com/world/2013/oct/03/edward-snowden-files-john-lanchester*

8 16 July Tweet, Mike Savage, 10:22 PM – 16 Jul 13

9 If we consult not a search engine but a more traditional library data-base, the time frame expands: as noted, publications with the phrase 'digital sociology' in them have appeared from 2009 onwards. If we broaden our search beyond the literal term, it expands furhter still as related labels, such as 'Cybersociology' (Wouters, 2003), have been around longer. In 2004, someone used the term 'pre-digital sociology', suggesting its opposite was on the author's mind.

10 Markoff, J. Government Aims to Build a 'Data Eye in the Sky', *New York Times*, 10 October, 2011, http://www.nytimes.com/2011/10/11/science/11predict.html.

11 'In 2005, PhD student Nathan Eagle at MIT Media Lab was already thinking along similar lines. He and his advisor Alex Pentland put up a website called 'reality mining' ('MIT Media Lab: Reality Mining') and wrote how the new possibilities of capturing details of peoples' daily behavior and communication via mobile phones can create sociology in the 21st century ('Sociology in the 21st Century'). To put this idea into practice, they distributed Nokia phones with special software to 100 MIT students who then used these phones for nine months – which generated approximately 60 years of 'continuous data on daily human behavior' (Manovich, 2011, p. 464).

12 A researcher on Pentlands project went so far as to declare: 'Phones can know,' [..] 'People can get this god's-eye view of human behavior.' Hotz, R, What They Know: The Really Smart Phone, *Wall Street Journal*, 23 April 2011

13 http://www.theguardian.com/commentisfree/2014/jul/07/facebook-study-science-experiment-research

14 Healy B. (2015) Facebook button lets users tell friends they voted in UK election, Mashable, 5 May 2015, http://mashable.com/2015/05/05/facebook-vote-button-uk-election/

15 See also Hunt, E. (2016) 'Three black teenagers': anger as Google image search shows police mugshots', *Guardian* 9 June, https://www.theguardian.com/technology/2016/jun/09/three-black-teenagers-anger-as-google-image-search-shows-police-mugshots

16 This paragraph and the next draw on an internal document prepared by the Centre for Interdisciplinary Methodologies in May 2016, with Celia Lury, Nerea Calvillo, Michael Dieter, and Nathaniel Tkacz.

17 See also Mearian, L. 'Insurance company now offers discounts – if you

let it track your Fitbit.' *Computer World*, 17 April 2015, http://www.com
puterworld.com/article/2911594/insurance-company-now-offers-discou
nts-if-you-let-it-track-your-fitbit.html
18 https://www.fixmystreet.com/
19 As John Hopkins asked on Nettime quoting an app tag line: 'Get the
ACLU's Mobile Justice app and keep justice within reach.' Where is this
going? John Hopkins, 'Apps to Record Police Put Power in the Public's
Hands' Nettime discussion list, 26 October 2015.
20 Im grateful to Mathieu Jacomy for enlightening discussions about adjust-
able methods.
21 This can also help to clarify the difference between digital methods
and computational methods. While the latter refers to the application
of methods developed in computing, digital methods deploy wider
digital infrastructures for purposes of social and cultural enquiry across
disciplines (Rogers, 2013). Digital methods sit at the interface between
social research, media and technology studies, computing and social
life.
22 'Capita [Private contractor] is provided with a "regular data drop"
[from UKBA] containing information on people including mobile
phone numbers who have a "negative outcome" on the Home Office
immigration database.' It is claimed that Capita had contacted *39,100
individuals by text*, while acknowledging that this figure is 'provisional
and subject to change'. The numbers are almost certainly much higher'
Back, L. and S. Sinha (2013) Welcome to Britain. Go Home. And have
a pleasant journey, *Open Democracy*, 16 October 2013. http://www.
opendemocracy.net/ourkingdom/les-back-and-shamser-sinha/welcome-
to-britain-go-home-and-have-pleasant-journey
23 Note that the blurring of boundaries is a more general feature of digital
social life: part of what is going on in the examples above is 'the collapse
of context' – the effect identified by Helen Nissenbaum (2004) that
online networked media make it difficult to control which of our social
performances become available to which audiences.
24 It is important to note that the methodological frameworks of computational social science are rarely purely representational, but partly derive
their promise from a different source: the promise to act on behaviours
and intervene in social life, to nudge, guide and influence through
interactive technologies. Representationalism seems to figure among the
methodological assumptions of computational social science only insofar
as it is necessary to support the wider experimentalist project. There
seems to be a general consensus that significant progress can be made in
computational social science while leaving the broader methodological
architecture of scientific empiricism undisturbed – to go quick, that 'we
can do it' by following the formula: 'we measure behaviour (digitally),
know it by analysing it (digitally), and then act on it (digitally)'. It is this
methodological framework that I and other digital sociologists argue is in

much deeper trouble than computational social scientists are prepared to acknowledge.

25 I myself have been trained in the latter field.

26 The reduction of problems of interactivity to problems of bias is also problematic in an ethical sense: To address issues of bias, researchers are increasingly tempted to access social data via commercial routes (purchasing data via services like GNIP) so that they get access to 'total data sets'. While such strategies are not necessarily avoidable, they do result in other kinds of 'buy-in', namely into the methodological frameworks that are embedded in digital platforms (see Chapter 3).

27 Of course, there were sociologists in the era of 'Internet research" who affirmed the empirical capacities of the Internet, not least those involved in the development of digital social research methods, such as online survey research. However, as I will discuss in Chapter 3, this work generally operated within a digitization of methods framework, and sidestepped methodological issues like the ambiguity of the digital as both topic and resource of social research.

28 A related possibility for digital sociology would be to 'switch frames' between the different approaches to "digital' sociology, between the digital as object and the digital as instrument. Sociologists have studied how social actors 'switch frames' in social life on an ongoing basis, for example, between treating the technology as instrument – 'a window on the world' – to technology as artefact in the world (when technology breaks down, for example.) Should sociology do the same? The practice of 'switching frames' is remarkably prevalent in digital social research, where researchers may move effortlessly from grand critiques of the 'ideological bias' of the Internet to the careful examination of a data visualization, showing an actor network located with online methods. While this may work in practice, it does not pass muster as a methodology.

29 The viability of this distinction has been called into question by philosophers and sociologists of science such as Mike Lynch (1991), drawing on the work of holistic philosopher of science Pierre Duhem (1996).

30 The examples discussed here were posted on 23 January 2013 (and archived on that day by the Internet archive): http://web.archive.org/web/20130123205135/http://actualfacebookgraphsearches.tumblr.com/

31 http://actualfacebookgraphsearches.tumblr.com/

2   What makes digital technologies social?

1 In an early reflection on the opportunities for social research opened up by the Facebook Application Programming Interface, Rieder proposed that social media make social connections available for analysis and manipulation concluding in a poetic mode that in a utopian (or dystopian) future, Facebook might qualify as the 'incarnation of sociality'

Rieder, B (2007) 'from application to infrastructure (and a little ANT)', http://thepoliticsofsystems.net/2007/10/

2 https://www.ibm.com/social-business/us-en/

3 '[S]uccessful entrepreneurship is about using frontier technologies to address human need and ambition. It understands it is part of society and owes a debt to the culture and public infrastructure that create it.' Hutton, W. (2013) In Silicon Valley I saw the virtues of the new economy, *Guardian*, 14 September http://www.theguardian.com/commentisfree/2013/sep/14/californian-capitalism-can-teach-britain

4 But it is also true that in 2009 a sociologist was able to write that the question of what makes social media social was still to be broached (Fuchs, 2009).

5 This is the influential definition of social networking sites provided by boyd and Ellison (2007): 'web-based services that allow individuals to (1) construct a public or semi-public profile within a bounded system, (2) articulate a list of other users with whom they share a connection, and (3) view and traverse their list of connections and those made by others within the system'.

6 With thanks to Marsha Rosengarten for suggesting this example.

7 The full quote reads 'I said I'm not fond of definitions, but I woke up this morning with the start of one in my head: Web 2.0 is the network as platform, spanning all connected devices; Web 2.0 applications are those that make the most of the intrinsic advantages of that platform: delivering software as a continually updated service that gets better the more people use it, consuming and remixing data from multiple sources, including individual users, while providing their own data and services in a form that allows remixing by others, creating network effects through an "architecture of participation", and going beyond the page meta-phor of Web 1.0 to deliver rich user experiences.' Tim O'Reilly (2005) Web 2.0: Compact Definition? 1 October 2005, http://radar.oreilly.com/2005/10/web-20-compact-definition.html

8 It is tempting to make this claim, as we could then offer a clean diagno-sis, namely, the rise of social platforms coincided with the demise of the public Web, an argument that would go along with Hannah Arendt's rather moralizing distinction between the public (heroic, democratic) and the social (mundane, conventional|). However I prefer to fudge this distinction. As I will discuss in Chapter 5, insofar as the social Web in spite of its shortcomings is still configurable as a participatory Web, it is also capable of supporting democratization, not just of society and politics, but of knowledge.

9 The formatted and/or structured quality of digital networked data is precisely what renders these platforms so attractive as a source of data for computational social science (Marres and Weltevrede, 2013). Many of the well-known examples of computational social science heavily rely on formatted data: like the analysis of reply chains, edits on Wikipedia

or hashtags. This type of research does not analyse unstructured data – such as raw text – but structured data. Not so much the 'naturalism', but rather the formatted quality of digital networked data, and of digitally enabled sociality, held the key to many of the early successes of digital social science.

10 Fyuki Kurasawa made this important point during the workshop on cosmopolitan methods in Paris (December 2014).

11 The full quote reads: 'Our study of an operations room led to a substantial reconceptualization of the construct of information system. [..] rather than a network of computer-based workstations in which information is stored, we observed an array of partial, heterogeneous devices brought together into coherent assemblages on particular occasions of work. To be made useful, these devices needed to be read in relation to an unfolding situation. Technologies, in this view, are constituted through and inseperable from the specifically situated practices of their use' Suchman et al., 1999, p. 399 .

12 It offers an excellent example of a process of translation as well as the demise of translation processes as a viable content dynamic on Twitter.

13 This idea of augmentation has inspired cybernetic fantasies: 'Social computing systems could eventually lead to an expansion of Dunbar's number. What if we develop social computing systems that are so efficient in maintaining relationships that they support richer and more complex social structures than our poor neo-cortexes can maintain on their own? Would such a society be better in fundamental ways than existing societies?' (Riedl, 2011)

14 I find the concept of 'augmentation' is of limited use in understanding experimentalism, as it is too flat and generic. This concept transposes onto social life the technological metaphor of 'augmented reality' without considering the specificity of social worlds.

15 'At its heart, PYMK is a link prediction problem: binary classification on whether a member will connect with another. For example, one of the first things to look at is friends-of-friends, or triangle listing (or triangle closing). Here, if Alice knows Bob and Bob knows Carol, then maybe Alice knows Carol. http://data.linkedin.com/projects/pymk With thanks to Sarietha Engelbrecht, who discussed this example in her DS final project.

16 Such intersections between digital technology and sociology are remarkable for various reasons, but one is that they remind us that sociology is certainly capable of leaving an enduring trace in the world. The implementation of PYMK is also interesting insofar as it demonstrates the ability for sociological methods to operate across different scales: Simmel's work on triads is usually grouped in the categories of micro-sociology and qualitative methods, but the LinkedIn implementation is in the opposite category. This surely is not just a positive accomplish-

ments (though it also is), but the digital implementation of sociology does render this field of knowledge newly responsible in digital societies: as sociological methods prove increasingly 'implementable,' they may acquire a dangerous efficacy. These methods may turn, for example, into instruments of social discrimination, as when the analysis of Facebook networks was proposed as a method for detecting depressive tendencies.

17 In a commentary presented at the symposium on the New Socialism, December 2014, University of Warwick.

18 Some sociologists refer to this dynamic as performativity, but I prefer interactivity to highlight that it is a distributed dynamic, involving various actors and entities.

19 http://www.ft.com/cms/s/0/d6daedee-706a-11e5-9b9e-690fdae72044.html#axzz3pDUwhSmb

20 This 'implementation' of ethnomethodology's important insight is accompanied by several ironies. For one, Garfinkel's definition of 'social method', to 'account for social life as part of social life', was supposed to bring to an end the study of the social – or at least, it was presented as a way to ceremonially dismantle its status as a distinct discipline, i.e. sociology. Yet as a consequence of the 'socialization' of digital infrastructures, practically the opposite seems to be transpiring. The proliferation of accounting devices that render mundane moments and informal interaction recordable and thereby accountable – the ethnomethodological proposition – is accompanied by loud re-assertions of 'the social', as well as for social science. Secondly, ethnomethodologists had claimed that the formats for accounting 'for everyday life as part of everyday life', were readily available in and as social life, but today these have become in and of themselves rather intense objects of design, investment, promotion, dare I say, creation, generation, and so on. As such, digital sociology also challenges some aspects of ethnomethodology.

21 A number of general sociological statements are then applicable to digital platforms: the pursuit of empirical social research is made possible by the methodical character of social life, a claim that ethnomethodologists had advanced several decades ago (Cicourel, 1964). Furthermore, in this digital methods for social research are no different from older forms of media-based sociology: successful social research methods of the past, like statistical analysis and the opinion poll were highly dependent on the media and information infrastructures in the society in which they were developed, like the evolving state bureaucracy of the nineteenth century and the daily news media of the twentieth century (Hacking, 1990).

22 For un-expected forms of interaction to come about – as, happened for example, when the anthropologist Gabriella Coleman (2015) met a notorious Anonymous hacker in the streets of New York – depends on the mobilization of great resources.

23 http://www.techtimes.com/articles/12840/20140812/twitter-acknowled
   ges-14-percent-users-bots-5-percent-spam-bots.htm#sthash.0rGsWiZP.
   dpuf
24 As noted, computational social science tends to bracket reflexivity: in
   their view the advantage of digital networked data is that they make it
   possible to *dispense* with the opinions, and views, perspectives of research
   subjects, and to consider only their digitally recorded behaviours.
   Newman and Watts (2007) praise online data for their objectivity, which
   'survey instruments [. . .] not only are onerous to administer, but also
   suffer from inaccurate or subjective responses of subjects (Newman and
   Watts, 2007, p. L-5).

3   Do we need new methods?

 1 Google Correlate runs on top of Google Trends, which allows you to
   query 'how often a particular search-term is entered relative to the total
   search-volume across various regions of the world' http://www.google.
   com/trends/correlate/faq
 2 I will argue that a lot *more* is involved in the configuration of Internet
   devices as 'sociological machines' than is often assumed, and that
   this 'more' is where sociologists can make a valuable contribution.
   Today, search engines still fail the sociological test, lacking certain
   formative capacities that are crucial to the doing of social enquiry. But
   this failure is not final. Rather than dismissing these tools, we must
   ask: what is required before such devices can serve as sociological
   machines?
 3 http://www.theguardian.com/uk/interactive/2011/dec/07/london-riots-
   twitter
 4 Mills, C. (2013) The Great British Class Fiasco, the Oxford Sociology Blog
   http://oxfordsociology.blogspot.co.uk/2013/04/the-great-british-class-fia
   sco.html. For an overview of the debate, see http://soc.sagepub.com/site/
   British_Social_Class/British_Social_Class_Homepage.xhtml
 5 With thanks to Sebastian Giessmann for discussing his ongoing research
   on Moreno with me.
 6 As such, the idea of 'data-driven' research doesn't describe the data practices of digital social research particularly well. Digital social research is
   not any less theoretical than non-digital social research, it simply derives
   its concepts – its 'ontology' – not only from social theory but rather from
   its research apparatus (Bowker et al., 2009).
 7 Project data also appear to have been used, among others, as part of Ted
   Cruz Presidential Campaign. http://www.theguardian.com/us-news/2015/
   dec/11/senator-ted-cruz-president-campaign-facebook-user-data
 8 Other examples include work by Wolfram: 'More than a million
   people have now used our Wolfram | Alpha Personal Analytics for
   Facebook. And as part of our latest update, in addition to collecting

some anonymized statistics, we launched a Data Donor program that allows people to contribute detailed data to us for research purposes.' http://blog.stephenwolfram.com/2013/04/data-science-of-the-facebook-world/

9 My own digital research project on Internet Governance also made use of interactive methods: In this study, we consulted experts and advocates in Internet Governance in order to map these issues using Twitter analysis. We subsequently involved these experts and advocates in the interpretation of our issue visualizations. http://www.issuemapping.net/Main/WCITProfiles

10 Deborah Lupton (2014) writes: 'Titles such as 'digital social research' and computational social science'. . .are used to refer to work.. focused on the collection and use of data and tools to analyse these data. Followers adopt an approach that is largely drawn from computer science.' (p. 17)

11 The next section draws on Marres, N. and C. Gerlitz (2016) Interface methods: Renegotiating Relations Between Digital Research, STS and Sociology, *Sociological Review*.

12 Harvey, Reeves and Ruppert (2013) have proposed that socio-technical devices should not be understood as mere gadgets, but as 'complex and unstable assemblages that draw together a diversity of people, things and concepts in the pursuit of particular purposes, aims, and objectives'.

13 My use of the term 'interface' draws on the work of Lucy Suchman (2007a) and Celia Lury (2004), both of whom have drawn attention to interfaces as key sites for the negotiation of epistemic divisions of labour. As an in-between, interfaces allow for dynamics of multi-valence, in which tools, data and methods can be connected in various ways and to enable various analytic and normative purposes.

14 Similarly, co-word analysis is less solidly a sociological method than it may appear to be at first sight. When the method was developed in the 1980s, it presented in rudimentary form a methodology that was later to be called 'actor-network theory', one focused on the detection and analysis of the changing relations between heterogeneous entities over time (Latour, 2005). However, digital implementations of co-occurrence today call into question the specificity of the approach. Indeed, a survey of the wider literature on co-word analysis reveals that the method is taken up in diverse fields such as scientometrics, software engineering and communication studies (Danowski, 2009), where it is framed as deriving from innovation studies and/or scientometrics more broadly defined. What is of critical importance for us, at this juncture, is that our 'own' method comes to appear rather less solidly anchored in familiar scholarly traditions: the methodological uncanny affects our 'own methods.'

15 This includes the Issue Mapping and Co-Word Machine workshops

that I organized at Goldsmiths, University of London in May 2012 – both funded by the ESRC Digital Social Research Programme – as well as the Digital Methods Summer School hosted by the New Media group at the University of Amsterdam in July 2012. See www.issue mapping.net

16 We collected our data for this study with T-CAT, the online Twitter data Capture and Analytics Toolset developed by the Digital Methods Group at the University of Amsterdam (Borra and Rieder, 2014). This toolkit includes The Associational Profiler, a tool for co-hashtag and co-word analysis developed as part of the ESRC-funded project Issue Mapping Online led by myself (www.issuemapping.net)

17 Insofar as digitization involves changing relations between data, technology, users and research tools, it brings into focus a classic sociological argument about the nature of method in social enquiry: namely the proposition first formulated by Aaron Cicourel (1964) that the 'methods' of social enquiry are best understood as a distributed accomplishment: *method is not just something that social researchers implement by way of research design on their object of study. The very viability of social method depends on mutual coordination between research subjects, measures, social practices, analytic categories, data formats and so on.* This is a holistic understanding of method, and one that explicitly recognizes the significance of non-methodical elements like practices and technical formats among its constitutive components. This understanding of method, however, was developed many decades ago, and the idea of 'interface methods' itself presents only a continuation of methodological debates in social science. As I hope to show in the next chapter, digital social research offers special opportunities for re-activating and perhaps expanding Cicourel's analysis. As he argued, the aim of sociological methodology should be 'to achieve a more basic level of interaction between theory, method and data.'

4   Are we researching society or technology?

1 With thanks to Anne Helmond who pointed me to this figure in December 2012: the original link now references another figure (about hashtags on Facebook). https://csmt2012.wordpress.com/midterm-memes/

2 This chapter draws on Marres (2015) Why map issues? On controversy analysis as a digital method, *Science, Technology and Human Values*, and Marres, N. and D. Moats (2015), 'Mapping controversies with social media: the case for symmetry' *Social Media and Society*, Special Issue Culture Digitally, T. Gillespie and H. Postigo (eds), 2056305115604176.

3 To address these issues of bias, researchers are increasingly tempted to access social data via commercial routes (purchasing data via services like GNIP), resulting in other kinds of 'buy-in'.

4 They add: 'In addition, most of the data analysed is self-reported and some is deliberately incorrect.' (p. 14)

5 This problem of the 'influence of the setting' (Garfinkel, 1967) and efforts to contain it by extracting empirical phenomena from the settings in which they occur, are relevant to a wide range of social research methodologies, including survey methods (Savage, 2010) and content analysis (Herring, 2009).

6 There are other differences: precautionists tend to work with stable data sets, while those who affirm the biases of settings are attracted by the dynamic data sets that online platforms make available.

7 There is of course also the question of language: as e-waste is an English term, it shouldn't surprise us that English-speaking regions are more prominently represented on this map.

8 There are various possible ways to address the problem: one might conduct a comparison between image collections associated with different key-words. And if this were feasible, one could compare the locations of e-waste with locations of a set of randomly chosen collections of Flickr images.

9 Hine notes: 'The transcript – of interaction in a chat forum – recorded both the key strokes which I had entered, and the information which had appeared on my screen during the interview. It was thus a kind of hybrid document, part of my own making, part of information entered into the machine by other participants and by programmers, and the whole passed through the filter of the machine. I was therefore unsure just what kind of data this was (p. 11).' Hine, C. (1994) Virtual Ethnography, paper presented at the conference When Science Becomes Culture, Montreal, http://www.cirst.uqam.ca/pcst3/pdf/Communications/hine.pdf

10 Lee, D. 'Dislike' button coming to Facebook BBC news, 16 September 2015 http://www.bbc.co.uk/news/technology-34264624

11 One way of understanding these proliferating problems of bias is in terms of a *trade-off* in digital social research: what researchers gain in terms of the volume of social data they have access too, and the analytic capacity of the instruments brought to bear on them, they pay for in terms of ceding control over research design and methodology to digital media technologies.

12 Of course, there are many elements besides devices that inform Twitter use including context and thematic focus (Bruns and Stieglitz, 2012), as such the ambiguity I am foregrounding here needs to be dis-aggregated further, but my aim in this chapter is to clarify the methodological problem of ambiguity.

13 Rieders 5 categories are 'descriptive analysis of users, motivations for using Facebook, identity presentation, the role of Facebook in social interactions, and privacy and information disclosure' (Rieder, 2013).

14 Such delineations of the empirical object of social media analysis tend to contain ambiguity by definitional means and do not engage with it as a

constructive empirical question (what are we mapping?). In his paper on Facebook research (2013), Rieder adopts a similar solution.

15 The project findings are available at http://www.pewinternet.org/2014/02/20/mapping-twitter-topic-networks-from-polarized-crowds-to-community-clusters/ (Smith, et al., 2014)

16 This study was conducted during the Digital Methods Summer Shool at the University of Amsterdam in the Summer 2013. Like the study reported in Chapter 3, we captured and analysed Twitter Data using T-CAT, the Twitter Analytics Toolkit developed by Erik Borra and Bernard Rieder (2014). The full study is archived at: https://wiki.digital-methods.net/Dmi/DetectingTheSocials

17 This Twitter set was based on two queries – 'privacy' and 'surveillance' – and includes all tweets containing these words between 6 and 12 June 2013, the period in which the NSA leak occurred. David Moats and I initially included both terms as it seemed the Snowden leaks resonated across the two topics.

18 This point also relates to a feature of ANT discussed in Chapter 3: taking up tools of online data analysis, it is impossible to operate in a purely descriptive register, following links wherever they may lead, as actor-network theorists had once suggested we do. Such a descriptive approach here literally becomes impossible: there is little we can describe about opaque hairballs. *The only way to conduct social research with digital platforms is to actively participate in the configuration of the empirical apparatus.*

19 The URL sequencer tool first expands all tiny URLs, including those that were truncations of already shortened URLs, and resolves them back to their original sources (t.co/XFDFS --- > tiny.url/SFDSFS --? BBC.co.uk/FDSFSDS). It then arranges every tweet in which a URL is shared in a given data set in time order. To analyse these URL shares qualitatively would be a challenge because of the amount of repetition due to the presence of RSS bots and Retweets. The URL sequencer identifies similar deployments of a URL by stripping away @ mentions and URL truncation to compare the core text and separates the types into columns. This allows the researcher to identify variations and modifications which may be consequential for how the URL is shared.

20 Co-hashtag network pre (top) and post (bottom) Snowden, Courtesy of Hjalmar Carlsen,5 May-4 June 2013, 20.085 Tweets containing 'my privacy', 13 June-13 July 2013, 21.165 Tweets containing 'my privacy'.

5 Who are digital sociology's publics?

1 In the case of digital platforms like Twitter and Facebook, the historical 'newness' of digital participation is then overstated twice over: the

'newness' claimed for these platforms also covers up the extent to which digital networked media prior to Web 2.0 platforms already were participatory (Coleman, 2012).

2 The notion of the 'audience' has been under fire from multiple directions: fragmentation of the mass society, marketing techniques bent on the segmentation of the audience.

3 This paragraph draws on Lezaun, J., N. Marres, and M. Tironi (forthcoming) Experiments in Participation, the Handbook of Science and Technology Studies, C. Miller, U. Felt et al. (eds). Cambridge (Mass): MIT Press.

4 The assumed traceability of publics raises further critical questions about the appropriation and *recognition* of the labour of participation. Scholars in science and technology studies have argued that knowledge production is inherently participatory: research subjects actively contribute to the process of enquiry, but this labour of participation and the associated contributions as a rule do not get recognized in science (Leigh Star and Strauss, 1999; Irani et al., 2013). Importantly, this is not to say that science is necessarily exploitative, but rather, that epistemic presumptions about methodological sovereignty do not make it possible to acknowledge these contributions. Digital architectures – with their traceability of contributions and affordances for collaboration, feedback and address, potentially make it possible to address these issues. Could trace-ability translate into epistemic recognition of the contribution of participation to knowledge?

5 Howard, P. (2011) Project on Information Technology and Political Islam. http://philhoward.org/project-on-information-technology-and-political-islam/

6 Vasagar, J. (2016) Singapore banks examine use of Facebook IDs for transfers *Financial Times*, 3 July. http://www.ft.com/cms/s/0/b2dd2cd8-3f39-11e6-8716-a4a71e8140b0.html#axzz4DQd5CWWU

7 – ability signals the capacity of digital arrangements to produce these effects. As such their societal 'impact' and significance partly resides in the generation of potentialities (Lury and Marres, 2015).

8 The normative understanding of participation stipulates autonomy as a requirement in two ways: (1) participation is a good in itself, which does not need to serve other instrumental purposes besides itself, as people participate for participations sake (2) the conduct of participation requires a relatively autonomous sphere, where participants are free from the influence of the particularities of everyday life and powerful interests (Nash, 2009).

9 With thanks to Kristin Asdal for suggesting this connection.

10 I found this slogan in the header of a job advert for a 'quantitative data analyst to help implement our big data initiative'. For me, this communication strengthened my risk assessment that the coming digital knowledge democracy could well go hand-in-hand with the

continuation of established hierarchies of knowledge, such as those that value quantitative over qualitative knowledge. https://docs.google.com/document/d/19nboMDpw7p_Ye8g3Hf_S_OwpxA2ts3z2SmpgbTX_1E/edit

11 My typology is inspired by other typologies of digital participation such as Kelty's (2012) and Haklay (2013). With thanks to João Porto de Albuquerque.

12 Knight, J. 'Big Data and Adminstrative Data', Big data – Social Data, 10 December 2015, University of Warwick's Q-Step Centre, http://www2.warwick.ac.uk/fac/cross_fac/q-step/newsevents/eventslist/fssbd/

6 Does digital sociology have problems?

1 https://en.wikipedia.org/wiki/Facebook_real-name_policy_controversy#cite_note-EFF-27

2 https://en.wikipedia.org/wiki/Facebook_real-name_policy_controversy#cite_note-EFF-27

3 Julia Turner: 'Everything you were angry about on social media' Slate, 17 December 2014 http://www.slate.com/articles/life/culturebox/2014/12/the_year_of_outrage_2014_everything_you_were_angry_about_on_social_media.html

4 The Science and Technology Select Committee (2016), 'The Big Data Dilemma': Fourth Report of Session 2015-1610 February http://www.publications.parliament.uk/pa/cm201516/cmselect/cmsctech/468/468.pdf

5 https://www.britsoc.co.uk/equality-diversity/statement-of-ethical-practice

6 http://aoir.org/reports/ethics2.pdf

7 Another problematic consequence of the growing demands for ethical standards in digital research, is the bifurcation of the space of enquiry, risking the re-establishment of strict divisions between institutionally vetted and non-official forms of enquiry.

8 Slee, T. (2011) 'Internet-Centrism 3 (of 3): Tweeting the Revolution (and Conflict of Interest)' 22,September, http://whimsley.typepad.com/whimsley/2011/09/earlier-today-i-thought-i-wasdoomed-to-fail-that-part-3-of-this-prematurely-announced-trilogy-was-just-not-going-to-getwr.html#paper2

9 I am grateful to Matthias Orlikowksi for discussions of this point.

10 Watts, D. (2014) Stop Complaining About the Facebook Study, it's a golden age for research, *Guardian*, 7 July, http://www.theguardian.com/commentisfree/2014/jul/07/facebook-study-science-experiment-research

References

Abdel-Rahman, N. (2015). New media and Egyptian cyberactivism: The role of Facebook in Egyptian politics and the 'revolution'. Doctoral dissertation, Sociology, University of Lancaster.

Abbott, A. (2011). Googles of the past: Do keywords really matter? Annual Lecture of the Department of Sociology, Goldsmiths, 15 March.

Adkins, L. and Lury, C. (2011). Introduction: Special measures. Special Issue on Measure and Value. *The Sociological Review*, *59*(s2): 5–23.

Akrich, M. and Latour, B. (1992). A summary of a convenient vocabulary for the semiotics of human and nonhuman assemblies. In *Shaping Technology/Building Society Studies in Sociotechnical Change*, W. Bijker and J. Law (eds) Cambridge: MIT Press: pp. 259–64.

Amoore, L. and Piotukh, V. (2015). Life beyond big data: Governing with little analytics. *Economy and Society*, *44*(3): 341–66.

Anderson, C. W. (2011). Deliberative, agonistic, and algorithmic audiences: Journalism's vision of its public in an age of audience transparency. *International Journal of Communication*, *19* (5): 529–47.

Andrejevic, M. (2014). Big data, big questions: The big data divide. *International Journal of Communication*, *8*: 1673–89.

Arvidsson, A. (2011). General sentiment: How value and affect converge in the information economy. *The Sociological Review*, *59*(s2): 39–59.

Arvidsson, A. and Colleoni, E. (2012). Value in Informational Capitalism and on the Internet. *The Information Society*, *28*(3): 135–150.

Ashmore, M., MacMillan, K. and Brown, S. D. (2004). It's a scream: Professional hearing and tape fetishism. *Journal of Pragmatics, 36* (1): 349–74.

Athique, A. (2013). *Digital Media and Society: An Introduction.* Cambridge: Polity.

Back, L. (2010). Broken devices and new opportunities: re-imagining the tools of qualitative research, National Centre for Research Methods, working paper.

Back, L. (2012). Live sociology: social research and its futures. *The Sociological Review*, *60*(S1): 18–39.

Back, L. and Puwar, N. (eds). (2012). *Live Methods*. Wiley-Blackwell.

Baker, P. and Potts, A. (2013). 'Why do white people have thin lips?' Google and the perpetuation of stereotypes via auto-complete search forms. *Critical Discourse Studies*, *10*(2): 187–204.

Barocas, S., Hood, S. and Ziewitz, M. (2013). Governing algorithms: A provocation piece. *Available at SSRN 2245322*.

Bastian, M., Heymann, S. and Jacomy, M. (2009). Gephi: an open source software for exploring and manipulating networks. *ICWSM*, *8*, 361–2.

Becker, H. (1963). *Outsiders*. New York: The Free Press.

Beer, D. (2012, 31 August). Using Social Media Data Aggregators to Do Social Research. *Sociological Research Online*.

Beer, D. and Burrows, R. (2007). Sociology and, of and in Web 2.0: Some initial considerations. *Sociological Research Online*, *12*(5) http://www.socresonline.org.uk/12/5/17.html

Beer, D. and Burrows, R. (2013). Popular culture, digital archives and the new social life of data. *Theory, Culture and Society*, *30*(4): 47–71.

Bell, D. (1976). The coming of the post-industrial society. *The Educational Forum*, 40 (4): 574–9.

Berker, T., Hartmann, M. and Punie, Y. (2005). *Domestication of Media and Technology*. London: McGraw-Hill Education.

Bialski, P. (2016). Fields of anonymity: A mapping of discourses around trackability, tracelessness, and accountability in programming worlds. Paper presented during the symposium on Non-knowledge and Digital Culture, University of Leuphana, Lunenburg, 26 January.

Birkbak, A. (2013). From networked publics to issue publics: Reconsidering the public/private distinction in web science. In *Proceedings of the 5th Annual ACM Web Science Conference*. ACM: pp. 24–32.

Birkbak, A. and Carlsen, H. B. (2015). The public and its algorithms. In *Algorithmic Life: Calculative Devices in the Age of Big Data*. L. Amoore and V. Piotukh (eds). London and New York: Routledge: pp. 21–34.

Boellstorf, T. and Mauer, B. (2015). *Data – Now Bigger and Better!* Chicago: Prickly Paradigm Press.

Bond, R. M., Fariss, C. J., Jones, J. J., Kramer, A. D., Marlow, C., Settle, J. E. and Fowler, J. H. (2012). A 61-million-person experiment in social influence and political mobilization. *Nature*, *489*(7415): 295–8.

Borra, E. and Rieder, B. (2014). Programmed method: Developing a toolset for capturing and analyzing tweets. *Aslib Journal of Information Management*, *66*(3): 262–78.

Borra, E., Weltevrede, E., Ciuccarelli, P., Kaltenbrunner, A., Laniado, D., Magni, G. and Venturini, T. (2015). Societal controversies in Wikipedia articles. *Proceedings of the 33rd Annual ACM Conference on Human Factors in Computing Systems*, ACM: pp. 193–6.

Boshmaf, Y., Muslukhov, I., Beznosov, K. and Ripeanu, M. (2011).

The social bot network: When bots socialize for fame and money. In *Proceedings of the 27th Annual Computer Security Applications Conference*, ACM: pp. 93–102.

Boullier, D. (2016). Big data challenges for the social sciences: From society and opinion to replications, Working paper, Social Media Lab, EPFL Lausanne, https://arxiv.org/ftp/arxiv/papers/1607/1607.05034.pdf

Bowker, G. C. (2005). *Memory Practices in the Sciences*. Cambridge, MA: MIT Press.

Bowker, G. C. and Star, S. L. (2000). *Sorting Things out: Classification and its Consequences*. Cambridge, MA: MIT Press.

Bowker, G. C., Baker, K., Millerand, F., and Ribes, D. (2009). Toward information infrastructure studies: Ways of knowing in a networked environment. *International Handbook of Internet Research*. Dordrecht: Springer Netherlands: pp. 97–117.

boyd, d. (2010). Social network sites as networked publics: Affordances, dynamics, and implications. *Networked Self: Identity, Community, and Culture on Social Network Sites*, Z. Papacharissi (ed.), London and New York: Routledge: pp. 39–58.

boyd, d. (2014). *It's Complicated: The Social Lives of Networked Teens*. New Haven: Yale University Press.

boyd, d. and Crawford, K. (2012). Critical questions for big data: Provocations for a cultural, technological, and scholarly phenomenon. *Information, Communication and Society*, 15(5): 662–79.

boyd, d. and Ellison, N. B. (2007). Social network sites: Definition, history, and scholarship. *Journal of Computer-Mediated Communication*, 13(1): 210–30.

Brauer, C. (2011). 'Netmodern: Interventions in digital sociology'. Doctoral dissertation, Goldsmiths, University of London.

Brown, B., McGregor, M. and Laurier, E. (2013). iPhone in vivo: Video analysis of mobile device use. In *Proceedings of the SIGCHI Conference on Human Factors in Computing Systems*. ACM: pp. 1031–40.

Bruns, A. (2008). *Blogs, Wikipedia, Second Life, and beyond: From Production to Produsage*. New York: Peter Lang.

Bruns, A., Burgess, J. and Mahrt, M. (2013). *Twitter and Society*. K. Weller and C. Puschmann (eds). New York: Peter Lang.

Bruns, A. and Stieglitz, S. (2012). Quantitative approaches to comparing communication patterns on Twitter. *Journal of Technology in Human Services*, 30: 160–85.

Bucher, T. (2013). The friendship assemblage: Investigating programmed sociality on Facebook. *Television and New Media*, 14(6): 479–93.

Burgess, J., Galloway, A. and Sauter, T. (2015). Hashtag as hybrid forum: The case of #agchatoz. In N. Rambukkana (ed.), *Hashtag Publics*. New York: Peter Lang.

Burke, P. (2012). *A Social History of Knowledge II: From the Encyclopaedia to Wikipedia*. Cambridge: Polity.

Button, G. and Dourish, P. (1996). Technomethodology: Paradoxes and possibilities. *Proceedings of the SIGCHI conference on Human Factors in Computing Systems*, ACM: pp. 19–26.

Callon, M. (1984). Some elements of a sociology of translation: domestication of the scallops and the fishermen of St Brieuc Bay. *The Sociological Review*, *32*(S1): 196–233.

Callon, M. (2006). Can methods for analysing large numbers organize a productive dialogue with the actors they study? *European Management Review*, *3*(1): 7–16.

Callon, M., Courtial, J., Turner W. and Bauin, S., (1983). From translations to problematic networks: An introduction to co-word analysis. *Social Science Information*, 22: 191–235.

Carlsen, H. A. B. and Birkbak, A. (2015). The World of Edgerank. *Computational Culture*, 15 January, http://computationalculture.net/article/the-world-of-edgerank-rhetorical-justifications-of-facebooks-news-feed-algorithm

Carnap, R. (1995) [1961]. *An Introduction to the Philosophy of Science*, M. Gardner (ed). Dover Publications.

Carrigan, M. (2016). *Social Media for Academics*. London: Sage.

Castellani, B. (2014). Complexity and the failure of quantitative social science. *Focus*, 8 (8) http://discoversociety.org/2014/11/04/focus-complexity-and-the-failure-of-quantitative-social-science/

Castelle, M. (2013). 'Relational and non-relational models in the entextualization of bureaucracy'. *Computational Culture: a Journal of Software Studies* 3, http://computationalculture.net/article/relational-and-non-relational-models-in-the-entextualization-of-bureaucracy

Castells, M. (1996). *The Rise of the Network Society: The Information Age: Economy, Society, and Culture* (Vol. 1). New York: John Wiley and Sons.

Chilvers, J. and Kearnes, M. (eds). (2015). *Remaking Participation: Science, Environment and Emergent Publics*. London and New York: Routledge.

Christensen C. (2013). Wave-riding and hashtag-jumping. *Information, Communication and Society*, (16): 646–66.

Christin, A. (2015). 'Sex, scandals, and celebrities'? Exploring the determinants of popularity in online news. *Sur le journalisme/ About journalism/ Sobre jornalismo*, *4*(2): 28–47.

Cicourel, A. V. (1964). *Method and Measurement in Sociology*. New York: Free Press.

Clough, P. T., Gregory, K., Haber, B. and Scannell, R. J. (2015). The datalogical turn. *Non-Representational Methodologies: Re-Envisioning Research*, P. Vanninni (ed.), London and New York: Routledge, pp. 146–64

Cohen, S. (2002 (1972)). *Folk Devils and Moral Panics: The Creation of the Mods and Rockers*. London and New York: Routledge.

Coleman, G. (2012). *Coding Freedom: The Ethics and Aesthetics of Hacking*. Princeton: Princeton University Press.

Coleman, G. (2014). *Hacker, Hoaxer, Whistleblower, Spy: The Many Faces of Anonymous*. London and New York: Verso Books.

Conte, R., Gilbert, N., Bonelli, G., Cioffi-Revilla, C., Deffuant, G., Kertesz, J. and Nowak, A. (2012). Manifesto of computational social science. *The European Physical Journal Special Topics*, *214*(1): 325–346.

Couldry, N. (2012). *Media, Society, World: Social Theory and Digital Media Practice*. Cambridge: Polity.

Couldry, N. and J. van Dijck (2015). Researching social media as if the social mattered. *Social Media and Society*, *1*(2): 2056305115604174.

Couldry, N. and Powell, A. (2014). Big Data from the bottom up. *Big Data and Society*, *1*(2): 2053951714539277.

Crampton, J. W., Graham, M., Poorthuis, A., Shelton, T., Stephens, M., Wilson, M. W. and Zook, M. (2013). Beyond the geotag: Situating 'big data' and leveraging the potential of the geoweb. *Cartography and geographic information science*, *40*(2): 130–139.

Crawford, K. (2013). Hidden biases in big data, *Harvard Business Review* https://hbr.org/2013/04/the-hidden-biases-in-big-data/

Crawford, K. (2014). The test we can – and should – run on Facebook, *The Atlantic*, 2 July, http://www.theatlantic.com/technology/archive/2014/07/the-test-we-canand-shouldrun-on-facebook/373819/

Crawford, K. and Gillespie, T. (2016). What is a flag for? Social media reporting tools and the vocabulary of complaint. *New Media and Society*, *18*(3): 410–28.

Crossley, N. (2008). Pretty connected: The social network of the early UK punk movement. *Theory, Culture and Society*, *25*(6): 89–116.

Crossley, N. (2010). *Towards Relational Sociology*. London and New York: Routledge.

Danowski, J. (2009). Inferences from word networks in messages. *The Content Analysis Reader*. K. Kippendorf and M. A. Bock (eds), Thousand Oaks, CA: SAGE, pp. 421–429.

Dányi, E. (2006). Xerox project: Photocopy machines as a metaphor for an 'open society'. *The Information Society*, *22*(2): 111–15.

Davies, W. (2015a). *The Happiness Industry: How the Government and Big Business Sold Us Well-Being*. London and New York: Verso Books.

Davies, W. (2015b). The return of social government. From 'socialist calculation' to 'social analytics'. *European Journal of Social Theory*, *18*(4): 431–50.

Dean, J. (2001). Publicity's secret. *Political Theory*, *29*(5): 624–50.

Dennis, K. and Urry, J. (2009). *After the Car*. Cambridge: Polity.

Derksen, M. and Beaulieu, A. (2011). Social technology. *The Handbook of Philosophy of Social Science*, 703–19.

Deutsch, K. W., Markovits, A. S. and Platt, J. R. (eds). (1986). *Advances in the Social Sciences, 1900–1980: What, Who, Where, How?* Lanham, MD: University Press of America.

Deville, J. (2015). *Lived Economies of Default: Consumer Credit, Debt Collection and the Capture of Affect*. London and New York: Routledge.

Deville, J. and L. van der Velden (2015). Seeing the invisible algorithm: The practical politics of tracking the credit trackers. *Algorithmic life: Calculative Devices in the Age of Big Data*, Amoore, L. and Piotukh, V. (eds), London and New York: Routledge: pp. 87–105.

Dewey, J. (1991 (1927)). *The Public and Its Problems*. Athens: Swallow Press and Ohio University Press.

Dickel, S. (forthcoming) Responsibilization made easy. Assembling Crowdworkers for Science. In *TechnoScienceSociety Technological Reconfigurations of Science and Society*, S. Maasen, C. Schneider, S. Dickel (eds). Sociology of Science Yearbook, Delft: Kluwer.

Didier, E. (2009). *En quoi consiste l'Amérique ? Les statistiques, le New Deal et la démocratie*. Paris: La Découverte.

Dijck, J. van (2013). *The Culture of Connectivity: A Critical History of Social Media*. Oxford: Oxford University Press.

Diminescu, D. (2012). Introduction: Digital methods for the exploration, analysis and mapping of e-diasporas. *Social Science Information*, 51(4): 451–8.

Duhem, P. (1996). *Essays in the History and Philosophy of Science*, trans. R. Ariew and P. Barker, Indianapolis: Hackett.

Dourish, P. and Bell, G. (2011). *Divining a digital future: Mess and mythology in ubiquitous computing*. Cambridge, MA: MIT Press.

Driscoll, K. (2012). From punched cards to 'big data': A social history of database Populism. *communication+ 1*, 1(1): 1–33.

Driscoll, K. and Walker, S. (2014). Big data, big questions: Working within a black box: Transparency in the collection and production of big Twitter data. *International Journal of Communication*, 8 (20): 1745–64.

Eagle, N., A. Pentland, and D. Lazer (2009). Inferring social network structure using mobile phone data. *Proceedings of the National Academy of Sciences (PNAS)*, 106(36): 15274–8.

Edwards, A., Housley, W., Williams, M., Sloan, L. and Williams, M. (2013). Digital social research, social media and the sociological imagination: Surrogacy, augmentation and re-orientation. *International Journal of Social Research Methodology*, 16(3): 245–60.

Espeland, W. N. and Stevens, M. L. (1998). Commensuration as a social process. *Annual Review of Sociology*, 24: 313–43.

Ezrahi, Y. (1990). *The Descent of Icarus: Science and the Transformation of Contemporary Democracy*. Cambridge, MA: Harvard University Press.

Fish, A., Murillo, L. F., Nguyen, L., Panofsky, A. and Kelty, C. M. (2011). Birds of the Internet: Towards a field guide to the organization and governance of participation. *Journal of Cultural Economy*, 4(2): 157–87.

Forlano, L. and Halpern, M. (2015). Reimagining work: entanglements and frictions around future of work narratives. *The Fibreculture Journal*, (26): 33–59.

Fuchs, C. (2009). Information and communication technologies and society: A contribution to the critique of the political economy of the internet. *European Journal of Communication*, 24(1): 69–87.

Gabrys, J. (2014). Programming environments: Environmentality and citizen sensing in the smart city. *Environment and Planning D: Society and Space*, 32(1): 30–48.

Garfinkel, H. (1984 [1967]). *Studies in Ethnomethodology*. Cambridge: Polity.

Galloway, A. R. (2014). The cybernetic hypothesis. *differences*, 25(1): 107–31.

Garcia, D. (2014). From tactical media to the neo-pragmatists of the web. *Leonardo Electronic Almanac*, 20(1): 124–35.

Garcia, D. and Lovink, G. (1997). The ABC of tactical media. *first distributed via the nettime listserv*.

Geismar, H. (Forthcoming). The instant archive. In the *Routledge Companion to Digital Ethnography*. L. Hjorth, H. Horst, A. Galloway and G. Bell (eds), London and New York: Routledge.

Gerlitz, C. and Helmond, A. (2013). The like economy: Social buttons and the data-intensive web. *New Media and Society*, 15(8): 1348–65.

Gerlitz, C. and Lury, C. (2014). Social media and self-evaluating assemblages: On numbers, orderings and values. *Distinktion: Scandinavian Journal of Social Theory*, 15(2): 174–88.

Gerlitz, C. and Rieder, B. (2013). Mining one percent of Twitter: Collections, baselines, sampling. *M/C Journal*, 16(2). http://journal.media-culture.org.au/index.php/mcjournal/article/view/620Rieder

Giddens, A. (1987). *Social Theory and Modern Sociology*. Cambridge: Polity.

Giessmann, S. (2009). Ganz klein, ganz gross. Jacob Levy Moreno und die Geschicke des Netzwerkdiagramms. *Medien in Zeit und Raum. Massverhältnisse des Medialen*, I Koster and K. Schubert (eds). Bielefeld: Transcript Verlag: pp. 267–92.

Gieryn, Th. (2006). City as truth-spot laboratories and field-sites in urban studies. *Social Studies of Science*, 36 (1): 5–38.

Gill, N. and Bialski, P. (2011). New friends in new places: Network formation during the migration process among Poles in the UK. *Geoforum*, 42(2): 241–9.

Gillespie, T. (2013). What social bots tell us about social media. *Culture Digitally*. 2 April. http://culturedigitally.org/2013/04/what-socialbots-tell-us-about-social-media/

Gillespie, T. (2010). The politics of 'platforms'. *New Media and Society*, 12(3): 347–64.

Gillespie, T., Boczkowski, P. J. and Foot, K. A. (2014). *Media Technologies: Essays on Communication, Materiality, And Society*. Cambridge, MA: MIT Press.

Ginsberg, J., Mohebbi, M. H., Patel, R. S., Brammer, L., Smolinski, M. S. and Brilliant, L. (2009). Detecting influenza epidemics using search engine query data. *Nature*, 457(7232): 1012–14.

Girard, M. and D. Stark (2007). Socio-technologies of Assembly: Sensemaking and demonstration in rebuilding Lower Manhattan. *Governance and Information Technology: From Electronic Government to Information*

Government. D. Lazer and V. Mayer-Schoenberger (eds). Cambridge, MA: MIT Press: pp. 145–76.

Gitelman, L. (2013). *Raw Data is an Oxymoron*. Cambridge, MA: MIT Press.

Gitelman, L. (2014). *Paper Knowledge: Toward a Media History of Documents*. Durham, NC: Duke University Press.

Given, J. (2006). Narrating the digital turn: Data deluge, technomethodology, and other likely tales, *Qualitative Sociology Review*, 1 (2): 54–65.

Goffman, E. (1978). *The Presentation of Self in Everyday Life*. Harmondsworth.

Goldberg, G. (2016). Antisocial media: Digital dystopianism as a normative project, *New Media and Society*, *18* (5): 784–99.

Gonzalez-Polledo, E. (2016). Chronic media worlds: Social media and the problem of pain communication on Tumblr. *Social Media and Society*, 2(1): 2056305116628887.

Goodwin, C. (1994). Professional vision. *American Anthropologist*, *96*(3): 606–33.

Grommé, F. (2015). Turning aggression into an object of intervention: Tinkering in a crime control pilot study. *Science as Culture*, *24*(2): 227–47.

Gross, A. (2015). The technical redoing and the aesthetic reordering of search keywords, Chapter 3, In Data types and functions: A study of framing devices and techniques, Doctoral dissertation, University of Warwick, pp. 82–118

Gross, M. and Krohn, W. (2005). Society as experiment: Sociological foundations for a self-experimental society. *History of the Human Sciences*, *18*(2): 63–86.

Gruzd, A. and Haythornthwaite, C. (2011). Networking online: Cybercommunities. *The SAGE Handbook of Social Network Analysis*. London: Sage: pp. 167–79.

Guggenheim, M. (2012). Laboratizing and de-laboratizing the world changing sociological concepts for places of knowledge production. *History of the Human Sciences*, *25*(1): 99–118.

Guggenheim, M. (2015). The media of sociology: tight or loose translations? *British Journal of Sociology*, *66* (2), 345–72

Haber, B. (2016). 'Queer Facebook? Digital sociality and queer theory' In *Digital Sociologies*. Bristol: Policy Press.

Habermas, J. (1991 (1962)). *The Structural Transformation of the Public Sphere: An Inquiry into a Category of Bourgeois Society*, trans. Th. Burger. Cambridge, MA: MIT Press.

Hacking, I (2000). *The Social Construction of What?* Cambridge, MA: Harvard University Press.

Hacking, I. (1990). *The Taming of Chance*. Cambridge: Cambridge University Press.

Haklay, M. (2013). Citizen science and volunteered geographic information: Overview and typology of participation. *Crowdsourcing Geographic Knowledge*, D. Sui, S. Elwood and M. Goodchild (eds). Dordrecht: Springer Netherlands: pp. 105–22.

Halavais, A. (2013). Structure of Twitter: Social and technical. *Twitter and Society*, Weller, K., Bruns, A., Burgess, J., Mahrt, M. and Puschmann, C. (eds). New York: Peter Lang: pp. 29–42.

Halewood, M. (2014). *Rethinking the Social Through Durkheim, Marx, Weber and Whitehead*. London: Anthem Press.

Halford, S., Pope, C. and Weal, M. (2013). Digital futures? Sociological challenges and opportunities in the emergent semantic web. *Sociology*, *47*(1): 173–89.

Haraway, D. J. (1997). *Modest– Witness@ Second– Millennium. FemaleMan– Meets–OncoMouse: Feminism and Technoscience*. Cambridge, MA: MIT Press.

Haraway, D. (2010). When species meet: Staying with the trouble. *Environment and planning. D, Society and space*, *28*(1): 53.

Harvey, P., Reeves, M. and Ruppert, E. (2013). Anticipating failure: transparency devices and their effects. *Journal of Cultural Economy*, *6*(3): 294–312.

Healy, K. Public sociology in the age of social media, *Perspectives on Politics*, forthcoming.

Healy, K. (2015). The performativity of networks. *European Journal of Sociology*, *56*(02): 175–205.

Heclo, H. (1978). Issue networks and the executive establishment. *The New American Political System*. A. King (ed.) Washington, DC: American Enterprise Institute for Public Policy Research.

Herring, S. C. (2009). Web content analysis: Expanding the paradigm. In *International handbook of Internet research*. J. Hunsinger, L. Klastrup, M. Allen (eds). Dordrecht: Springer Netherlands: pp. 233–49.

Hine C. (2015). Mixed methods and multimodal research and internet technologies. *The Oxford Handbook of Multimethod and Mixed Methods Research Inquiry*. Hesse-Biber S.N., Johnson R. B. (eds). Oxford : Oxford University Press, pp. 503–21.

Hine, C. (2000). *Virtual Ethnography*. London and New York: Sage.

Hine C. (2012). Headlice eradication as everyday engagement with science: An analysis of online parenting discussions. *Public Understanding of Science*, 23 (5): 574–91.

Hochman, N. and Manovich, L. (2013). Zooming into an Instagram city: Reading the local through social media. *First Monday*, *18*(7). http:www.firstmonday.org/article/view/4711/3698

Hogan, B. (2010). The presentation of self in the age of social media: Distinguishing performances and exhibitions online. *Bulletin of Science, Technology and Society*, 30(6): 377–86.

Hogan, B., Carrasco, J. A. and Wellman, B. (2007). Visualizing personal networks: Working with participant-aided sociograms. *Field Methods*, *19*(2): 116–44.

Housley, W., Procter, R., Edwards, A., Burnap, P., Williams, M., Sloan, L. and Greenhill, A. (2014). Big and broad social data and the sociological imagination: A collaborative response. *Big Data and Society*, *1*(2): 2053951714545135.

Howard, P., Duffy, A., Freelon, D., Hussain, M., Mari, W. and Mazaid, M. (2011). Opening Closed Regimes: What Was the Role of Social Media During the Arab Spring? Project on Information Technology and Political Islam, working paper.

Innes, H. (1951). *The Bias of Communication*. Toronto: Toronto University Press.

Introna, L. D. and Nissenbaum, H. (2000). Shaping the Web: Why the politics of search engines matters. *The Information Society*, *16*(3): 169–85.

Irani, L. (2015). Hackathons and the making of entrepreneurial citizenship. *Science, Technology and Human Values*, *40*(5): 799–824.

Irani, L. C. and Silberman, M. (2013). Turkopticon: Interrupting worker invisibility in amazon mechanical turk. *Proceedings of the SIGCHI Conference on Human Factors in Computing Systems*. ACM: pp. 611–20.

Jackson, S. J., Gillespie, T. and Payette, S. (2014). The policy knot: Re-integrating policy, practice and design in CSCW studies of social computing. *Proceedings of the 17th ACM Conference on Computer Supported Cooperative Work and Social Computing*. ACM: pp. 588–602.

Jacomy, M. (2015). L'analyse visuelle de réseaux. *I2D–Information, données and documents*, *52*(2): 60–1.

Jenkins, H. (2012). *Textual poachers: Television fans and participatory culture*. London and New York: Routledge.

Jiménez, A. C. (2014). The right to infrastructure: A prototype for open source urbanism. *Environment and Planning D: Society and Space*, *32*(2): 342–62.

Jones, S. (ed.). (1998). *Doing Internet Research: Critical Issues and Methods for Examining the Net*. New York: Sage Publications.

Keegan, B., Ahmed, M. A., Williams, D., Srivastava, J. and Contractor, N. (2010). Dark gold: Statistical properties of clandestine networks in massively multiplayer online games. *Social Computing. IEEE Second International Conference*, pp. 201–8.

Kelly, J. (2010). Parsing the online ecosystem: Journalism, media, and the blogo-sphere. *Transitioned media: A Turning Point in the Digital Realm*, G. Einav (ed.). New York: Springer: pp. 93–108.

Kelty, C. (2005). Geeks, social imaginaries, and recursive publics. *Cultural Anthropology*, *20*(2): 185–214.

Kelty, C. M. (2008). *Two Bits: The Cultural Significance of Free Software*. Durham, NC: Duke University Press.

Kelty, C. (2012). From participation to power. *The Participatory Cultures Handbook*. Delwiche, A. and Henderson, J. (eds). New York and London: Routledge.

Kelty, C., Panofsky, A., Currie, M., Crooks, R., Erickson, S., Garcia, P. and Wood, S. (2015). Seven dimensions of contemporary participation disentangled. *Journal of the Association for Information Science and Technology*, 66(3): 474–88.

Kennedy, H. (2016). New data relations and the desire for numbers. In *Post, Mine*, Repeat. Basingstoke: Palgrave: pp. 221–36.

Kennedy, H. and Moss, G. (2015). Known or knowing publics? Social media data mining and the question of public agency. *Big Data and Society*, 2(2): 2053951715611145.

Kitchin, R. (2014). *The Data Revolution: Big Data, Open Data, Data Infrastructures and their Consequences*. London: Sage.

Knoblauch, H., B. Schnettler, J. Raab (2006). Video analysis: Methodology and methods. *Qualitative Audiovisual Data Analysis in Sociology*. Knoblauch, H., B. Schnettler, J. Raab, and H. Soeffner (eds) Frankfurt am Main et al.: Peter Lang: pp. 9–28

Knorr-Cetina, K. (2009). The synthetic situation: Interactionism for a global world. *Symbolic Interaction*, 32(1): 61–87.

Knorr-Cetina, K. (2014). 2 Scopic media and global coordination: The mediatization of face-to-face encounters. *Mediatization of communication*, K. Lundby (ed.). Berlin/Boston: De Gruyter: pp. 39–61.

Knox, H., Savage, M. and Harvey, P. (2006). Social networks and the study of relations: networks as method, metaphor and form. *Economy and Society*, 35(1): 113–40.

Kosinski, M., Stillwell, D. and Graepel, T. (2013). Private traits and attributes are predictable from digital records of human behavior. *Proceedings of the National Academy of Sciences*, 110(15): 5802–5.

Langlois, G., Elmer, G., McKelvey, F. and Devereaux, Z. (2009). Networked publics: The double articulation of code and politics on Facebook. *Canadian Journal of Communication*, 34(3): 415–34.

Langlois, G. and Elmer, G. (2013). The research politics of social media platforms. *Culture Machine*, 14: pp. 1–17.

Lasén, A. and Martínez de Albeniz, I. (2011). An original protest, at least. Mediality and participation. *The Cultures of Participation. Media Practices, Cultures and Literacy*. H. Greif and A. Lasén (eds). Berlin: Peter Lang, pp. 141–58.

Lash, S. (2002). *Critique of Information*. London and New Dehli: Sage.

Latour, B. (1987). *Science in Action: How to Follow Scientists and Engineers Through Society*. Cambridge: Harvard University Press.

Latour, B. (1993). *We Have Never Been Modern*. C. Porter (trans.). Cambridge: Harvard University Press.

Latour, B. (1998). Thought experiments in social science: From the social contract to virtual society' 1st virtual society? Annual Public Lecture, London: Brunel University.

Latour, B. (1999). On recalling ANT. *The Sociological Review*, 47(S1): 15–25.

Latour, B. (2005). *Reassembling the Social. An introduction to Actor-Network Theory*. Oxford: Oxford University Press.

Latour, B., Jensen, P., Venturini, T., Grauwin, S. and Boullier, D. (2012).

'The whole is always smaller than its parts' – a digital test of Gabriel Tardes' monads. *The British Journal of Sociology*, *63*(4): 590–615.

Latour, B. and Woolgar, S. (2013 [1979]). *Laboratory Life: The Construction of Scientific Facts*. Princeton: Princeton University Press.

Laurier, E., Lorimer, H., Brown, B., Jones, O., Juhlin, O., Noble, A. and Weilenmann, A. (2008). Driving and 'passengering': Notes on the ordinary organization of car travel. *Mobilities*, *3*(1): 1–23.

Law, J. (2004). *After Method: Mess in Social Science Research*. London and Routledge.

Law, J. (1994). *Organizing Modernity*. Oxford: Blackwell.

Law, J. and Ruppert, E. (2013). The social life of methods: Devices. *Journal of Cultural Economy*, *6*(3): 229–40.

Law, J. and Urry, J. (2004). Enacting the social. *Economy and Society*, *33*(3): 390–410.

Lazarsfeld, P. (1975). *An Introduction to Applied Sociology*, Praeger.

Lazer, D., Kennedy, R., King, G. and Vespignani, A. (2014). The parable of Google flu: traps in big data analysis. *Science*, *343*(6176): 1203–5.

Lazer, D., Pentland, A. S., Adamic, L., Aral, S., Barabasi, A. L., Brewer, D. and Jebara, T. (2009). Life in the network: the coming age of computational social science. *Science 323*(5915): 721.

Lee, R. M. (2000). *Unobtrusive methods in social research*. Milton Keynes: Open University Press.

Lee, R. M., Fielding, N. and Blank, G. (2008). The internet as a research medium: An editorial introduction to the Sage Handbook of Online Research Methods. *The SAGE Handbook of Online Research Methods*, Lee, R. M., Fielding, N. and Blank, G. (eds). London: Sage, pp. 3–20.

Leigh Star, S. and A. Strauss (1999). Layers of silence, arenas of voice: The ecology of visible and invisible work. *Computer Supported Cooperative Work* (CSCW) 8(1–2): 9–30.

Lewis, K. (2015). Three fallacies of digital footprints. *Big Data and Society*, *2*(2): 2053951715602496.

Lezaun, J. (2007). A market of opinions: The political epistemology of focus groups. *Sociological Review* (55): 130–51.

Lezaun, J. (2011). Offshore democracy: Launch and landfall of a sociotechnical experiment. *Economy and Society*, *40*(4): 553–81.

Lezaun, J., N. Marres and M. Tironi (forthcoming) Experiments in participation. In *The Handbook of Science and Technology Studies*, 4th edn, C, Miller, U. Felt et al. (eds). Cambridge, MA: MIT Press.

Lezaun, J., and Soneryd, L. (2007). Consulting citizens: Technologies of elicitation and the mobility of publics. *Public Understanding of Science*, *16*(3): 279–97.

Licoppe, C. (2004). 'Connected' presence: The emergence of a new repertoire for managing social relationships in a changing communication technoscape. *Environment and Planning D: Society and Space*, *22*(1): 135–56.

Licoppe, C. (2016). Mobilities and urban encounters in public places in the age of locative media. seams, folds, and encounters with 'pseudonymous strangers'. *Mobilities*, *11*(1): 99–116.

Licoppe, C., Diminescu, D., Smoreda, Z. and Ziemlicki, C. (2008). Using mobile phone geolocalisation for 'socio-geographical' analysis of co-ordination, urban mobilities, and social integration patterns. *Tijdschrift voor economische en sociale geografie*, *99*(5): 584–601.

Lievrouw, L. (2014). Materiality and media in communication and technology studies: An unfinished project. *Media technologies: Essays on communication, materiality, and society*, T. Gillespie, P. J. Boczkowski, and K. Foot (eds). Cambridge, MA: MIT Press, pp. 21–51.

Lippmann, W. (2002 (1927)). *The Phantom Public*. New Brunswick and London: Transaction Publishers.

Livingstone, S. (2008). 'Taking risky opportunities in youthful content creation: Teenagers' use of social networking sites for intimacy, privacy and self-expression. '*New Media and Society*', 10 (3): 393–411.

Livingstone, S. M. and Lunt, P. K. (1994). *Talk on Television: Audience Participation and Public Debate*. Psychology Press.

Lovink, G. (2008). The society of the query and the Googlisation of our lives. A tribute to Joseph Weizenbaum. *Eurozine*. http://www. eurozine. com/articles/2008-09-05-lovink-en. html

Lupton, D. (2014). *Digital Sociology*. London and New York: Routledge.

Lury, C. (2012). Going live: Towards an amphibious sociology. *The Sociological Review*, 60(S1): 184–97.

Lury, C. (2004). *Brands: The Logos of the Global Economy*. London and New York: Routledge.

Lury, C. and Marres, N. (2015). Notes on objectual valuation. In *Making Things Valuable*, M. Kornberger, L. Justesen, A. Koed Madsen and J. Mouritsen (eds), Oxford: Oxford University Press.

Lury, C. and Wakeford, N. (eds). (2012). *Inventive Methods: The Happening of the Social*. London and New York: Routledge.

Lynch, M. (1993). *Scientific Practice and Ordinary Action: Ethnomethodology and Social Studies of Science*. Cambridge: Cambridge University Press, pp. 154–8.

Lynch, M. (1991). Method: Measurement – ordinary and scientific measurement as ethnomethodological phenomena. *Ethnomethodology and the Human Sciences*, G. Button (ed.), Cambridge: Cambridge University Press, pp. 77–108.

Mackenzie, A. (2005). Problematising the technological: The object as event? *Social Epistemology*, 19(4): 381–99.

Mackenzie, A., Mills, R., Sharples, S., Fuller, M. and Goffey, A. (2015). Digital sociology in the field of devices. *Routledge International Handbook of the Sociology of Art and Culture*, L. Hanquinet and M Savage (eds). London: Routledge: pp. 367–382.

MacKinnon, L. (2015). Love's algorithm: The perfect parts for my machine.

Algorithmic life: Calculative Devices in the Age of Big Data, Amoore, L. and Piotukh, V. (eds), London and New York: Routledge: pp. 161–75.

Madianou, M. and Miller, D. (2013). Polymedia: Towards a new theory of digital media in interpersonal communication. *International Journal of Cultural Studies*, 16(2): 169–87.

Mandiberg, M. (2012). Introduction. *The Social Media Reader*. New York: NYU Press, pp. 1–12.

Manovich, L. (2011). Trending: The promises and the challenges of big social data. In *Debates in the Digital Humanities*, M. Gold (ed.), Minnesota: University of Minnesota Press, pp. 460–75.

Marres, N. (2006). Net-work is format work: Issue networks and the sites of civil society politics. In *Reformating Politics: Information Technology and Global Civil Society*, J. Dean, J. Anderson, and G. Lovink (eds). London and New York: Routledge, pp. 3–17

Marres, N. (2011). The costs of public involvement: Everyday devices of carbon accounting and the materialization of participation. *Economy and society*, 40(4): 510–33.

Marres, N. (2012a). The redistribution of methods: On intervention in digital social research, broadly conceived. *The Sociological Review*, 60(S1): 139–65.

Marres, N. (2012b). The experiment in living. In *Inventive Methods: The Happening of the Social*. C. Lury and N. Wakeford (eds). London and New York: Routledge, pp. 76–94.

Marres, N. (2012c [2015]). *Material Participation: Technology, the Environment and Everyday Publics*, Basingstoke: Palgrave Macmillan.

Marres, N. (2015). Why map issues? On controversy analysis as a digital method. *Science, Technology and Human Values*, 40(5): 655–86.

Marres, N. and Gerlitz C. (forthcoming). On social media as experiments in sociality. In *Inventing the Social*. N. Marres, M. Guggenheim and A. Wilkie (eds), Mattering Press.

Marres, N. and Gerlitz, C. (2016). Interface methods: Renegotiating relations between digital research, STS and Sociology. *Sociological Review*, 64 (1): 21–46.

Marres, N. and Lezaun, J. (2011). Materials and devices of the public: An introduction. *Economy and society*, 40(4): 489–509.

Marres, N. and Moats, D. (2015). Mapping controversies with social media: The case for symmetry. *Social Media+ Society*, 1(2), T. Gillespie and H. Postigo (eds), 2056305115604176.

Marres, N. and Rogers, R. (2000). Depluralising the Web, re-pluralising public debate – the case of the GM food debate on the Web. In *Preferred Placement: Knowledge Politics on the Web*. Maastricht: Jan van Eyck Akademie: pp. 113–136.

Marres, N. and Weltevrede, E. (2013). Scraping the social? Issues in live social research. *Journal of Cultural Economy*, 6(3): 313–35.

Marres, N. and Weltevrede, E. (2015). Scraping the social? Issues in real-time social research. In *La Médiatisation de l'Évaluation / Evaluation in the Media*. J. Bouchard, É. Candel, H. Cardy and G. Gomez-Mejia (eds) Berlin: Peter Lang.

Marres, N., M. Guggenheim, and A. Wilkie (eds), *Inventing the Social*. Mattering Press, forthcoming.

Mayer, K. (2012). Objectifying social structures: Network visualization as means of social optimization. *Theory and Psychology*, *22*(2): 162–78.

Mayer-Schoenberger, V. and Cukier, K. (2013). *Big Data: A Revolution That Will Transform How We Live, Work and Think* (London: John Murray).

Mazanderani, F. and Brown, I. (2011). Privacy as a practice: exploring the relational and spatial dynamics of HIV-related information seeking. In *Computers, Privacy and Data Protection: an Element of Choice*. Dordrecht: Springer Netherlands: pp. 251–68.

McKelvey, F. R. (2014). Algorithmic media need algorithmic methods: Why publics matter. *Canadian Journal of Communication*, *39*(4): 597–613.

McRobbie, A. and S. Thornton (1995). Rethinking 'moral panic' for multi-mediated social worlds, *The British Journal of Sociology* 46 (4): 559–74.

Merton, R. K. (1968). The Matthew effect in science. *Science*, *159*(3810): 56–63.

Miller, D. and D. Slater (2001). *The Internet: An Ethnographic Approach*. Oxford: Berg.

Miller, P. and Rose, N. (2008). *Governing the Present: Administering Economic, Social and Personal Life*. Cambridge: Polity.

Moats, D. (2015). Mapping controversies with Wikipedia: The case of Fukushima. Doctoral diss., University of London, Goldsmiths, UK.

Moor, L. (2011). Neoliberal experiments: Social marketing and the governance of populations. *Inside Marketing: Practices, Ideologies, Devices*, D. Zwick and J. Cayla (eds). Oxford: Oxford University Press: pp. 299–319.

Morley D. and K.-H. Chen (eds) (1996). *Stuart Hall: Critical Dialogues in Cultural Studies*, London: Routledge.

Morozov, E. (2013). *To Save Everything, Click Here: Technology, Solutionism, and the Urge to Fix Problems That Don't Exist*. London: Penguin.

Munk, A. (2013). A field guide to the web: Techno-anthropology and the digital natives. In *What Is Techno-anthropology?* T. Borsen and L Botin (eds). Aalborg, Denmark: Aalborg Universitetsforlag, pp 91–116.

Murthy, D. (2008). Digital ethnography an examination of the use of new technologies for social research. *Sociology*, *42*(5): 837–55.

Murthy D. (2013). *Twitter: Social Communication in the Twitter Age*. Cambridge: Polity.

Murthy, D., Gross, A., Takata, A. and Bond, S. (2013). Evaluation and development of data mining tools for social network analysis. In *Mining Social Networks and Security Informatics*. Dordrecht: Springer Netherlands: pp. 183–202.

Mützel, S. (2009). Networks as culturally constituted processes: a comparison of relational sociology and actor-network theory. *Current Sociology*, *57*(6): 871–87.

Mützel, S. (2015). Facing big data: Making sociology relevant. *Big Data and Society*, 2(2): 2053951715599179

Myers, N. (2006). Animating mechanism: Animations and the propagation of affect in the lively arts of protein modelling. *Science Studies*, 19(2): 6–30.

Narayanan, A. and B. Zevenbergen (2015). No encore for encore? Ethical questions for web-based censorship measurement, Data and Society Institute, New York.

Nash, K. (2009). *Contemporary Political Sociology: Globalization, Politics and Power*. London: Wiley and Blackwell.

Neff, G. and D. Nafus (2016). *The Quantified Self*. Cambridge, MA: MIT Press.

Nelkin, D. (1992). *Controversy: Politics of Technical Decisions*. New York and Dehli: Sage.

Newman, M., Barabási, A. and Watts, D., (2007). *The Structure and Dynamics of Networks*, Princeton, NJ: Princeton University Press.

Niederer, S. (2013). 'Global warming is not a crisis!': Studying climate change skepticism on the web. *Necsus, European Journal of Media Studies* 2 (1): 83–112.

Niederer, S. (2016). Networked content analysis. The case of climate change. Doctoral dissertation, University of Amsterdam.

Niederer, S. and van Dijck, J. (2010). Wisdom of the crowd or technicity of content? Wikipedia as a sociotechnical system. *New Media and Society*, 12(8): 1368–87.

Nissenbaum, H. 2004. Privacy as contextual integrity. *Washington Law Review* 79 (1): 101–39

Nold, C. (2015). micro/macro prototyping, *International Journal of Human-Computer Studies* (81): 72–80.

Orton-Johnson, K. and Prior, N. (eds). (2013). *Digital Sociology: Critical Perspectives*. Basingstoke: Palgrave Macmillan.

Osborne, T. and N. Rose (1999). Do the social sciences create phenomena? The case of public opinion research. *British Journal of Sociology (50)*: 367–96.

Oudshoorn, N. and Pinch, T. (2003). *How Users Matter: The Co-Construction of Users and Technology (inside Technology)*. Cambridge, MA: the MIT Press.

Papacharissi, Z. (2015). We have always been social. *Social Media+ Society*, 1(1): 2056305115581185.

Pasquale, F. (2015). *The Black Box Society: The Secret Algorithms that Control Money and Information*. Cambridge, MA: Harvard University Press.

Passmann, J. and Gerlitz. C. (2014). Good platform-political reasons for bad platform-data. Zur sozio-technischen Geschichte der Plattformaktivitäten Fav, Retweet und Like. Media Kontrolle. Working paper.

Passoth, J.-H. (2015). Mit Stift und Papier in digitalen Welten? *Die qualitative Analyse internetbasierter Daten*. D. Schirmer, N. Sander, and A. Wenninger (eds). Wiesbaden: Springer Fachmedien: pp. 261–80.

Pateman, C. (1989). Feminist Critiques of the Public/Private Dichotomy. In *The Disorder of Women*. Stanford: Stanford University Press, pp. 118–40.

Pentland, A. (2014). *Social Physics: How Good Ideas Spread – the Lessons from a New Science*. London: Penguin.

Pearce, W. K. Holmberg, I. R. Hellsten, and B. Nerlich (2014). 'Climate change on Twitter: Topics, communities and conversations about the 2013 IPCC Working Group 1 Report.' PLoS One 9:e94785. doi:10.1371/journal.pone.0094785.

Perng, S. Y., Buscher, M., Halvorsrud, R., Wood, L., Stiso, M., Ramirez, L. and Al-Akkad, A. (2012). Peripheral response: Microblogging during the 22/7/2011 Norway attacks, *Proceedings of the 9th International ISCRAM Conference*, L. Rothkrantz, J. Ristvej and Z. Franco (eds),.Vancouver, Canada.

Petersen, K. (2014). Producing space, tracing authority: Mapping the 2007 San Diego wildfires. *The Sociological Review* 62 (s1): 91–113.

Plantin, Jean-Christophe. (2015). The politics of mapping platforms: Participatory radiation mapping after the Fukushima Daiichi disaster. *Media, Culture and Society* 37 (6): 904–21.

Popper, K. (2002 (1945)). *The Open Society and Its Enemies: Volume 1: The Spell of Plato*. London: Routledge.

Postill, J. and Pink, S. (2012). Social media ethnography: The digital researcher in a messy web. *Media International Australia*, *145*(1): 123–34.

Powell, A. (2014). 'Datafication', transparency, and good governance of the data city. *Digital Enlightenment Yearbook 2014: Social Networks and Social Machines, Surveillance and Empowerment*, K. O'Hara, M-H.C. Nguyen, P. Haynes (eds), IOS Press, pp. 215–26.

Procter, R., Vis, F. and Voss, A. (2013). Reading the riots on Twitter: Methodological innovation for the analysis of big data. *International journal of social research methodology*, *16*(3): 197–214.

Recuber, T. (2015). Self-destruction as self-preservation: Digital suicide notes and the commemoration of the self. Paper presented at the Annual Meeting of the American Sociological Association. Chicago, IL.

Rieder, B. (2012). What is in PageRank? A historical and conceptual investigation of a recursive status index. *Computational Culture* (2), http://hdl.handle.net/11245/1.375851.

Rieder, B. (2013). Studying Facebook via data extraction: The Netvizz application. In *Proceedings of the 5th annual ACM web science conference*. ACM: pp. 346–55.

Riedl, J. (2011). The promise and peril of social computing. *Computer*, *1*(44): 93–5.

Riemens, P. (2002). Some thoughts on the idea of 'hacker culture'. Cyber Society Live, Online Discussion List, 31 May.

Ritzer, G. and Jurgenson, N. (2010). Production, consumption, prosumption: The nature of capitalism in the age of the digital 'prosumer'. *Journal of consumer culture*, *10*(1): 13–36.

Rogers, R. (2009). The end of the virtual–digital methods. Inaugural Address, University of Amsterdam.

Rogers, R. (2013). *Digital Methods*. Cambridge, MA: MIT press.

Rogers, R. and Marres, N. (2000). Landscaping climate change: A mapping technique for understanding science and technology debates on the World Wide Web. *Public Understanding of Science*, *9*(2): 141–63.

Rohle, T. (2007). Desperately seeking the consumer: Personalized search engines and the commercial exploitation of user data. *First Monday*, *12*(9). http://dx.doi.org/10.5210/fm.v12i9.2008.

Rommes, E., Oost, E. V. and Oudshoorn, N. (1999). Gender in the design of the digital city of Amsterdam. *Information, Communication and Society*, *2*(4): 476–95.

Rorty, R. (1980). *Philosophy and the Mirror of Nature*. Princeton, NJ: Princeton University Press.

Ruppert, E. (2013). Rethinking empirical social sciences. *Dialogues in Human Geography*, *3*(3): 268–73.

Ruppert, E., P. Harvey, C. Lury, A. Mackenzie, R. McNally, S. Baker, Y. Kallianos, C. Lewis (2015). Socialising big data: From concept to practice, *CRESC Working Paper* No. 138 February.

Ruppert, E., J. Law and M. Savage (2013). Reassembling social science methods: The challenge of digital devices. *Theory, Culture and Society*, *30*(4): 22–46.

Ruths, D. and Pfeffer, J. (2014). Social media for large studies of behaviour. *Science*, *346*(6213), 1063–4.

Sandvig, C. (2014). Are you a political junkie and felon who loves blenders? *Accountability and Algorithms Conference*, 28 February, New York University.

Sarawagi, S. (2007). Information extraction. *Foundations and Trends in Databases*, 1 (3): 261–377.

Sassen, S. (2002). Towards a sociology of information technology. *Current Sociology*, *50*(3): 365–88.

Savage, M. (2009). Contemporary sociology and the challenge of descriptive assemblage. *European Journal of Social Theory*, *12*(1): 155–74.

Savage, M. (2010). *Identities and Social Change in Britain Since 1940: The Politics of Method*. Oxford: Oxford University Press.

Savage, M. and Burrows, R. (2007). The coming crisis of empirical sociology. *Sociology*, *41*(5): 885–99.

Savage, M., Devine, F., Cunningham, N., Taylor, M., Li, Y., Hjellbrekke, J. and Miles, A. (2013). A new model of social class? Findings from the BBC's Great British Class Survey experiment. *Sociology*, *47*(2): 219–50.

Savage, M., F. Devine, N. Cunningham, S. Friedman, D. Laurison,

A. Miles, H. Snee and M. Taylor (2014). On Social Class, Anno 2014 *Sociology* 49 (6): 1011–30.

Schinkel, W. (2016). Smart charisma and the imagination of futurity, paper presented at the launch of the Centre for Public Imagination, Rotterdam, 16 June.

Schneider, S. M. and Foot, K. A. (2005). Web sphere analysis: An approach to studying online action. In Hine, C. (ed.), *Virtual Methods: Issues in Social Research on the Internet*. Oxford, New York: Berg, pp. 157–70.

Schwartz, H. (1979). Data: Who needs it? Describing normal environments – examples and methods. *Analytic Sociology*, 2(1): A4–C12.

Scott, J. (2012). *Social Network Analysis*. London: Sage.

Schick, L. and Winthereik, B. R. (2013). Innovating relations – or why smart grid is not too complex for the public. *Science and Technology Studies, 26* (3), 82–102.

Schmidt, J. (forthcoming) Late-modern technology? On technoscientific knowledge, self-organizing technosystems, and the loss of control in Synthetic Biology. In *TechnoScienceSociety: Technological Reconfigurations of Science and Society*, S. Maasen, C. Schneider, S. Dickel (eds) *Sociology of Science Yearbook*, Delft: Kluwer.

Seaver, N. (2015). The nice thing about context is that everyone has it. *Media, Culture and Society*, 37(7): 1101–9.

Sharma, S. (2013). Black Twitter?: Racial hashtags, networks and contagion. *New Formations: A Journal of Culture/Theory/Politics*, 78(1): 46–64.

Shaw, R. (2015). Big data and reality. *Big Data and Society*, 2(2): 2053951715608877.

Shirky, C. (2009). *Here Comes Everybody (There Goes The Audience): The Power of Organizing Without Organizations*. New York: Penguin.

Shklovski, I., Mainwaring, S., Skúladóttir, H. and Borgthorsson, H. (2014). Of leakiness and creepiness in app space: User perceptions of privacy and mobile app use. *Proceedings of the 2014 ACM Conference on Human Factors in Computing* (Toronto, Canada, 2014). ACM: pp. 2347–56.

Simonite, T. (2012). What Facebook knows. *Technology Review, 115*(4): 42–8.

Simonson, P. and Weimann (2003). Critical research at Columbia: Lazarsfeld's and Merton's 'Mass communication, popular taste, and organized social action' *Canonic Texts in Media Research: Are There Any? Should There Be? How About These?* E. Katz, J. D. Peters, T. Liebes, and A. Orloff (eds). Cambridge: Polity: pp. 12–38.

Skeggs, B. and Yuill, S. (2016). The methodology of a multi-model project examining how Facebook infrastructures social relations. *Information, Communication and Society*, 19(10), 1356–72.

Slater, D. (2002). Social relationships and identity online and offline. *Handbook of New Media: Social Shaping and Consequences of ICT*. Lievrouw, L. and Livingstone, S. (eds) London: Sage Publications: pp. 533–46.

Smith, M., Rainie, L., Schneiderman, B. and Himelboim, I. (2014). Topic Networks: From Polarized Crowds to Community Clusters, 20 February.

Snee, H., Hine, C., Morley, Y., Roberts, S. and Watson, H. (2015). *Digital Methods for Social Science*. Basingstoke: Palgrave MacMillan.

Snow, C. P. (1959). Two cultures. *Science, 130*(3373): 419–20.

Soneryd, L. (2016). Technologies of participation and the making of technologized futures. In *Remaking Participation: Science, Environment and Emergent Publics*. J. Chilvers and M. Kearnes,(eds).. London and New York: Routledge: pp 144–61.

Stengers, I. (1996). *Cosmopolitiques*, Paris: La découverte and Les Empêcheurs de penser en rond.

Suchman, L. A. (1987). *Plans and Situated Actions: The Problem of Human-Machine Communication*. Cambridge: Cambridge University Press.

Suchman, L. (1997). Centers of coordination: A case and some themes. *Discourse, Tools and Reasoning*. Berlin and Heidelberg: Springer: pp. 41–62.

Suchman, L. (2007a). *Human-Machine Reconfigurations: Plans and Situated Actions*. Cambridge: Cambridge University Press.

Suchman, L. (2007b). Agencies in technology design: Feminist reconfigurations. Unpublished manuscript.

Suchman, L., Blomberg, J., Orr, J.,Trigg, Randall (1999). Reconstructing technologies as social practice. *The American Behavioral Scientist* 43 (3): 392–408.

Terranova, T. (2006). The concept of information. *Theory, Culture and Society, 23*(2/3): 286–8.

Terranova, T. (2011). Free Labor. *The New Media and Technoculture Reader*. M. Lister and S. Giddings (eds). London and New York: Routledge, pp. 350–6.

Thelwall, M., Sud, P. and Vis, F. (2012). Commenting on YouTube videos: From Guatemalan rock to el big bang. *Journal of the American Society for Information Science and Technology, 63*(3): 616–29.

Thelwall, M., K. Vann, and R. Fairclough (2006). Web issue analysis: An integrated water resource management case study. *Journal of the American Society for Information Science and Technology, 57* (10): 1303–14.

Thielmann, T. (2012). Taking into account. Harold Garfinkels Beitrag zür eine Theorie sozialer Medien. *Zeitschrift für Medienwissenschaft* (6): 85–102.

Thomas, W.I and D.S. Thomas (1928). *The Child in America: Behavior Problems and Programs*. New York: Knopf: 571–2.

Thompson, J. B. (2011). Shifting boundaries of public and private life. *Theory, Culture and Society, 28*(4): 49–70.

Thrift, N. and French, S. (2002). The automatic production of space. *Transactions of the Institute of British Geographers, 27*(3): 309–35.

Tkacz, N (2014). *Wikipedia and the Politics of Openness*, Chicago: University of Chicago Press.

Tufekci, Z. (2014a). Big questions for social media big data: Representativeness, validity and other methodological pitfalls. *arXiv preprint arXiv:1403.7400*.

Tufekci, Z. (2014b). What happens to #Ferguson affects Ferguson: Net neutrality, algorithmic filtering and Ferguson. *Message*, 14 August.

Turner, F. (2013). *The Democratic Surround: Multimedia and American Liberalism from World War II to the Psychedelic Sixties*. Chicago: University of Chicago Press.

Uprichard, E. (2012). Being stuck in (live) time: The sticky sociological imagination. *The Sociological Review*, 60(S1): 124–38.

Uprichard, E. (2013). Describing description (and keeping causality): The case of academic articles on food and eating. *Sociology*, 47(2): 368–82.

Uprichard, E., Burrows, R. and Byrne, D. (2008). SPSS as an 'inscription device': from causality to description? *The Sociological Review*, 56(4): 606–22.

Venturini, T., and D. Guido (2012). 'Once upon a text': An ANT tale in text analysis. *Sociologica*, 62(3). doi:10.2383/72700.

Venturini, T. M. Jacomy, D. Pereira (2014). Visual Network Analysis, Sciences Po MediaLab, working paper, http://www.tommasoventurini.it/wp/wp-content/uploads/2014/08/Venturini-Jacomy_Visual-Network-Analysis_WorkingPaper.pdf

Vis, F. (2013). A critical reflection on Big Data: Considering APIs, researchers and tools as data makers. *First Monday*, 18(10). http://ojs-prod-lib.cc.uic.edu/ojs/index.php/fm/article/view/4878/3755

Wagner-Pacifici, R., Mohr, J. W. and Breiger, R. L. (2015). Ontologies, methodologies, and new uses of Big Data in the social and cultural sciences. *Big Data and Society*, 2(2), 2053951715613810.

Wajcman, J. (1991). *Feminism Confronts Technology*. Cambridge: Polity.

Wajcman, J. and Jones, P. K. (2012). Border communication: Media sociology and STS. *Media, Culture and Society (34)*: 673–90.

Wakeford, N. (2016). Don't go all the way: Revisiting 'misplaced concretism'. *Boundary Objects and Beyond: Working with Leigh Star*. G. Bowker, S. Timmermans, A. Clarke, and E. Balka (eds). Cambridge, MA: MIT Press, pp 69–84.

Watts, D. (2004). The 'new' science of networks. *Annual Review of Sociology* (30): 243–270.

Webber, R. J., Butler, T. and Phillips, T. (2015). Adoption of geo-demographic and ethno-cultural taxonomies for analysing Big Data. *Big Data and Society*, 2(1): 2053951715583914.

Weber, M. (1968 (1905)). *Economy and Society: An Outline of Interpretative Sociology*. Berkeley and Los Angeles: University of California Press.

Weltevrede, E. (2015). Repurposing digital methods: The research affordances of platforms and engines. Doctoral dissertation, University of Amsterdam.

Weltevrede, E., Helmond, A. and Gerlitz, C. (2014). The politics of real-time: A device perspective on social media platforms and search engines. *Theory, Culture and Society*, *31*(6): 125–50.

Wilkie, A., Michael, M. and Plummer-Fernandez, M. (2014). Speculative method and twitter: Bots, energy and three conceptual characters. *The Sociological Review*, *63*: 79–101.

Woolgar, S. (2002). *Virtual Society?: Technology, Cyberbole, Reality*. Oxford: Oxford University Press.

Woolgar, S. and Neyland, D. (2013). *Mundane Governance: Ontology and Accountability*. Oxford: Oxford University Press.

Wouters, P. (2003). Cybersociologie-een beknopt kookboekje. *Amsterdams Sociologisch Tijdschrift*, 30(1/2): 274–300.

Wyatt, S. (2008). Feminism, technology and the information society: Learning from the past, imagining the future. *Information, Community and Society*, *11*(1): 111–30.

Wynn, J. R. (2009). Digital sociology: Emergent technologies in the field and the classroom. *Sociological Forum* 24, (2): 448–56.

Wynne, B. (2008). Public participation in science and technology: performing and obscuring a political–conceptual category mistake. *East Asian Science, Technology and Society: International Journal* (1): 99–110.

Ziewitz, M. (2016). Governing algorithms myth, mess, and methods. *Science, Technology and Human Values*, *41*(1): 3–16.

Index